THE ENGLISH POOR LAWS,
1700–1930

11/9/18

1 2 FEB 2014

1 6 NOV 2018

R01180

Social History in Perspective

General Editor: Jeremy Black

Social History in Perspective is a series of in-depth studies of the many topics in social, cultural and religious history.

PUBLISHED

Please note that a sister series, *British History in Perspective*, is available.

Social History in Perspective
Series Standing Order
ISBN 0–333–71694–9 hardcover
ISBN 0–333–69336–1 paperback
(outside North America only)

You can receive future titles in this series as they are published by placing a standing order. Please contact your bookseller or, in case of difficulty, write to us at the address below with your name and address, the title of the series and the ISBN quoted above.

Customer Services Department, Macmillan Distribution Ltd
Houndmills, Basingstoke, Hampshire RG21 6XS, England

THE ENGLISH POOR LAWS, 1700–1930

Anthony Brundage

First published 2002 by
PALGRAVE
Houndmills, Basingstoke, Hampshire RG21 6XS
and
175 Fifth Avenue, New York, N.Y. 10010
Companies and representatives throughout the world

PALGRAVE is the new global academic imprint of
St. Martin's Press LLC Scholarly and Reference Division and
Palgrave Publishers Ltd (formerly Macmillan Press Ltd).

ISBN 0–333–68270–X hardback
ISBN 0–333–68271–8 paperback

This book is printed on paper suitable for recycling and made from fully managed and sustained forest sources.

A catalogue record for this book is available from the British Library.

Library of Congress Cataloging-in-Publication Data
Brundage, Anthony, 1938–
    The English poor laws, 1700–1930 / Anthony Brundage.
        p. cm. – (Social history in perspective)
    Includes bibliographical references and index.
    ISBN 0-333-68270-X
        1. Poor laws–England–History. 2. Poor–England–History. 3. Public welfare–England–History. I. Title. II. Series.

    HV249.E89 B78 2001
    362.5–dc21   2001036095

10   9   8   7   6   5   4   3   2   1
11   10   09   08   07   06   05   04   03   02

Printed in China

CONTENTS

1

INTRODUCTION: APPROACHING ENGLISH POOR LAW HISTORY

Point of Entry

In 1895, a six-year-old boy, together with his mother and older brother, was admitted to the Lambeth Workhouse. The mother, a former vaudeville star separated from her hard-drinking actor husband, had permanently lost her singing voice, a misfortune that quickly turned to tragedy, as it brought a sudden end to her comfortable income. She struggled mightily against the inexorable descent into pauperism, selling her clothes and belongings one by one, and toiling as a dressmaker in a succession of flats she and her sons moved to, each smaller and meaner than the last. In the end, in spite of her efforts, she was forced to throw herself and her family on the mercies of the Lambeth poor law guardians. The boys, at first excited by the prospect of a new adventure, were soon chastened by the regimented rigour of workhouse life, and saddened by forced separation from their mother, who was assigned to the women's ward. Further isolation occurred when the brothers were transferred to the Hanwell School for Orphans and Destitute Children. This was especially hard on the younger boy, for he was not only separated further from his mother but from his brother as well. Harsh discipline, with floggings for minor infractions, was the order of the day at Hanwell, and the boy was overjoyed when, the next year, his mother secured the family's discharge, and managed for a while to keep them financially afloat. Freedom proved short-lived, however, and before long they were back in the workhouse. When his mother, finally overwhelmed by depression and mental instability, was committed to an asylum, the authorities compelled his father to care for the boy (his brother was soon in training for the navy). Life with his father, who died of alcoholism

1

within a few years, proved far from idyllic, but the boy was soon launched upon his life's work.

What should we make of this incident in the childhood of Charlie Chaplin, which he relates so matter-of-factly in his autobiography?[1] Professionally, it may well have been a godsend. His immersion in the workhouse afforded him close observation of the world of London pauperdom, providing vital source material for his most famous film character, 'The Little Tramp'. The poignancy of his portrayal of the tramp's dogged determination to maintain some semblance of dignity in the face of adversity and injustice would probably not have been possible without his incarceration in the workhouse. In other roles as well, Chaplin skewered the sometimes formal, sometimes casual cruelties of those with property and authority, a turning of the tables that surely grew out of his poor law experiences. Widening the lens on this experience just a little, it is probably also true to say that the impact of the workhouse on Chaplin's mother was considerably more devastating than it was for him. Possibly she would have been overwhelmed by mental illness anyway, but arguably, the searing sense of loss and helplessness as all the trappings of affluence and respectability were stripped from her and her sons was a major factor in its onset.

Assessing the impact of the poor law on these individual lives in late nineteenth-century London is a daunting task, and it becomes necessary to employ words like 'possibly', 'probably', 'surely', and 'arguably'. How much more difficult it is when we take a panoramic view, attempting to grasp the impact of the poor law on the lives of the many millions of men, women, and children caught up in its structures and operations over the last three centuries. This is the dilemma of the poor law historian, especially one who attempts a broad survey. Even writers employing a narrower geographic, chronological, or topical framework must confront the problem of generalizing from their case studies. It is, of course, possible to write about the poor laws from an institutional or administrative perspective, or to use a political framework, or to employ the language of number, making sophisticated analyses of the wealth of historical statistics relating to the poor laws. Such works have necessarily to abandon any real engagement with the actual fabric of the lives of those caught up in the poor law system. Nonetheless, many valuable studies along these lines have been published, and their findings are incorporated into this book. Even using an institutional lens, however, does not dispose of the problem of how 'typical' any set of policies might have been. For example, would Chaplin and his family have been treated the same way in, say, Manchester, or south Wales? As we shall see, any generalizing statement about the poor laws runs up against significant regional and local variations.

The dilemma for the writer of a survey text covering a span of more than two centuries is to convey something of the complexity and significance of the poor laws, without losing sight of the individual human dimension. The organization of the book is a straightforward, chronological one. Topically, it is structured around the main institutional and political events that transformed the poor law system from a highly localized, parochial relief system to a major central government department with many ancillary services. At the same time, a determined effort has been made to keep in sight the individual lives that were affected, both for good and ill, by engagement with the poor laws. This includes people in the upper and middle classes who took an active part in the system, for the poor law experience was, in essence, an often troubled, sometimes anguished relationship between the comfortable and the desperate. Not that the poor were simply passive recipients of the policies of those in authority; rather, they were often shapers, and sometimes active opponents, of a system that was central to many of their lives.

This study is necessarily a work of synthesis, an attempt to blend together material and interpretations from hundreds of more specialized books and articles. Poor law history has been a lively field, and there are a number of contested interpretive points. These disputes are not foregrounded in the subsequent narrative chapters, but rather briefly alluded to, with citations and elaboration in the endnotes for those who wish to pursue any given issue. To have done otherwise, with the names and theories of historians competing for the reader's attention with the historical events and players, would have rendered unwieldy an already complex story, especially for those receiving their first systematic exposure to the poor laws. However, in the remainder of this chapter, an attempt has been made to provide the reader with some sense of the broad outlines of poor law historiography.

A Wealth of Approaches to Poor Law History

The earliest important works on poor law history tended to be in the nature of surveys of major administrative and relief policy developments. The key work in the nineteenth century was George Nicholls's *History of the English Poor Law* (1854). Nicholls, who also wrote books on the Irish Poor Law and the Scottish Poor Law, was a leading poor law reformer, associated with the development of the deterrent workhouse. He had also served as one of the three Poor Law Commissioners under the New Poor Law of 1834. His advocacy of harsh cutbacks and deterrent strategies in poor relief is evident throughout his book, though it is still useful for factual administrative information. Even more thorough and comprehensive in coverage is Sidney and Beatrice Webb's *English Poor Law History* (1927–29). This indeed is the great classic in the field, still widely cited and an indispensable starting point for all serious researchers, though the Webbs' polemical purposes must always be kept in mind.[2] Like Nicholls, the Webbs too had a very practical interest in the poor laws, but as would-be abolitionists rather than defenders. As Fabian socialists and leading figures in the Labour Party, they sought to replace the poor law's 'framework of repression' with a 'framework of prevention', thus adumbrating the Welfare State. While many, perhaps most, subsequent authors had some political or ideological stance vis-à-vis the poor laws, their works were usually not so obviously partisan as that of Nicholls or the Webbs. Two exceptions should be noted: important books with a clear ideological stance, both works of Marxist inspiration that treat the poor law as a key ingredient of the capitalist transformation of Britain's society, economy, and culture. Karl Polanyi's *The Great Transformation* (1944) and E. P. Thompson's *The Making of the English Working Class* (1963) are valuable in their own right, and should be read by anyone with a serious interest in the wider currents of social and economic change of which the poor laws were a part.

The remainder of this discussion on poor law historiography focuses on the various approaches that have been taken by scholars during the past half-century, without mentioning specific authors in the text. Leading representatives of each approach or interpretive school are cited, and sometimes discussed in the endnotes. From this, the reader should be able to gain an idea of the variety of approaches that have been taken to poor law history, and be able to assign to the most appropriate category those titles in the Bibliography section at the end of the book that are not mentioned in the endnotes to this chapter.

One obvious reason for the flowering of interest in poor law history during the last 50 years is the creation of the British Welfare State in the years following the Second World War. This dramatic change in government structure and policy led historians to inquire into the origins of the transformation. This gave rise, from the 1950s into the 1970s, to a considerable debate on the so-called 'Victorian Revolution in Government', with some historians denying that the change was as revolutionary as others claimed. Although many areas of government growth were addressed in this body of scholarship, the poor laws were central to almost everyone's account.[3] And most of the contributions to this body of scholarship strongly buttressed the notion of an almost inevitable, linear progression from the poor law to the Welfare State. Such 'Whiggish' notions of steady progression towards the present state of things has grown markedly out of fashion during the last couple of decades.

Historians have been particularly active in studying the economic effects of the poor laws. Since so much of the impetus for reforming the system in the eighteenth and nineteenth century was driven by fears of the negative effects of mandatory poor relief on England's economy, this is hardly surprising. Most historians interested in these issues have focused on specific topics, such as the laws of settlement (which determined the parish from which an indigent person could claim relief), the system of relief allowances-in-aid-of-wages, or the effect of the poor laws on economic development.[4] Because the period of the late eighteenth and early nineteenth centuries, when the poor law system was considered to be in crisis, coincides with the foundational age of classical economics, some writers have viewed the poor laws through the lens of intellectual history, examining closely the ideas of leading thinkers.[5] The late nineteenth century, another period of intellectual ferment with profound consequences for the poor laws, has also attracted scholarly attention. Here, the focus is quite different, dealing with the effects of modernizing movements in the social sciences (including economics), the 'New Liberalism', and the social settlement movement.[6]

Other writers have been primarily concerned with the political dimensions of poor law history. This has by no means been confined to parliamentary politics; there have been many studies of the complex political manoeuvrings at the local level as well. Some of the issues raised in these works are the degree to which the landed elite took an active part in poor law reform, the nature of their motives, and how much centralization of government was associated with major reforms like the New Poor Law of 1834.[7] Important studies of labourers' resistance to poor law reform are an important addition to the political literature.[8] There are also significant political studies of later periods as well, though the focus is quite different because England by the late nineteenth century had become highly urbanized. Studies of the urban poor law, and of new social programmes like pensions and unemployment insurance that had their major impact in cities, thus tend to concentrate on the late nineteenth and early twentieth centuries.[9]

Most of the foregoing studies are concerned chiefly with the activities of political and social elites, or with the day-to-day operation of the system by local officials. With the growing prominence of social history in the last 30 years, however, many writers began to look at the poor law from the 'bottom up', making the poor themselves the focus rather than those who legislated or administered. A proliferation of studies of women, children, family maintenance on poor relief, and the like have turned poor law scholarship decisively away from an earlier emphasis on political and administrative history.[10] Many recent authors are concerned to impart a sense of agency to the poor, an aspect most clearly developed by Lynn Hollen Lees in her impressive recent book, *The Solidarities of Strangers* (1998). More specialized works have also been written on particular aspects of poor relief, such as medical care, education, assisted emigration, lunacy, or vagrancy.[11] There have been a number of important studies of the workhouse, some of them applying postmodernist theories like that of Michel Foucault, according to which the workhouse is best viewed as part of the 'carceral archipelago' of modern society, designed to produce submission and conformity.[12] Another scholarly growth sector is in the relationship between the poor laws and charity, a topic virtually ignored until recently.[13]

The foregoing will, it is hoped, help the reader to place the subsequent chapters in some scholarly context. A narrative survey like this is built on the foundations of the secondary literature available to the author. A similar work written 20 years ago would very likely have had less to say on social historical issues in general, especially on women and children, and marginalized groups like vagrants and the insane. Administrative and political perspectives would have been dominant, and a 'Whiggish' sense of progression towards the Welfare State would have been evident. Relatively little attention would have been paid to the poor law's relation to philanthropy. And the poor would have been shown in a more passive light, except on those relatively few occasions when they engaged in violent or menacing resistance. One written 20 years from now will necessarily have a somewhat different, perhaps substantially different, configuration, because the author will be able to draw upon many new specialized studies, employing fresh perspectives and innovative methodologies. One of the great satisfactions of any historian is being involved in the continual reworking of old categories and paradigms, and the constant injection of new approaches to and interpretations of the past. This is especially true of the poor law historian, thanks to the large number of dedicated and creative scholars in the field. A word should be said about the terminology employed in this book. Readers may wonder about the switching between the singular 'poor law' and the plural 'poor laws', the latter appearing in the title and here and there throughout the text. Contemporaries tended to use both the singular and plural forms, and the correct usage often depends on context. Since the poor relief system was not created by a single law but rather by hundreds of enactments over several centuries, the plural seems altogether fitting. This is even more true when we consider that key aspects of poor relief were not statutory at all, but were 'laws' created at the local level by magistrates and other officials. On the other hand, in spite of this complexity, it is useful to think of all these disparate elements as components of a single system – the poor law – hence the appropriateness of the singular form. In the rest of the book, usage is tailored to the context, though in many cases, either form would be correct. Another term that is used, the 'Old Poor Law', came into usage after 1834, with the passage of the Poor Law Amendment Act (the 'New Poor Law'). Thus the term refers to any aspect of poor relief between the first Elizabethan enactment (1597) and the 1834 statute.[14]

Another matter that requires explanation is why only the English poor laws (which also applied to Wales) are treated in this book. What of Ireland and Scotland? To begin with, there was no Irish poor law until 1838. Before then, helping the destitute in that country took the form of either private almsgiving or the charitable distributions of the Catholic Church and other organizations. With the passage of the Irish Poor Law in 1838, Ireland did acquire a system of public relief, but one that was far more centralized than its English counterpart. It was also more draconian in its operations, with the dreaded workhouse as the only resort for those seeking public relief. In Scotland, there was not a truly public system in operation until 1845. While a 'Scottish Poor Law' had been in existence for centuries, it was really a structured distribution of charity to the poor through the Kirk (Church of Scotland) Sessions, with a seldom used back-up power of assessing local landowners if the voluntary donations proved inadequate. Elements of this system remained in place even after the passage of the Scottish Poor Law of 1845, so that there continued to be significant departures from relief policies in England. Because of major differences between the English poor law and the relief systems of Ireland and Scotland, which are in turn based on distinctive political, economic, religious, and cultural factors, a book on poor relief throughout the British Isles would have to be considerably longer than the present volume. Yet there were important points of intersection between the three systems, such as the vexing problem of how to deal with Irish and Scottish paupers in England, and the influence of Scottish practice on the English New Poor Law, and these are covered in the book.

2

THE POOR LAWS IN THE EIGHTEENTH CENTURY: CHANGING PATTERNS OF RELIEF IN A MATURING CAPITALIST SYSTEM

The Parochial Basis of the Old Poor Law

Tudor England, beset by myriad economic, political, religious, and diplomatic crises, grappled with frightening levels of privation and social disorder. A solution of sorts was finally fashioned at the end of Elizabeth's reign, when Parliament passed the Poor Law of 1597, amending it in 1601. While by no means the first parliamentary enactment on poor relief,[1] the Elizabethan Poor Law was the first to set up a mandatory system of publicly financed poor relief throughout England and Wales. It also established a basic administrative framework that persisted largely unchanged for two centuries. The parish was made the local unit of poor law administration and taxation, with relief and 'setting to work' of the poor in the hands of the churchwardens and overseers of the poor named annually by the local justices of the peace. In practice, the office usually went by rotation among the farmers and other householders of the middling rank, magistrates usually confirming the names submitted to them by parish vestries. Although each of the more than 15 000 parishes (townships in the North) was responsible for the maintenance of its own indigent, considerable difficulty arose in determining which parish was chargeable in certain cases. Whenever there was any doubt about a pauper's place of birth or residence, overseers attempted to reduce the burden of their own community's poor rates by shunting the applicant off to another parish. In 1662

9

Parliament attempted to deal with this problem by passing the Act of Settlement, which facilitated the return of paupers to their rightful parishes.[2] Removal to the parish of one's settlement, by the order of two magistrates, could be carried out against anyone not resident for 40 days or occupying premises worth £10 a year. Furthermore, removal could be carried out not only against actual paupers but those 'likely to be chargeable'. The statute was the beginning of the legislature's attempts to provide every man, woman, and child in England and Wales with a clearly defined legal settlement in one place and to establish the criteria for removal. Additional laws over the next 35 years modified the settlement code by adding additional 'heads of settlement', such as apprenticeship, being hired for a year, serving in a parish office, or paying poor rates.[3] Women acquired the settlement of their husbands, children that of their parents. In 1697, irremoveability was conferred on non-indigent sojourners bearing a certificate from their parish acknowledging responsibility for their maintenance. The purpose of these late seventeenth-century enactments was both to regulate labour migration and to reduce litigation between parishes. It was to prove far more successful with the former than the latter.

Once the terms and conditions of eligibility for poor relief were well understood, overseers seem to have proved quite adept at working the system to their advantage. Magistrates, however, refused to simply rubber-stamp a parish's application for an order of removal, often inquiring closely into a pauper's background and circumstances. In counties as different as Kent and Yorkshire, a considerable amount of magisterial time was devoted to removals,[4] suggesting that this was broadly true throughout the country. Less politically divided courts of quarter sessions once the Hanoverian dynasty was firmly established also meant that fewer magistrates' orders were overturned on appeal.[5] Thus, in spite of the absence of central government supervision and the widespread impression that eighteenth-century local government was inefficient, an effective mechanism for the surveillance and regulation of labour migration was clearly in place.[6]

Poorhouses and Workhouses

If the regulating of migration and hence the burden of the poor rates led to the refining of the settlement laws, the practical problems of relieving the settled poor led to the adoption of the workhouse. The

Poor Law of 1601 had expressed the need for 'necessary places of habitation' for 'poor impotent people', and it was through local experimentation in the seventeenth century that the first ratepayer-supported poorhouses and workhouses were developed. The most straightforward reason for their emergence was the problem of aged and impotent paupers unable to care for themselves. When possible, relatives were pressed to assume the obligation, another stipulation of the 1601 law. For those without nearby relations a parish residence of some kind was the answer, often a large cottage or small house capable of holding several paupers and whatever full- or part-time superintendents and caregivers might be required.

A very different reason for the creation of local workhouses was the perceived need for an institution for the able-bodied. This was in part a deterrent against the 'sturdy rogues' who, many believed, were all too willing to forsake work and throw themselves on the ratepayers. Here, the Elizabethan laws were cited, for the able-bodied were required to be 'set to work' by parish authorities. In practice, however, this had often proved too difficult and costly, especially in smaller rural parishes, requiring as it did gathering the requisite materials, organizing the work, providing supervision, and (often) acquiring or building a structure for these activities. It did prove possible in urban parishes and, eventually, in clusters of rural parishes. Isolated, sometimes short-lived experiments in certain districts from the 1630s broadened into more vigorous and sustained efforts beginning with Bristol workhouse in 1696. A number of other towns, chief among them Exeter, Hereford, Colchester, King's Lynn, Gloucester, and Plymouth, followed Bristol's example over the next couple of decades.[7]

For some, workhouses were seen as a device for harnessing idle labour and reforming character. Late seventeenth-century advocates of the workhouse like Matthew Hale and Josiah Child, after examining institutions in Holland and other countries, advocated unions of parishes, suggesting that the workhouses formed could turn a profit for the parishes.[8] Such schemes viewed the unemployed poor as a potential national resource; workers therefore needed only the proper organization to be made both productive and happy.[9] A generation of experience, however, proved that it was impossible to turn a profit from the sale of pauper-produced goods.[10] Moreover, by the early eighteenth century attitudes towards the poor were beginning to harden in some quarters, as reflected in the views of commentators like John Locke, Bernard Mandeville, and Daniel Defoe. Labourers, increasingly seen as lazy, shiftless, and dissolute, could only be kept to their tasks by the relentless pressure of necessity. England's mandatory system of poor relief was, therefore, potentially subversive of the wholesome discipline of the unfettered market. In such circumstances the deterrent aspect of the workhouse came to the fore, and seemed an effective safeguard against the utter breakdown of labour discipline.

With the spread of such ideas through the governing class, advocacy of the workhouse appeared in Parliament. An Act of 1723 empowered parishes to build workhouses or to contract paupers out to private institutions; indigent relief applicants refusing to enter could be denied all further parochial sustenance. In the words of the statute,

> in case any poor person or persons ... shall refuse to be lodged, kept, or maintained in such house or houses, such poor person or persons so refusing shall be put out of the book ... and shall not be entitled to ask or receive collection or relief from the churchwardens and overseers of the poor of the same parish, town, or township.[11]

Thus, more than a century before the New Poor Law, the legislature had articulated fully one of the two linchpins of the 1834 reform, the workhouse test. The implications of this policy shift are far-reaching. Under its operation, poor law officials no longer needed to inquire into an applicant's character or situation. An 'offer of the house' would function as a self-acting test of destitution, a doctrine in tune with an advancing free market ethos.

In practice, the operation of the 1723 law was more modest. To begin with, most parishes did not avail themselves of it. Furthermore, while the act provided for the union of parishes to build a workhouse, this was seldom done; most of the new workhouses were built by single parishes. While some towns did combine parishes for a common workhouse under the act, most of the new unions were established by local Acts of Parliament, as had been done at Bristol in 1696. The advantage to this method was that the union of parishes was vested with the privileges of a corporation.[12] Since most of the new structures under the act were erected by individual rural parishes, they often amounted to little more than poorhouses, housing a small number of mostly aged paupers. In such communities, institutional deterrence of the able-bodied obviously could not be effective, even if this had been paramount in the minds of the overseers, which seems doubtful. The pure workhouse test, devoid of personal considerations and questions of character, was an austere abstraction appealing mostly to intellectuals and theorists. An example is Thomas Alcock, a clergyman opposed to compulsory maintenance of the poor altogether, who asserted in a 1752 pamphlet that, if the poor laws were to continue, unions of parishes offered the prospect of more rigorous administration. This was due, Alcock claimed, to the ability to confront the pauper with the stark offer of admission to a well-regulated workhouse:

> For to be sent to the Poor-House, however well they might be taken care of there, would look like a Sort of Exile, and be deem'd some Hardship and Punishment: And many that now live lazily on Monthly Pay, in order to avoid going thither, would be content to labour, and fare harder, and make a Shift to subsist.[13]

Such views, uncommon in the mid-eighteenth century, would become more widespread by the early nineteenth.

'Farming Out' and Outdoor Relief

One aspect of the 1723 law that does appear to have been widely used was that allowing parishes to farm out the maintenance of their settled paupers to private contractors. This was a well-established administrative expedient for such local government functions as lighting streets, conveying vagrants, and transporting convicts.[14] Contractors could bid for the right to provide comprehensive relief (both indoor and outdoor), management of the parish's workhouse inmates, or for some particular function, such as managing pauper lunatics or children. Workhouse contracting was the most common method resorted to, giving rise to a number of private establishments, often at a considerable distance, and frequently ill-managed and oppressive.[15] Parish authorities seem to have been pleased with the system on the whole, as it offered both financial savings and lighter administrative burdens.

In the numerous parishes where the poor were not farmed out, and in others where such contracting was for only certain classes of paupers, overseers had their hands full. They were of course responsible for assessing and collecting the poor rates, itself often an onerous task. When it came to providing poor relief, their labours began with determining an applicant's settlement, and securing a removal order if the settlement was elsewhere. If the removal was contested, this might well entail considerable time giving testimony to the local magistrates or even to quarter sessions. Even when there was no doubt as to settlement, difficult decisions often had to be made. If the applicant was able-bodied, should he or she be given outdoor relief or offered the workhouse (assuming the parish had one)? This invariably involved calculations as to the relative costs of each course of action. In most cases it was found cheaper to grant outdoor relief, especially if the pauper had a wife and children. Even with single men, if the applicant's distress was seen to derive from seasonal unemployment, it was usually cheaper to tide him over with outdoor relief. This is why able-bodied men are few and far between in workhouse registers.

In most parishes, the largest number of recipients were the aged, infirm, and children unable to provide for themselves, and most of these were on outdoor relief. Usually the overseers ordered a weekly pension, often no more than a shilling, to be paid indefinitely. Thus the parish pay book contained a number of long-term recipients of smallish pensions, which certainly were insufficient for maintenance. In the northern counties, payments were even less.[16] Obviously, the parish was providing what was calculated to be a sum sufficient for maintenance provided that relatives, or perhaps neighbours or friends, lodged the pauper or provided additional support. Where it was known to overseers that aged applicants had children or other close relatives capable of supporting them, they applied for a maintenance order to the justices, who usually assented. An order by the Breconshire quarter sessions in 1767 is typical:

> Evan John Howell of the said Parish of Ystradgunlais Yeoman and Elizabeth his wife being poor Impotent and Aged and unable to maintain themselves and being now chargeable to the Inhabitants of the said Parish and it is appearing to this Court that John Evan their son of the same Parish is a Person of Ability and capable of maintaining his Father and Mother It is Ordered that he do pay into the Hands of the Churchwardens and Overseers of the Poor of the said Parish the Sum of One Shilling and Eight pence Weekly towards the support of his said Parents until further Orders.[17]

Applicants considered 'deserving' were sometimes provided with a few extras, such as clothing, fuel, and tobacco.[18] Kinship networks, well known to everyone in small rural communities, were an integral part of the process. In large towns, where the overseers were not acquainted with many of the applicants, identifying relatives who could be incorporated into the relief picture was far more problematic. Because parish records were incomplete and many have not survived, it is difficult to determine the percentage of the population in receipt of relief in the eighteenth century. While it varied considerably from place to place, and the south and east saw a larger percentage of people on relief than the north and west, it has been estimated that, on average, in any given five-year period, one in five inhabitants of a parish would apply for relief.[19]

Childbirth and Child-rearing

Children, or rather a complex array of issues starting with pregnancy and continuing through birth and child-rearing, posed a special challenge for poor law officials. For a married woman whose husband was on parish pay, an additional child often meant simply an increased allowance. Major difficulties arose, however, for unmarried women. Once they were with child, every effort was made by overseers and magistrates to determine paternity, and hence financial responsibility. An elaborate body of 'bastardy' law consumed a good deal of official and judicial business. Most people took a dim view of illegitimacy, though an early seventeenth-century law that had stipulated a one-year sentence to the house of correction for 'every lewd woman which shall have any bastard which may be chargeable to the parish', seems to have become little used.[20] Although they usually no longer had to suffer incarceration, pregnant single women were still treated brutally by officials. Overseers often bribed women to go elsewhere to deliver their children. Sometimes they were abducted and dumped in another parish when their time drew near. Of course, such desperate expedients merely encouraged further litigation between parishes.

Once the child was born, it 'belonged' to the parish unless its paternity could be determined. This led to badgering of mothers by both overseers and magistrates to disclose the father's name. If they were successful, an affiliation order could then be issued on the man, requiring him to pay a regular amount to reimburse the parish for the child's maintenance. If the man denied paternity, it could lead to appeals and further judicial business and expense. The parish authorities were chiefly interested in reducing the burden on the ratepayers, and only secondarily in trying to enforce communal moral standards. Throughout the eighteenth century, moralists increasingly denounced the corrupting tendencies of the bastardy laws. Chief among these were the inducement to blackmail, lying, and worst of all, female wantonness.[21]

In many instances, parishes did find themselves saddled with the maintenance of bastard children and, as always, sought the cheapest solution. Boarding out to a foster family or admission to the workhouse were two options, but both courses of action were sometimes more expensive than apprenticing a child. Strictly speaking, apprenticeship only became an option when a child approached adolescence, though informal arrangements with farmers and other local employers were often entered into when a child was younger. Parishes advertised for apprenticeships and were quite willing to pay several pounds to those willing to assume the burdens (and of course profit from the children's labour). Very little inquiry was made into the character and circumstances of those offering apprenticeships to parish children, nor was any follow-up conducted to ensure compliance with the terms of the agreement. The corruption and brutality attendant upon such a scheme of things led one critic in 1732 to rail against 'the very bad practice in parish officers who to save expense are apt to ruin children by putting them out as early as they can to any sorry masters that will take them, without any concern for their education and welfare'.[22] This was but one of many charges against the system of parochial administration that would lead to demands for a major overhaul.

A particularly glaring evil in regard to public provision for children became evident in London. The large, unsanitary workhouses of the metropolis proved lethal to children, leading the philanthropist Jonas Hanway to champion their cause. He compiled statistical evidence showing that nearly half the infants admitted to London workhouses in the 1750s died before their second birthday. This revelation led to Hanway's Act of 1762, which required the boarding out of London parish children in the suburbs or countryside.[23] Hanway's successful campaign shows the overlapping of charity and poor law reform, especially with regard to children. Throughout the eighteenth century, philanthropists shared poor law reformers' desire to strengthen the sinews of national power. A mercantilist, pre-Malthusian concern to foster an increase of a healthy population and thus augment the labour force and military is a marked feature of the era. Institutions like Thomas Coram's Foundling Hospital and Hanway's Marine Society, in addition to saving lives and reforming character, also sought to add to the number of 'useful hands', especially in the merchant marine and navy.[24] At least among poor law reformers, this attitude would change dramatically by the early nineteenth century, as growing fears of a 'surplus population' became dominant.

Medical Care

The Elizabethan Poor Law had specified that care was to be provided for the 'Lame, Impotent, Old, and Blind', and medical care was therefore an area of major concern for parish officials. In addition to the chronic diseases of old age, there were the shorter-term conditions afflicting able-bodied labourers and children, as well as the necessity of providing such services as midwifery. Even if they had not been statutorily obliged to provide care, it was clearly in the interest of the ratepayers that the able-bodied be returned to productivity as quickly as possible. Local doctors, 'nurses', midwives, and bonesetters entered into parochial contracts to provide the needed treatments, sometimes on a case-by-case basis, sometimes annually for all the settled poor of the parish. Thus in Woodstock, Oxfordshire, in 1758, the vestry agreed 'to give Mrs. Southern two guineas and a half for the cure of James Smith's leg; one guinea to be paid immediately and the other guinea and a half so soon as we are fully satisfied of ye cure'.[25] Wooden legs, trusses, leeches, even a violin for a blind boy so he could earn a living figure among the things and treatments covered by some parishes. A stay in a hospital or infirmary (neither of which necessarily provided the most salubrious environment in the eighteenth century) was also sometimes sanctioned.[26] While towns with infirmaries were in a position to provide more extensive services than the usual small parochial outlays for practitioners, medicines, and special diets, a recent study of the Shrewsbury infirmary suggests limited use by poor law authorities.[27] As population grew during the latter half of the eighteenth century, it became more and more common for vestries to resort to medical contracting to cover all settled indigent parishioners.[28]

A related area requiring the overseers' attention was mental illness. A feeble-minded person, typically listed as an 'Idiot' in the parish books, was usually looked after locally by a caretaker hired by the parish. Dangerous 'Lunatics' were often thought to require institutionalization, which generally meant removal to a distant facility. Bethlem (or Bedlam) in London was the major hospital for the insane, but during the latter half of the century about 50 institutions were established, many of them catering to paupers.[29] While some of these provided a modicum of decent care, the general standard was rather low. Still, a mentally ill pauper was apt to be better provided for in a specialist institution. Because of the relatively high charges of most asylums, many lunatics were kept in the parish workhouse, often chained so that they would not disrupt the staff and other inmates.[30] Thus at Ashbury, Berkshire, parish officials paid local workmen 'to help chain Mary Hays'.[31] It is hard to avoid the conclusion that the typical parish workhouse of the eighteenth century, with its lack of wards for different categories of pauper and the total absence of professional staff, was a dismal, often brutal abode. Even where treatment was more generous, with decent dietaries and extras for the aged, this was as apt to be the result of inefficiency and corruption as it was to spring from any humanitarian impulse.

Attempts to Broaden the Administrative Area

The foregoing account will give some idea as to the operation of the poor laws in the middle of the eighteenth century. It was an intensely localized system, with major control over the lives of the indigent lodged in the hands of parochial small fry in thousands of small districts. Oversight by magistrates was by no means negligible, and where local justices took an active hand, intervention, frequently on behalf of the poor, was not uncommon. Nonetheless, Parliament ignored the poor laws most sessions, and it was only with difficulty that legislators could be stirred to action. There was no single glaring incident that roused them. Some were affected by the steady accretion of publicized abuses of paupers and the misuse of public monies. Others were moved by a perception that poor relief recipients, rather than being abused, were in fact coddled. Those willing to consider reforming the poor laws were a disparate lot, ranging from protectors of the poor to champions of the ratepayers, or – as the latter would no doubt have preferred – advocates of discipline and morality. Virtually all agreed, however, that any reform would have to expand the area of management beyond the parish.

Some bold reformers wished to adopt no smaller an area than the county. Thus in 1751 Henry Fielding, the novelist and London police magistrate, advocated one enormous workhouse for the whole of Middlesex. The proposed institution would have been in fact a combined workhouse and prison, capable of holding no fewer than 5000 paupers and 1000 convicts.[32] That his proposal appeared in his *Enquiry into the Causes of the Late Increase of Robberies* shows the close connection that some reformers made between paupers and criminals.[33] Although other reformers periodically suggested the county as the natural administrative unit, most Englishmen were unwilling to countenance such a major overhaul, preferring more moderate reforms that would maintain some semblance of localism.

As we have seen, various local Acts of Parliament, starting with Bristol in 1696, had grouped parishes into unions for workhouse purposes. The 1723 statute sought to facilitate such unions of parishes, but most of the workhouses built under its provisions were by individual parishes. One of the most persistent champions of further reform was William Hay, MP, who repeatedly urged the substitution of the county, hundred, or some other area for the parish. In 1735, he succeeded in convincing the House of Commons to pass a series of resolutions approving the principle of unions of parishes capable of supporting large workhouses. These establishments would not only be havens for the aged, infirm, and orphans but also places where the able-bodied could be set to work. However, a bill incorporating these features presented by Hay in the following session failed to pass, though it did get through the second reading and committee stage.[34]

The issue languished for the next decade and a half. When it resurfaced, the initiative once again (and far more effectively) lay with local forces. In certain parts of the country, notably East Anglia and Shropshire, landowners began moving vigorously to group parishes for workhouse purposes. While this might appear to be simply a return to the local act process used early in the century, this time the incorporations were in rural districts rather than towns, and the lead was taken by country gentlemen. The Suffolk hundreds of Carlford and Colneis were aggregated in 1756. Over the next 23 years, nine other unions of parishes were formed, which accounted for about half the parishes in the county. The movement spread to neighbouring Norfolk, but seemed to lose momentum as the poor displayed a marked resistance to the more restrictive outdoor relief policies pursued by the incorporations. Elite opinion in the county also appears to have been divided.[35] Nonetheless, the incorporated hundreds of East Anglia were a distinctive feature of the eighteenth-century poor law. Their sumptuous workhouses, called houses of industry, provided ample dietaries and generally humane treatment.[36] These 'Pauper Palaces', as critics dubbed them, persisted into the post-1834 regime, though of course their generous proclivities would be trimmed by the severe regulations of the New Poor Law.

In administrative terms, one of the most striking features of the poor law incorporations of the era was the transfer of authority away from parish overseers to elected and appointed guardians of the poor. There was an obvious concern to vest control of poor relief in more capable – which is to say socially superior – hands. While the Elizabethan law had stipulated that overseers were to be chosen from the 'substantial house-holders', in practice those of superior station had 'preferred to pay a fine rather than undertake so troublesome a task'.[37] Overseers, drawn from the ranks of local farmers and tradesmen, were believed to lack the requisite judgement and perspective to conduct wise administration of the poor laws. Taking their place in the newly formed incorporations were men of a superior stamp, drawn chiefly from the landed gentry, the upper ranks of the tenant farmers, and the magistracy. The Flegg incorporation in Norfolk, formed by a local Act of Parliament in 1775, was typical. In addition to JPs, those occupying land of at least £80 in rateable value, or possessing an estate worth at least £30 in one of the incorporated hundreds or worth £200 anywhere in the county, were qualified to act as guardians.[38]

While rural incorporations such as those in East Anglia (as well as Shropshire and the Isle of Wight) were the only practical results of the reform campaign during the period, the national discourse on the failings of the parochial system continued. A host of pamphleteers assailed the shortcomings and misdeeds of overseers, sometimes on the grounds of their alleged softness on cunning paupers. Pointing to the success of the East Anglian incorporations, Samuel Cooper in 1763 advocated the establishment of 'hundred houses' throughout the kingdom. In 1760, Josiah Tucker made a suggestion that anticipates the principle adopted by the New Poor Law in 1834: creating poor law unions by combining all parishes within a six-mile radius of each market town.[39] In other pamphlets, every variety of administrative district from the county to the hundred was proposed, as well as every funding means from compulsory assessments to charitable donations to lotteries and tontine schemes.[40] In 1764, Dr Richard Burn, a Westmorland rector and author of an influential legal manual for magistrates, weighed in with his *History of the Poor Laws*. Burn's history, the first of its kind, was a vehicle for critiquing the ideas of his contemporaries as well as for suggesting his own reforms. He declared the county to be far too large and unwieldy a district to ever find favour with country gentlemen. Favouring the hundred as the unit of administration, he called for the replacement of parish officers by a salaried general overseer named by the justices for each hundred.[41] Most subsequent reformers tended to agree with Burn that, in addition to expanding the administrative area, some professionalizing of poor relief services was essential.

Thomas Gilbert's Reforms

In the closing years of the American Revolutionary War, national attention again was directed to reform of the poor laws. The prospect of demobilized soldiers and sailors returning to the labour market,[42] coupled with certain structural changes in the economy attendant upon the enclosure movement and the early stages of industrialization, imparted a new sense of urgency. Thomas Gilbert, MP for Lichfield, presented an important bill to the House of Commons in 1782. Patterned closely after an earlier bill of his that had narrowly failed to pass in 1765, it provided for a major overhaul of the local administrative system of relief. Parishes, by a vote of two-thirds of their major landowners and ratepayers, were empowered to join together in poor law unions for the purpose of building and maintaining a workhouse. In these Gilbert unions, overseers were to be superseded by a magistrate-appointed paid guardian in each parish, chosen from a list submitted by the parishioners. Most controversially, able-bodied labourers were excluded from the union workhouse, which was to lodge only the aged, impotent, and children. The parish guardian was to find work for the unemployed able-bodied; failing that, the parish was required to provide outdoor relief. Once the bill passed, parishes seemed slow to avail themselves of it, and Gilbert's attempt in 1786 to make the law mandatory failed. Nevertheless, the pace of permissive adoptions of the law picked up after the turn of the century, and by the eve of the New Poor Law, 924 parishes, almost all of them rural, had combined themselves into 67 Gilbert Act unions. These were entirely in the East, South-east, and Midlands.[43] Thus by the end of the eighteenth century there were two sets of largely rural poor law unions in existence: one created by the local act process, the other under the terms of Gilbert's Act. Both were created by permissive legislation; neither was subject to central government superintendence. In this, they reflected a new kind of localism, albeit one considerably expanded from the original parochial base. In both cases, the authority of parish overseers had been removed and discretionary power was lodged, in effect, in the hands of the magistrates, country gentlemen, and better-off tenant farmers of the district.

In spite of his inability to get a compulsory version of his 1782 Act through Parliament in 1786, Gilbert did manage to get two other important bills enacted that year. One measure required overseers throughout the country to report poor law expenditures for the years 1783–85, thus providing the first national database of relief statistics that might be used by subsequent reformers. These 'Gilbert returns' were to be frequently cited in future sessions. A companion measure required ministers and churchwardens to provide information on all parochial charities, indicating how close poor law and philanthropy were linked in the minds of some reformers.[44] The indefatigable Gilbert returned to the fray in 1787, this time with a bill that would have established something like county-wide poor relief in England and Wales. His scheme called for relief to be in the hands of paid district agents, superintended by district committees meeting once a month and county committees meeting once a quarter. Both committees were to be drawn from the upper classes. Cries of protests from around the country led to the dropping of the bill, but it had its supporters, including a visionary Lancashire country gentleman who saw it as a stepping stone to a truly national system of relief: 'The Poor would then be supported out of a National purse, [and] the whole Kingdom would be but as one Parish, where every Englishman had the same right to a settlement, as to the rights of a subject.'[45]

Open and Close Parishes

One thing that was not changed by Gilbert's Act of 1782, even in districts that chose to adopt it, was the parochial basis of financial assessment. For the purpose of building a workhouse, each parish in a Gilbert union was assessed according to its rateable value. When it came to operating and maintenance costs, however, the assessment was based on the number of paupers each parish had in the workhouse. This made a crucial difference in the amount of poor rates each parish had to pay, for the number of paupers differed markedly from one parish to the next. The number of paupers in a parish was in proportion to the size of the labouring population residing there. Parishes with fewer resident workers tended to have fewer paupers and hence lower poor rates. One determinant of labourers' residential patterns was the division of landownership. So-called close parishes in which the land was owned by one or only a few could limit the number of resident labourers; open parishes, with a considerable number of small landowners, found this difficult. Many poor law writers in the eighteenth century commented adversely on major landowners pulling down cottages. As Roger North complained in his 1753 *Discourse on the Poor*:

> It is another very great destruction of People, as well as an Impediment to the Recruit of them, that Gentlemen of late years, have taken up an Humour of Destroying their Tenements and Cottages, whereby they make it impossible that Mankind should inhabit upon their Estates. This is done sometimes barefaced, because they harbour the Poor that are a charge to the Parish.[46]

Large landowners (or their major tenants) who could control the size of their parishes' populations by such means had an obvious advantage in terms of poor rate assessments. A labourer forced into adjacent parishes might still have a settlement in the place whence he was evicted, in which case he was often provided with non-resident relief when unemployed. Nonetheless, over time, other heads of settlement such as hiring, apprenticeship, bastard children, and so on, tended to work to the disadvantage of open parishes. As such communities became increasingly pauperized, the greater size, visibility, and perceived turbulence and immorality of their poor fuelled the debates on the poor laws. It is important not to make too much of the contrast between open and close parishes. Many parishes could not be so tidily classified. Moreover, many major landowners and tenant farmers were not disposed to pull down cottages. Nor is it likely that most country gentlemen were motivated first and foremost by a desire to reduce their own and their tenants' poor rates. A strong paternalistic commitment, not just to the poor, but to the wider community, was an important value for many country gentlemen, both as landowners and as magistrates. The spread of humanitarianism, though sometimes exaggerated,[47] also played a part. Simple inertia and lack of concern were at work with others. The point is that a simplistic notion of the primacy of economic interest can obscure a much more complex and interesting array of attitudes towards the poor among the upper classes.

The Effects of Quickening Economic Change

The reform movements discussed above were being played out against a backdrop of wider economic change: the enclosure movement, the decline of cottage industry, and the beginnings of industrialization. While these played an important role in changing the patterns of pauperism and the relative burdens of poor rates, one must be careful. To begin with, there were wide regional disparities, some districts remaining comparatively unaffected until well into the nineteenth century. Furthermore, even where change was under way, older values, attitudes, and policies sometimes proved remarkably durable. With these caveats in mind, it is possible to discern some elements of economic development that were having a marked, and in some cases catastrophic effect on the poor.

The population expanded far more rapidly in the latter half of the eighteenth century, increasing by nearly 50 per cent to a figure of 8.7 million by 1801. While there is evidence of an even faster rate of growth in industry and agriculture, the distribution of the fruits of this increase was extremely uneven. Moreover, the changes wrought in production adversely affected labourers' standards of living. The decline of cottage production of textiles, for example, removed an important source of income in some districts. The advance of capitalist methods of agriculture tended to the proletarianization of farm workers. Previously, labourers were hired by the year (thus gaining a settlement) and frequently housed (when single) with their employers. Now they were becoming ordinary wage workers, and had to shift for themselves in regard to housing. Furthermore, the ability to raise part of their own produce was severely curtailed by the effects of the enclosure movement, which eradicated commons' rights for labourers.[48]

Employment opportunities in the textile industry and other new urban enterprises offered the prospect of some relief to overcrowded rural parishes with large relief rolls. However, many settled paupers were loath to give up the security represented by the weekly parish pension. An effort to encourage pauper migration was made by some rural parishes like Hanwell, Middlesex, where the overseers called a meeting of all the paupers to inform them of openings for children in a worsted spinning mill in Nottinghamshire. Even though families were threatened with being removed from the pension list, the great majority refused to send their children away.[49] Most paupers were determined not to break up their families; they also knew their rights under the poor law and the likelihood that they would prevail in any appeal to magistrates. While there was a certain amount of voluntary migration by young unmarried workers or entire families to the new factory towns in the North and Midlands, conditions there were far from secure.

Unemployed workers in industrial communities found it difficult to gain settlements and had to petition their rural parish of origin for non-resident relief, though informal arrangements by which the parish of settlement remitted payments to an industrial township became increasingly common.[50] Failing that, they could be transported back to their parish by the town overseers. While sojourning labourers bearing certificates were exempt from removal, a recent study has revealed that these tended to be issued within a rather circumscribed geographic area.[51] The cumulative effect of these economic changes was not only a sense of precariousness and a decline in living standards, but an eroding of the social fabric. As patriarchal relations and accompanying patterns of deference withered with the growth of a capitalist market, relations between social classes hardened.

The 1790s: Dearth, War, and the Spectre of Revolution

In the final decade of the century a combination of adverse factors produced a sense of crisis in poor law management. Bad weather, bad harvests, the political and social upheavals across the Channel, and the outbreak of war with revolutionary France in 1793, exacerbated poor relief problems. Through the 1780s and early 1790s there had been relative prosperity and stable food prices. With growing unemployment, rising population, and higher food prices, poor rates soared. In 1776 the total poor relief burden had been just over £1.5 million; by 1803 it was more than £4 million. The average expenditure per head of population over these years went from 4s. 4d. to 8s. 11d.[52] To the issue of growing poor rates and a supposed decline of the work ethic among the poor was added a fear of their revolutionary potential. Even though landowners' incomes were generally on the rise, political instability and social disorder haunted the British upper classes. There was a marked conservative turn, even among many radical Whigs, and the repressive policies of the government of William Pitt the Younger drew widespread support. While endorsing measures to stifle dangerous radicalism and 'atheism', however, many members of Britain's elite sought to shore up the tattered social fabric through a revival of Christian spirit and the adoption of ameliorative policies at the local level. In poor relief, this translated into a marked tendency of magistrates, more of them than ever from the ranks of the Anglican clergy,[53] to stabilize conditions by supporting 'generous' relief policies. These liberal proclivities were also reflected in Parliament. At both the national and local level, policies were adopted that, according to later critics, had the effect of fuelling further demoralization and pauperization.

Parliamentary measures of the 1790s focused on two aspects of poor relief, workhouses and the law of settlement, both of which were markedly liberalized. By a 1795 statute, forced removal to the parish of settlement was not allowed until a person actually applied for relief. This reversed the long-standing law by which anyone likely to become chargeable could be removed. Many magistrates were inclined to implement this new measure. In August 1795, the justices of a Kent petty sessions ordered the parishes in their division to relieve the poor irrespective of settlements.[54] The following year saw an act explicitly forbidding the use of workhouses for the able-bodied. This was a repudiation of the 1723 Act, which, in the words of the new law,

> has been found to be inconvenient and oppressive, inasmuch as it often prevents an industrious poor person from receiving such occasional relief as is best suited to the peculiar case of such poor person and inasmuch as in certain cases it holds out conditions of relief injurious to the comfort and domestic situation and happiness of such poor persons.[55]

The author of the 1796 measure, Sir William Young, expressed his paternalism and strong belief in an organic hierarchical social order in a pamphlet published shortly afterward. By the system of forcing the able-bodied into workhouses, especially under the system of contracting out, 'the old chain which held together the country gentleman, the farmer, and the peasant, in the relations of magistrate, overseer, and pauper, is broken and rendered nugatory'.[56]

This pamphlet was addressed to Pitt, who had already signalled his intention to bring forth a comprehensive poor law bill. Young pointed out to the Prime Minister that Gilbert's Act of 1782 was founded on 'true and just principles', expressing the hope that it would be more widely adopted.[57] Thus, in addition to keeping workhouses for the aged, infirm, and children, and relaxing the law of settlement, the hope was for a measure expanding the administrative area considerably beyond the parish. In the event, Pitt's bill failed to secure passage. With his attention fixed on directing the British war effort and suppressing domestic radicalism, the premier was unable to devote the time and energy needed to produce an effective bill. The measure he introduced in 1796 was scarcely debated in the House of Commons, but drew considerable fire from local authorities throughout the country. It followed Gilbert's scheme in turning over control of poor relief to salaried county guardians. It would also have provided legislative sanction to a practice that was rapidly spreading: supplementing inadequate wages out of parochial poor relief funds.[58] The bill also called for a national poor law budget and regular reports from local authorities to the Privy Council,[59] centralizing elements that were responsible for much of the criticism directed against it.

The Allowance System

One of the policies Pitt's unsuccessful bill endorsed was the rapidly growing practice of granting allowances-in-aid-of-wages (hereafter referred to simply as allowances) that enabled labourers and their families to sustain themselves during difficult times. Lagging wages and increased food prices meant that more and more families, even with the principal breadwinners in full employment, were unable to make ends meet. With food prices on the rise, wages in the South and East were stuck at a rate of about 8s. 6d. a week.[60] Many parochial officials and justices viewed allowances as an acceptable solution to the dearth of the late 1790s. The alternative would have been to raise wages, an action that might have proved awkward to reverse once food prices had gone down. Another solution, Samuel Whitbread's minimum wage bill of 1795, though supported by the Whigs and by some magistrates, was considered too sweeping. Savagely attacked by Pitt, it was in fact the catalyst for announcing his own legislative plans.[61] In spite of rejecting both Pitt's and Whitbread's national schemes, however, elites in the countryside were attempting to stabilize poor relief and provide a more secure base of support for the labouring classes in their own localities.

While Pitt's and Whitbread's measures foundered on the shoals of county loyalties and other forms of localism, there was considerable support among the upper classes for raising wages. Wages, however, were paid in the countryside mainly by tenant farmers who were decidedly opposed to increasing their labourers' pay. While magistrates could still set wages under the Statute of Artificers of 1563, this power had fallen into disuse, and most were unwilling to revive it. Given this impasse, it was quite natural for gentry and clergy, in their capacity as magistrates, to effect the necessary increase in family income by ordering overseers to grant relief in addition to wages. Parish pay had of course always borne some relationship to the cost of living. In a rough and ready way, overseers and magistrates had generally taken into account the price of provisions, heating, and rent, as well as the size of a labourer's family in calculating the amount of outdoor relief. What is new about the 1790s is that this became much more precise and formalized, adopted across entire petty sessions districts and even counties, and enshrined in printed tables of benefits. Furthermore, under the 1795 Act it was much more difficult to compel the able-bodied to enter the workhouse, and thus many more paupers had to be accommodated by the allowance system, at least in those districts where the system became prevalent.

The most famous of all the local systematized allowance scales developed in the final decade of the century was in Berkshire. In May 1795, 20 justices, 7 of whom were clergymen, met at the Pelican Inn at Speenhamland, near Newbury. Forced to deal with unprecedented pauperism and the clear inability of labourers' families to subsist on the going wages of the area, the magistrates drew up an elaborate sliding scale of poor relief benefits:

> When the gallon loaf of second flour weighing 8 lb. 11 oz. shall cost 1s., then every poor and industrious man shall have for his support 3s. weekly, either produced by his own or his family's labour or an allowance from the poor rates, and for the support of his wife and every other of the family 1s. 6d.
>
> When the gallon loaf shall cost 1s. 4d., then every poor and industrious man shall have 4s. weekly for his own, and 1s. 10d. for the support of every other of his family.
>
> And so on in proportion as the price of bread rises or falls (that is to say) 3d. to the man and 1d. to every other of the family on every penny which the loaf shall rise above a shilling.[62]

This was later worked up in tabular fashion so that overseers had only to consult a printed table to determine the precise amount of the family dole for any combination of bread price, wage level, and family size.[63] The Speenhamland scale was by no means the first such device adopted by magistrates; a group of Dorsetshire justices had developed a similar one in 1792. Elaborate tables of relief had already been worked up by magistrates in Buckinghamshire and Oxfordshire. Even in Berkshire, there appear to have been earlier scales.[64] It was the action taken in May 1795, however, that became the most widely known, emulated, and castigated. Often, it was referred to as if it were an Act of Parliament: the 'Speenhamland bread law'. By the early nineteenth century, the 'Speenhamland System' was increasingly used as a term of iniquity by reformers who sought a complete cessation of allowances to the able-bodied.

In an important sense, the Speenhamland System rapidly became a bogeyman whose true dimensions were more modest than reformers and many later historians were willing to acknowledge. Far from being a pervasive form of poor relief, it was applied only in certain districts and only at certain times of the year. More common in the East and South than in the rest of the country, it was used chiefly in the slack season of the agrarian year. The problem of seasonal unemployment had become exacerbated with the decline of cottage industry and allotments for labourers to raise some of their own food, as well as the loss of commons rights attendant upon enclosure.[65] Changes in agricultural production also provided less employment for women in grain-producing areas.[66] Again, these factors were unevenly distributed; enclosure, for example, had far less impact in the North and West. The implicit labour contract in the grain-growing South and East featured seasonal layoffs and outdoor relief, while that in the livestock-farming North and West was based on full employment throughout the year.[67] In another sense, however, Speenhamland was indeed critical, both because it reflected how 'modernizing' market conditions impacted upon the poor laws, and because it was a major factor in the grand clash of ideas about poverty and poor relief that marked the 1790s. The actual effects of Speenhamland may have been less demoralizing and pauperizing than many critics claimed, and this issue will be taken up in the next chapter. However, because the late eighteenth-century Speenhamland critics played a powerful role in framing the debate leading up to the New Poor Law of 1834, we must now consider their contributions.

Economists, Philosophers, and Moralists

Britain's economy in the eighteenth century was undergoing major structural changes. Starting in the late seventeenth century, banking and financial institutions became increasingly complex and responsive to the needs of investors and entrepreneurs. By 1770, a significant percentage of the middle and upper classes were engaged in buying and selling of stocks and other financial instruments. With Britain's far-flung trade network and naval power, transactions of goods and securities had achieved a global reach. The owners of landed estates were not backward in this new economic activity, and agriculture itself became more and more a capitalist enterprise. As the acquisitive, individualist, and profit-maximizing values of a market economy reached ever deeper into the culture, older forms of economic and social organization were challenged. Values and institutions seen as impediments to the free flow of capital and labour became the targets of modernizing reformers. Thus not only did mercantilism, with its emphasis on government direction of economic activity, come in for sharp criticism, but so too did the poor laws. While a mandatory assessment for maintaining the nation's poor had been attacked earlier, it had usually been on moral grounds. The political economists of the late eighteenth century, however, often couched their arguments in the language of dispassionate scientific observation.

Adam Smith, professor at the University of Glasgow and a leading figure of the Scottish Enlightenment, produced the most influential analysis of the economy and provided a mode of analysis eagerly taken up by others. His masterly *Wealth of Nations* (1776) demolished the intellectual underpinnings of mercantilism, and was a clarion call to the sweeping away of all obstacles to free trade. In his wide-ranging consideration of all forms of economic activity, Smith naturally turned his attention to the poor laws. Unlike many later political economists, Smith had no quarrel with a system of mandatory public relief. He confined his treatment of the subject to the law of settlement, condemning its restriction of labour mobilty and inhibiting of wage rates. More importantly for Smith, the forcible removal of men and women involved no less a matter than fundamental human rights: 'To remove a man who has committed no misdemeanour from the parish where he chuses to reside, is an evident violation of natural liberty and justice.'[68] Furthermore, as other sections of the *Wealth of Nations* make clear, he was a consistent advocate of the labouring class, believing that the powers inherent in those who employed labour were often wielded in a collusive fashion against the best interests of society.[69] Few of his immediate successors were to exhibit the same concerns. Using Smith's mode of analysis but jettisoning his concern that it should be used to improve the lot of the poor, they were responsible for making economics into what came to be called the 'dismal science'.

An example of the new breed of economic writer is Joseph Townsend. A clergyman as well as an eminent geologist, Townsend published his *Dissertation on the Poor Laws* in 1786. From the outset, the author adopted a negative tone towards the poor, who, he declared, were under a decree of nature 'to fulfil the most servile, the most sordid, and the most ignoble offices in the community'. As to the measures designed to maintain them in times of distress, these, according to Townsend, did 'little more than give encouragement to idleness and vice'. The poor laws, 'so beautiful in theory, promote the evils they mean to remedy, and aggravate the distress they were intended to relieve'.[70] The only solution, for Townsend and the increasing numbers who considered their views to be grounded in science, was the abolition of mandatory assessment and relief. Only then could the wholesome discipline of the market take effect, bringing the poor face to face with harsh economic realities and the necessity of developing the qualities of character to survive.

An even better known critic, but one with an equally severe view of poor relief, was Edmund Burke. Although thought of chiefly as a philosophical conservative and arch-opponent of the French Revolution, Burke was an ardent disciple of Adam Smith. However, like Townsend, in regard to the poor laws he inverted Smith's sympathetic approach. He also continued the process of further abstracting the lower orders into a commodity, stripped of all individuality. Already the most eloquent intellectual bulwark of Pitt's counter-revolutionary policies, Burke turned his attention to poor relief in November 1795. In his '*Thoughts and Details on Scarcity*', he vigorously embraced an unfettered free-trade capitalism and denounced the woeful error of the allowance system. Nor was Speenhamland simply an aberration of an otherwise wholesome law: mandatory relief itself was iniquitous and destructive of social order. Moreover, a mandatory system deadened the charitable spirit, which he viewed as vital to maintaining social cohesion.[71] In spite of the poor laws' two-century history, Burke was unwilling to accord them the sort of 'prescriptive' right given to other institutions of long standing, such as aristocracy. His fear of the labouring classes, fuelled by the spectacle of bloody revolution in France and its all too likely exporting to England, made Burke a leading advocate of harshness towards the poor. That an ardent defender of the traditional social order should have so firmly discountenanced one of the hallowed underpinnings of that order – the poor laws – is one of many moral and intellectual anomalies of this turbulent age.[72]

The fullest treatment of the poor laws in the 1790s was Sir Frederic Morton Eden's *State of the Poor* (1797). Eden was a political economist whose views reflected both Smith's and Burke's critiques, yet he departed from them on key elements. Although not an extreme advocate of laissez-faire economics, he had a much more negative view of the poor laws than Smith. Whereas Smith had at least implicitly endorsed mandatory relief, confining his criticism to the settlement laws, Eden chose to base his attack on the wages-fund theory, which he derived from Smith's *Wealth of Nations*. This was a much more fundamental and devastating criticism. The finite amount which society at any point had available in its wages-fund was drained by the poor rates: 'To invest a public body with a part of that stock, which, for the sake of profit, sets the greater part of useful labour in motion, seems indeed repugnant to the sound principles of political economy.'[73] Thus, according to Eden, there was an inverse relationship between poor rates and wages. More ominously, the trend of rapidly rising poor relief threatened the very existence of the wages-fund, and general pauperization seemed the inescapable outcome of existing poor law policies.[74] Eden pronounced himself a disciple of Burke, though he was reluctant to embrace Burke's abolitionist position, preferring to keep a trimmed-down poor law while strongly encouraging Friendly Societies and other forms of working-class self-help.[75] Citing the arguments in Burke's *Reflections on the French Revolution* (1790), Eden pointed out that the long history of the poor laws had rendered relief a prescriptive right of the poor. As with monarchy, aristocracy, the Church, and other prescriptive institutions, the proper and prudent approach with admitted abuses was to reform and correct, not to abolish altogether. Yet, given the sweeping nature of Eden's critique, any reformation based on it was bound to be a drastic one.

As far as long-term influence on poor law policy is concerned, undoubtedly the most important of the economic writers of the late eighteenth century is Thomas Malthus. A clergyman and later professor of history and political economy, Malthus made a theory of inexorable population increase central to his attack on the poor laws. In the *Essay on Population* (1798), he set forth with icy logic and mathematical exactitude his 'irrefutable' doctrine: that human passions tended to augment the number of people at a geometric rate of increase, while the best that could be hoped for in the food supply was at an arithmetic rate of increase. By guaranteeing subsistence to all, the poor laws deeply aggravated this already melancholy prospect. The most pernicious policy was the allowance system, by which the amount of relief was pegged to family size, offering a powerful inducement to early, improvident marriages and reckless breeding. But the whole poor law system, even without family allowances, was for Malthus a disastrous interference with the wholesome if depressing dictates of nature. With little hope that the poor laws could be repealed, he wished they had never been enacted:

> The evil is perhaps gone too far to be remedied, but I feel little doubt in my own mind that if the poor-laws had never existed, though there might have been a few more instances of very severe distress, yet that aggregate mass of happiness among the common people would have been much greater than it is at present.[76]

Malthus's book was couched as a reply to William Godwin's *Essay Concerning Human Justice* (1793), a radical call for the levelling of society and the consequent ushering in of an age of universal peace and harmony. Inspired by the heady events of the early French Revolution, Godwin's essay was part of an outpouring of social criticism and utopian speculation that angered and frightened conservatives. Malthus's book was therefore not simply a reply to Godwin but a key text of the powerful counter-revolutionary movement which began in the 1790s. It was not only an attack on the levelling principles of the French Revolution, but also a repudiation of the yearnings for moral and material progress unleashed by the Enlightenment. In an important sense, the real target of Malthus's essay was Adam Smith rather than Godwin. The latter was something of a straw man, and at any rate by 1798, with the recent butcheries of the Terror and the corruption of the Directorate in France, the Godwinites were weakened and dispirited. Smith's insistence that material progress for all classes necessarily results from a free market was quite another matter, however. Malthus considered that a far too dangerous hope for anyone to entertain, and the *Essay on Population* is a systematic dashing of the hopes raised in the *Wealth of Nations*. Thus political economy, deflected from the bright visions of its founder, became the 'dismal science', and the poor laws were viewed in an unremittingly hostile light by its practitioners.[77]

If Malthus was the most influential writer of the period in shaping poor law policy over the next generation, Jeremy Bentham was perhaps more crucial in the long run. His views were certainly far more distinctive and original. If Malthus represented at least a partial repudiation of the Enlightenment, Bentham seemed to embody it; he was the quintessential English *philosophe*. A rigorous and unconventional thinker, eccentric in appearance and manner, he inspired a small band of followers, known as Philosophical Radicals, who made it their mission to change English laws and institutions. What inspired such devotion was Bentham's breathtaking audacity in stripping away from each component of national life its accumulated historical, religious, and cultural sanctity, and insisting that it prove its usefulness. The cold, searching glare of reason was turned upon the most hallowed institutions: the common law, criminal law, the judiciary, prisons, education, and the poor laws. All these and more were found wanting when measured by Bentham's 'felicific calculus', a precise reckoning of the pleasure and pain created by any policy or course of action. The legislator, according to Bentham, was to be guided solely by a determination to maximize happiness and minimize misery. Utility was the only valid yardstick. Bentham dedicated his life to rigorous scrutiny of existing institutions and the devising of new ones that would produce 'the greatest good for the greatest number'. An incomplete Constitutional Code and a host of reform schemes on specific government functions constitute his impressive, if sometimes baffling, legacy.

Several elements of Bentham's proposals are thought to have had considerable influence on the course of poor law reform in the nineteenth century. The first of these is centralization. In his constitutional blueprint to overhaul British government, Bentham created a central government minister for every function. One of these was an indigence relief minister, which has sometimes been cited as the model for the Poor Law Commissioners under the New Poor Law. Yet his proposal was not published until after the New Poor Law was passed, and the powers of his indigence relief minister – keeping statistics, inspecting workhouses, and offering advice to workhouse managers – were rather more modest than those of the new central board after 1834.[78] Yet, in asserting that poor relief was indeed a public responsibility requiring central government oversight, and thus challenging the abolitionists like Townsend, Burke, and Malthus, Bentham's role was critical.[79] His defence of the necessity of maintaining poor relief was based, characteristically, on rational rather than on moral grounds. Witnessing a person's death by starvation might be morally repugnant to some, but that was not the point for Bentham. A starving peasantry would be transformed into a turbulent, revolutionary mass, and no one's life or property would be secure. Voluntary charitable giving, often invoked by the abolitionists, was not only insufficient but insecure. Because givers exercised the power to discriminate between deserving and undeserving, and hence the power to decide who would live and who would die, philanthropy was not an effective bulwark against revolution.

Bentham denied that even government should try to discriminate between the deserving and the reprobate. There were only the indigent, henceforth to be distinguished from the mass of the ordinary poor who subsisted by their labour. The former were without resources, and hence the proper objects of poor relief.[80] Since all those without resources were to be relieved regardless of character, it was critically important to devise a system that would not operate as an inducement for the poor to cease working and join the indigent. For Bentham, the institution that would prevent this from occurring was the workhouse, which all the able-bodied would be required to enter as a condition of their relief. A workhouse test of this type would automatically weed out the merely work-shy from the truly indigent. This idea was of course not entirely new – the 1723 statute was based on something like it – but Bentham had in mind an entirely new type of workhouse. It was based on his long-term interest in prison design and inspired by a method invented by his brother Samuel to efficiently supervise workers in Russia. Bentham dubbed it 'Panopticon' (all-seeing), because it allowed a large number of inmates to be both seen and controlled by one or only a few supervisors. It was to be a huge polygonal structure designed on a radial principle with the inmates housed in rooms along the outer periphery; the supervisor was situated at the hub, able to see the inmates at any time and yet remain unseen himself. Since inmates under constant scrutiny could be controlled in ways never envisaged by earlier advocates of the workhouse, Panopticon also served as a reformatory for the reprobate. He also presented it as a wholesome place of refuge for the aged, infirm, and children, most of whom would also be required to enter. Careful classification by age, gender, infirmity, and so on would ensure that no vicious habits were transferred from the reprobate to the innocent and virtuous.[81] As Bentham summarized the benefits of his system both for the able-bodied and for others: 'Morals reformed, health preserved, industry invigorated, instruction diffused, public burthens lightened, Economy seated as it were upon a rock, the gordian knot of the Poor-Laws not cut but untied – all by a simple Idea of Architecture!'[82] For Bentham, Panopticon was thus a 'happiness maximizing' device, though historians have tended to focus on its totalitarian implications.[83]

Bentham's 'simple idea of architecture' was to have a significant influence on later workhouse design, though his scheme of harnessing it to a system of private contract did not. He believed strongly that major financial savings could be achieved through a proposed national network of 250 houses of industry built on the Panopticon principle. Farming out paupers had certainly been tried before, but Bentham's conception of the principle was as far removed from previous practice as Panopticon differed from a typical eighteenth-century workhouse.

He promoted a National Charity Company, directed by himself operating under contract to the government.[84] A system of well-regulated Panopticon workhouses, he claimed, could be made to realize a profit, and thus social peace could be maintained, poor rates lowered, and degraded characters reformed, all by a combination of the proper architecture and administrative arrangements. Although Pitt's government was at first favourably disposed and even provided a start-up grant to Bentham, in the end the plan was considered too radical and controversial. The comic-opera quality to some of these drawn-out manoeuvrings and outbursts, including Bentham's diatribes against King George III for allegedly blocking his grand project, should not obscure his great importance in poor law history. In spite of the fact that his private contracting ideas were rejected, no other thinker rivalled his intellectual reach on the topic of government organization and administrative methods.[85] If, indeed, as has been claimed, the 1790s witnessed the formulation of the modern concept of poverty,[86] all of the writers discussed here played a critically important role. Bentham's modernizing ideas on the forms and structures of government became more significant in the years after 1830; in the period from 1800 to 1830, which we turn to in the next chapter, the views of Smith, Townsend, Eden, and Malthus were more central.

3

DEBATES, EXPERIMENTS, AND REFORMS, 1800–1832

Evangelizing the Poor

When we consider the intellectual trajectory from Adam Smith to Malthus discussed in the last chapter, abolition of the poor laws might seem a likely outcome. And not surprisingly, the period from the beginning of the nineteenth century to the 1820s witnessed a great deal of abolitionist argument, both within and outside of Parliament. On the other hand, Bentham's work inclined in another direction: that it was possible to keep a mandatory system of relief and yet, through ingenious administrative arrangements and novel workhouse design, avoid the pauperizing effects of the old system. However, in spite of important differences between the increasingly abolitionist slant of the political economists and the administrative activist approach of Bentham, they shared a rationalist outlook. Their secular discourses were alike in abstracting the poor, discussing them in a manner that allowed the observer/reformer to keep both his physical and emotional distance. But a rapidly growing religious movement would have nearly as great an impact on poor law reform as the secular systems discussed: Evangelicalism. Through the latter half of the eighteenth century, a number of upper- and middle-class Britons embraced a deeply personal, emotionally charged form of Christian belief. A sharp break from the comfortable, undemanding creed of the Church of England and the more quiescent forms of Nonconformity, Evangelicalism placed stern demands on its adherents. Partly generated by the fear of social revolution, it not only enjoined close scrutiny of one's own behaviour and character, but stressed the importance of close involvement in the lives of the poor. The Evangelical mission, to create a more godly society as well as reform individual character, prefigured Victorian moral earnestness. Many Evangelicals were involved in movements like the anti-slavery programme or prison reform. Others sought to raise the spiritual tone of their own localities, starting of course with their social inferiors. Charitable enterprises, especially those having an educational function, drew Evangelicals to their ranks. Teaching in Sunday schools, visiting the sick, and providing charitable relief to the 'deserving' poor all offered ample scope for proselytizing among the lower orders. In this way discipline, thrift, sobriety, and other desirable traits could be nurtured, social bonds strengthened, and godless revolutionary levelling thwarted.

Evangelicalism had a profound effect on philanthropy in the nineteenth century. It infused charity with a pious, even sacred obligation to make sure that one's giving promoted the moral elevation of the recipient. Heedless donations to humanitarian causes and avoidance of painstaking inquiries were apt to produce more harm than good. Careful investigation into the character and circumstances of the objects of one's beneficence was therefore of critical importance.[1] These methods were also applied to the poor law recipients in the form of identifying the truly deserving, consigning the reprobate to the harshest, most deterrent policies that could be devised. In this sense, the Evangelical movement could work in harness with more secular attempts to trim relief, though in general it did not lend support to poor law abolition. Indeed, a strong case was made by Hannah More, one of the leading Evangelical writers of tracts to improve the moral condition of the poor, that the poor laws were an important component of the English constitution. In her 'Village Politics', written in the 1790s, she pointed out that English workers had no need of revolution because they enjoyed a well-established right to sustenance under the poor laws. The dialogue in this tract is between two labourers: Tom Hod, a confused but ardent disciple of Thomas Paine, and Jack Anvil, a sensible defender of the established order. Among the many advantages of the British system over that of revolutionary France enumerated by Jack to his misguided friend is a guarantee of poor relief:

> 'Twas but last year that you broke your leg, and was nine weeks in the Bristol Infirmary, where you was taken as much care of as a lord, and your family was maintained all the while by the parish. No poor-rates in France, Tom; and here there's a matter of two million and a half paid for the poor every year, if 'twas but a little better managed.[2]

It might be observed that while More presents the poor laws as a bulwark against revolution, in the final phrase of this passage she suggests the need for closer and more careful supervision. As an Evangelical, Hannah More was concerned not only to keep the poor quietly in their place, but to engage with them as individuals and bring about their moral regeneration. When applied to poor law administration, this was likely to result in deciding the type and quantity of relief on a case-by-case basis, not imposing 'self-acting' devices like the workhouse test. At the same time, Evangelical concerns about undermining individual character and family cohesion through profuse poor relief pointed towards sharp cutbacks.

Wartime Privations and the Slowing of Reform

Throughout the long war against Napoleonic France, which persisted with only brief interruptions until 1815, there was a marked reluctance on the part of Parliament to consider major poor law reforms. At the local level, too, few parish vestries or magistrates were inclined to undertake any bold initiatives. Probably a majority of the educated public did not embrace any reform scheme wholeheartedly, preferring either to keep the old system, largely out of inertia or a fear of touching off a revolution. On the whole, it seemed safer and easier to carry on with established methods of poor relief. Although conditions had improved slightly since the extreme dearth of the 1790s, poor rates continued to rise. A total national assessment of £5.3 million in 1802–3 had risen to £8.6 million by 1813.[3] Nonetheless, many agriculturalists were profiting handsomely from wartime prices, and rising poor rates, though irritating, seemed bearable. In many districts, the allowance system was providing real protection for the poor, though there were years of great suffering such as 1801 and 1812.[4] Even in this relatively placid climate, however, there was a continuing national dialogue as well as some attempts at poor law reform in Parliament.

One major step that Parliament did take in these years was to approve George Rose's motion for official returns on poor law expenditure for 1802–3. Since there had been no national statistics compiled since the Gilbert returns of the early 1780s, the new figures allowed legislators, as well as analysts and commentators, to see what had happened during the preceding 20 years. Total poor relief was shown to have doubled since 1783. More importantly, the returns showed expenditure per head of population was much higher in the South-east and Midlands, especially the cereal-growing areas where the allowance system was in wide use. While the national average was 9s. 7d. for all of England and Wales, there was striking regional variation. Sussex topped the list with 23s. 4d. per head, while Lancashire managed with a parsimonious 4s. 11d. More than 1 million persons received some poor relief during 1802–3, or about one in nine of the population according to the 1801 census. The official returns also provided valuable information about workhouses. In all, there were 3765 workhouses reported in the 14 611 parishes. Most of them must have been quite modest institutions, little more than traditional poorhouses. There was a total of 83 468 indoor paupers, an average of only 22 per house. The figures do show the tremendous preponderance of outdoor relief, for only one in 12 relief recipients were in some kind of workhouse. The reason is not far to seek: indoor relief was decidedly more expensive, amounting to a national average annual expenditure per pauper of £12 3s. 7d., while outdoor relief averaged £3 3s. 8d. While almost all commentators agreed that the returns indicated a growing crisis, there was little will to act.[5]

The poor law debates that did take place in the House of Commons show how Malthusian doctrine continued to spread through the political elite. In 1807, the Whig MP, Samuel Whitbread, who in the 1790s had championed a minimum wage policy, seemingly recanted his earlier beliefs, declaring that the tendency of all relief was to demoralize the poor and create overpopulation and offering a lengthy paean to Malthus. Yet, while admitting that the latter's principles had strongly bolstered abolitionism ('the prevailing sentiment'), Whitbread pushed instead for a major overhaul of the poor law.[6] The bill he introduced represented a return to the principle at work in measures like Gilbert's Act of 1782: replacing parochial small fry with men of greater social substance. He sought to make voting in parish vestries proportionate to the amount of property held, complaining that vestries were 'under the influence of popular clamour'[7] and that 'inconsiderable renters sometimes have it in their power to dispose of the parish money against the opinion of the more substantial and better informed inhabitants'.[8] If Whitbread had confined himself to this constitutional change (something like it came into operation on an optional basis in 1818), he might have stood a better chance. Instead he loaded his measure with fancy extras such as mandatory educational provisions (at a time when many conservatives feared working-class literacy) and a scheme to expand the use of parish cottages for the indigent. The measure drew criticism from many quarters, including from Malthus himself.

The Duke of Portland's government had no interest in the bill, and the large Tory majority in the House saw little merit in this Whig measure, so it was dropped after its second reading. But it aroused considerable interest in the country at large. While Malthus was rather polite and measured in his criticism, a more crude Malthusian assault on the bill came from J.B. Monck, who wrote: 'that the poor are such as we find them, swarming, indolent, improvident, discontented, dispirited, oppressed, degraded, vicious, is chiefly owing to the system of the Poor Laws'. Other authors took the opportunity to attack Malthusian doctrine and defend the traditional system of poor relief, though some of them lauded Whitbread's attempted revisions of the law.[9] A quite different angle was taken by William Cobbett, the 'poor man's friend' and editor of the radical *Political Register*, who denounced the bill for its elitist modifications of local voting rights. A champion of the 'democratic' nature of parish vestries, where the smallest ratepayer had a vote equal to that of the largest, Cobbett was alarmed at Whitbread's idea of plural voting rights for the well-to-do.[10] To Cobbett, such an innovation reflected the ominous oligarchic tendencies at work throughout the countryside, by which the poor were being systematically deprived of their historic rights. A Cobbettite defence of the traditional vestry was to be a mainstay of radical attacks on select vestries and ultimately on the system under the New Poor Law by which guardians were elected on a weighted property franchise.

On the wider theories of poverty and relief, one of the most influential writers of the age was Patrick Colquhoun, a Glasgow magistrate who had retired to London in 1789 and had become a police magistrate and respected governmental advisor. Resembling Bentham in his comprehensive linking of social issues, he advocated a 'system of police' under central government supervision by which the crime and indigence could be effectively countered. His fully elaborated views on these questions were presented in his *Treatise on Indigence* in 1806. In this book, the public was first introduced to an idea earlier discussed but not published by Bentham: the fundamental distinction between poverty and indigence. Poverty was the natural condition of the mass of humanity who were required to labour for their daily bread. Indigence, on the other hand, was the inability to make a living, even by working. It was therefore, indigence and not poverty that was the evil. The poor laws had confounded the two and devices like the allowance system were likely to eradicate the distinction completely. While granting that Malthus had developed an impressive analysis, Colquhoun refused to accept the abolitionist implications of the population principle. Like Bentham, he penned his faith on wise administrators and sound principle, the chief obstacle to whose benevolent sway was an ignorant and often corrupt localism. Like Bentham an advocate of an activist administration armed with constantly updated statistics, Colquhoun did not share Bentham's faith in the efficacy of indoor relief.[11]

The Poor Laws and Economic Development

In addition to the moral issues that were so central to the poor laws, contemporaries were vitally interested in the issue of their effects on economic development. The pure optimal model of development offered by the political economists posited unfettered movement of capital and labour. Wages, prices, and profits guided society to the best possible allocation of its resources, all without government direction or restraint. But the poor laws represented a survival of the now discredited mercantilist system by which a paternalist government deflected resources to policies thought to have overriding social importance. Whether one thought that the poor laws promoted ultimate societal collapse, or that they could be rendered useful through drastic reform, or indeed that they should be kept as they were, the question of the law's effect on economic development was critical. Beyond the immediate issue of the economic effect of the poor laws lay the question of whether maximum development had a privileged position; was it right and necessary that all which did not pass muster according to the calculus of the economists be swept away? These questions have proved equally compelling to historians.

Economic changes that had been under way in the eighteenth century continued, and even accelerated. In agriculture, the enclosure movement spread, especially in the South, East, and Midlands, with usually negative consequences for the labourers. While the additional work involved in enclosing the previously common fields did represent at least temporary employment opportunities, these were more than offset by the loss of the right to keep animals and to forage on what had been the village commons. With the disappearance of an important supplement to farm workers' wages, their position became more precarious. At the same time, rural handcraft industry was disappearing with the advance of factory production. This removed another important supplement to family incomes: the off-season earnings (often by wives) in textiles and other crafts. Cottage allotments, on which labourers had been able to raise their own vegetables, were also disappearing in the headlong rush by landowners and farmers to make every square inch of ground pay the maximum return.

Since wage income tended more and more to come from a single source – the male labourer's earnings – family incomes fell below subsistence levels with rising prices. As we have seen, rather than raise wages farmers preferred to supplement inadequate pay with outdoor relief. The resulting system of allowances continued to draw criticism for allegedly pauperizing and demoralizing the lower orders, but what real effect did the system have on economic development? This question involves an examination of how much the rapid population growth of the era offset the productivity gains in agriculture and industry. Furthermore, it invites inquiry into the connection between the allowance system and population growth. In short, it involves revisiting the proposition that to Malthus and many of his contemporaries was self-evident: allowances were a direct bounty on reckless reproduction, hence exacerbating the population crisis and increasing human misery and degradation. Furthermore, by subsidizing low wages, allowances retarded the growth of labour productivity. Throughout the nineteenth century and beyond, there was little questioning of these assertions, and even the Webbs agreed that the allowance system had been a disaster.[12] During the last generation, this view has been widely repudiated. Local variations and anomalies have been pointed out, along with a denial of any clear linkage between allowances and population growth. The revisionists portrayed allowances as but one of several policies adopted by parishes responding, not irrationally or inhumanely, to conditions in a lagging sector of the economy.[13] A corollary of this revisionist line is that the poor laws have been wrongly blamed for rapid population growth. Recently, however, the Malthusian case has been vindicated, and the rapid fertility rate increase in the first quarter of the nineteenth century linked to the widespread use of child allowances.[14]

The larger issue of the impact of the poor laws generally on economic development has also proved contentious, and tends to come back to the issue of regional variation. The system of relatively generous relief in cereal-growing counties in the final decades of the Old Poor Law has been defended not just in moral terms but for actually assisting the advance of agriculture. The outlays by ratepayers are said to have provided an incentive to employment. Moreover, as a system far in advance of any other society in Europe (none of which offered wage subsidies and family support), it helps explain Britain's economic primacy.[15] This view has been criticized both for exaggerating the degree of difference with other European societies and also for ignoring the enormous gap between a low-wage, high-relief South and East and a high-wage, low-relief North and West.[16] It is quite possible that historians will never resolve this issue. While a seemingly straightforward one that should be susceptible to econometric analysis, it turns out to be far more complex, associated as it is with a host of moral and social issues that not only deeply concerned contemporaries, but which continue to resonate powerfully at the start of the twenty-first century. What can be said with some certainty is that in the opening decades of the nineteenth century the principles of economics burrowed ever deeper into the culture and social values of middle- and upper-class Englishmen. To be sure, the older paternalist ethos continued to be a powerful strain, but found itself increasingly on the defensive. When major social and political upheavals could be laid at the door of a demoralizing system of poor relief, the arguments of those advocating the application of the 'rational' principles of the economists proved irresistible.

Post-war Dislocations and Demands for Reform

When Britain finally emerged victorious in the protracted and costly military struggle against Napoleonic France, the jubilant mood among Britain's ruling class was tempered by a realization that fresh dangers threatened, this time internal ones. Even during the war, there had been disquieting signs of worker disaffection, such as the attacks by Luddites on machinery, and sometimes on machine owners, in worsted and hosiery centres like Derby, Leicester, and Nottingham. The government, responding to fears that this movement could spread, threatening general revolution, had responded with military force and draconian laws. With the end of the war, and the inevitable economic dislocations compounded by a mass of demobilized soldiers and sailors seeking employment, the mood was unsettled and tense. Moreover, political grievances among the middle and lower classes had spread rapidly since the 1790s. Aristocratic corruption and misrule were assailed by a wide array of reformers and radicals. There was also a revival of the earlier movement to reform Parliament, to which even Pitt had given some support before the French Revolution and which had been muzzled by wartime laws restricting speech, press, and assembly. Lord Liverpool's Tory government, in which reactionaries like Lord Castlereagh held key positions, was determined to resist, and if necessary to suppress all those who sought to make government more responsive to the popular will. It is against this dark backdrop that renewed efforts by society's leaders to reform the poor laws unfolded.

With the onset of a post-war depression and the accompanying flooding of the labour market by returning veterans, relief costs surged and the proportion of wages paid out of the poor rates increased.[17] There had been an industrial slump in 1811, but a much more severe one after 1815 followed major cutbacks in government military procurement. Food prices, and hence agricultural profits, also began to decline sharply, so that farmers and landowners, who had been grudgingly willing to continue the old relief system during the previous era of high profits, began to have second thoughts. The sudden transition to a peacetime economy, plus a cyclical depression, created enormous anxieties among the upper classes. One of the responses of Parliament was to pass the 1815 Corn Law, which, though a clear violation of the principles of laissez-faire economics (and denounced by some economists as such), sought to shore up farm prices by excluding lower-priced foreign grain. When it came to the poor, however, no such deviation from economic orthodoxy, even one as embedded in tradition as the poor laws, was to be tolerated. If only the shield of the poor laws were removed, workers would be subjected to the wholesome discipline of market forces, and the economy could right itself. Not surprisingly, the national discourse on the poor laws, measured by the pamphlet literature after 1815, became highly active. And not surprisingly, the debates of these years represented the high-water mark of abolitionism.

Two classic abolitionist texts reappeared in 1817: a reprint of Joseph Townsend's 1786 *Dissertation on the Poor Laws*, and a fifth edition of Malthus's *Essay on Population*. Both served to stimulate discussion, especially the latter. Malthus had not been a crude abolitionist, and had even in 1807 denied that he desired to see the poor laws swept away altogether, but the 1817 edition of the *Essay* moved him closer to an unequivocal abolitionist line: 'The poor-laws tend in the most marked manner to make the supply of labour exceed the demand for it.' Unless they were abolished, he concluded, the cancerous spread of pauperism would continue.[18] A spate of ardent pleas for immediate abolition flowed from the pens of his followers, one from the Evangelical rector of a parish in Surrey, showing that religious zeal was by no means incompatible with the new 'science'.[19] A nuanced, more ably argued abolitionist position was taken by another Evangelical, John Bird Sumner, a widely respected writer on economic subjects for the Tory *Quarterly Review*. Sumner was later to become a key member of the Royal Commission on the Poor Laws of 1832–34, and ultimately Archbishop of Canterbury. He endorsed Malthus's principle, though expressing some reservations, and linked it with the plan of Divine Providence. Thus the poor laws, which depressed wages and inhibited virtue, were found wanting on both economic and theological grounds.[20] Many writers clamoured either for immediate or gradual abolition, while others directed their criticism at the allowance system, which had produced a profligate, work-shy, impudent workforce. As John Davison put it in his *Considerations on the Poor Laws* (1817):

> The labourer reckons half with his master, and half with the overseer. Towards his master he has neither the zeal nor the attachment he ought to have to his natural patron and friend, and with his parish he keeps up a dependence which has something in it at once abject and insolent.[21]

How skewed the 'debate' was to the abolitionist side is evident in the fact that the Whig *Edinburgh Review* supported it as enthusiastically as did the Tory *Quarterly Review,* though the latter, it must be noted, also published Coleridge's anti-Malthusian defence of the poor laws.[22] In 1817, Thomas Chalmers, an active figure in the Church of Scotland, and a charity reformer in his own parish in Glasgow, began contributing to the *Edinburgh*. Admired for his efforts to stamp out begging and make philanthropy more discriminating by careful inquiry and home visiting of applicants, Chalmers turned his caustic eye on the English poor laws in 1817. In arguing that the poor laws, from the very beginning, had subverted 'the natural order of human feelings', he echoed Edmund Burke. The only proper course was to move towards gradual abolition. Mandatory assessments should be phased out as those supported by them died. For the newly indigent, there was to be a fund raised by voluntary contributions only, thus removing the guarantee of relief, and of course with it a historic right of the English and Welsh. Under the suggested change, the character of applicants would be carefully evaluated, and only the deserving would receive help.[23] What Chalmers was suggesting was in fact a close approximation of the Scottish Poor Law, in which voluntary funds raised by donations in parish churches were distributed to those deemed deserving by a committee of the kirk sessions and the principal heritors (landowners). Those wishing to end the English poor laws found the Scottish system an attractive model, both because of its largely voluntary character and because major landowners played a dominant part in its management. In the decades before 1834, Scotland's way of managing the poor was often lauded, and the works of Colquhoun and Chalmers frequently cited.[24] The fourth edition of the *Encylopaedia Britannica* (1810) chimed in under its entry on 'Poor', reviling the English system and praising the Scottish.[25] In vain did a Cobbetite like James MacPhail assert that the English Poor Law was the most 'humane, Christian-like law in the world', pointing out that the poor in Scotland were miserable and half-starved.[26] Such traditional Christian injunctions on the duty to care for the poor, found also in the works of the great eighteenth-century theologian William Paley, carried less and less weight. Part of the reason is that the sons of the gentry had been imbibing at English universities a new theology that scoffed at Paley's notion that the poor were vested with 'natural rights'. In the influential teaching and writing of Edward Copleston of Oriel College, Oxford, the design of Providence was rather to be looked for in the working of the market and the principle of population.[27]

Before turning to parliamentary activity in the post-Napoleonic War era, two other writers should be considered: David Ricardo, the most noted economist of the day, and Jane Marcet, a popularizer who brought the discussion to a wider social circle. Ricardo, more akin to Bentham than to Malthus intellectually, treated the issue in an unremittingly scientific tone, devoid of any overt moralizing. Although Ricardo accepted that there might ultimately be a population crisis, he rejected Malthus's claim that poor relief was a pure waste of resources, pointing out that the tendency of the poor law was simply to shift overall capital resources to agriculture and away from other investments. In Ricardian terms, the result was apt to be an undesirable and far from optimum array of goods and services, though it was one that promoted a kind of equality. Ricardo made it simply a question of a policy choice: if equality at a lower overall material level was desired, then the poor law would promote such a course. If economic growth and material abundance were sought, curtailment if not abolition of poor relief was the answer. Although Ricardo himself thought that continuing the existing system was an incorrect choice, he did not frame it in the moralizing, apocalyptic terms of the Malthusians.[28] These important differences from Malthus may have appeared evident only to that small number whose intellects were deeply etched by the secular tenets of classical economics. For others it doubtless appeared simply that the country's most eminent economist had added his voice to the condemnation of the poor laws.

The mass of the literate public was more likely to be reached and persuaded by the work of Jane Marcet. Mrs Marcet's *Conversations on Political Economy*, which was written in a lively, lucid manner and aimed at the widest possible audience, appeared in 1816 and went through six editions by 1839. Cast as a dialogue between the knowledgeable Mrs B and the humane but naive Caroline, Marcet's book served as a kind of primer of political economy. Caroline is repeatedly made to see the error and ultimate tragedy of her soft-hearted ways, not least on the question of poor relief. She finally agrees with Mrs B that the poor laws must be abolished, though only after sufficient time for education and the moral example of their betters had prepared the lower orders for self-help. This softer version of Malthus's doctrine no doubt proved more palatable to the majority for whom sentiment and a sense of doing right were important components of any policy question.[29] Like two other women writers – Hannah More a decade earlier and Harriet Martineau a decade or so later – Marcet played a key role in popularizing the debate on the poor laws and making it a compelling issue.

Renewed Parliamentary Activity

The economic and social crises of the immediate post-war period put poor law reform back on the list of urgent matters for the country's political leaders. Economic malaise, dangerous radical movements like the Spenceans, and fresh cries for parliamentary reform may have persuaded some that it was best not to tamper with the system and enrage the lower classes. Many, however, believed that the various signs of economic, social, and political breakdown could be traced, at least in part, to a dysfunctional and corrupting poor law system. A House of Commons Select Committee on the Poor Laws, chaired by William Sturges-Bourne, was appointed in 1817. The two most important members of this 40-man committee were both country gentlemen and associates of the Tory reformer George Canning: Sturges-Bourne himself and Thomas Frankland Lewis. Sturges-Bourne was a key member of the Royal Commission on the Poor Laws of 1832–34, while Lewis was to become one of the three Poor Law Commissioners who administered the

New Poor Law. An alarmist Malthusian tone runs through the committee's report. After describing in some detail the defects of the existing system, the report concludes:

> unless some efficacious check be interposed, there is every reason to think, that the amount of the assessment will continue as it has done, to increase, till at a period more or less remote, according to the progress the evil has already made in different places it shall have absorbed the profits of the property on which the rate may have been assessed, producing thereby the neglect and ruin of the land, and the waste or removal of other property, to the utter subversion of that happy order of society so long upheld in these kingdoms.[30]

The evidence to back up this alarming claim was drawn from a single Shropshire town whose mines had recently failed.[31]

And yet the Commons' committee report did contain a policy prescription that bore important fruit: altering voting rights in parish vestries to favour large occupiers and owners. The committee anticipated that once select vestries composed of the major owners and occupiers controlled parish vestries, the administration of poor relief would be greatly improved. Showing the continuing importance of the Scottish example, the report declared that the way out of the poor law morass was to empower 'such a part of the vestry as may bear some analogy to the heritors and kirk session of Scotland'.[32] The Prime Minister, Lord Liverpool, disappointed that the Lower House's report did not contain a more comprehensive plan of reform, appointed a committee of the House of Lords. This body failed to come up with specific policy recommendations other than an 'improved system of management' (though they did not specify select vestries) and a simplification of the law.[33] Like the Commons' committee, however, that in the Upper House also expressed its admiration for the Scottish Poor Law. The Lords' committee published as an appendix to their own report one from the General Assembly of the Church of Scotland describing in detail the management of poor relief by heritors and kirk sessions.[34] The Foreign Secretary, Lord Castlereagh, had, a few months earlier, praised the system in Scotland, where 'the practice was for proprietors to assess themselves in what they deemed necessary for the support of those whom they themselves considered entitled to it'.[35] Select vestries seemed to many in Parliament to offer the best hope for a more rigorous and effective oversight of poor relief.

Select Vestries

The statutory results of these investigations were the two Select Vestries laws that passed in 1818 and 1819 and quickly became known as Sturges-Bourne's Acts, after their principal formulator. These laws represented the first major breakthrough in moving the parochial voting system in an oligarchic direction since Gilbert's Act of 1782. That statute, it will be recalled, provided that in parochial elections within the new Gilbert Act unions, the right to vote was weighted according to the rateable value of one's property. Gilbert had tried unsuccessfully to get the principle adopted throughout the country in 1786, as had Whitbread in his 1807 bill. Like the 1782 measure, Sturges-Bourne's Acts were permissive, that is they applied only in those parishes whose vestries voted to adopt the new provisions. Defending the first of his bills in the House of Commons, Sturges-Bourne declared that 'the object in view was to follow the analogy of the kirk-sessions in Scotland, as far as the very different system of poor laws in England would admit'.[36] The 1818 law provided that for electing select vestries, the following scale would be used: those occupying land of less than £50 rateable value could cast a single vote, while those with over £50 could cast an additional vote for each £25 of value, up to a maximum of six votes. Thus the major owners and occupiers would have six times as much political weight as the smallholders. The 1819 Act added resident clergymen as ex-officio members of the vestry. There was to be no 'self-acting' workhouse test applied by select vestries; rather, they were specifically enjoined to consider carefully each applicant's character and circumstances, distinguishing between 'the deserving and the idle, extravagant or profligate poor ...'.[37] To facilitate such rigour, there were also provisions for salaried overseers, better keeping of accounts, and building or enlarging workhouses. Finally, select vestries were less subject to magisterial interference. Under the 1819 Act, if a select vestry refused to grant relief, it would require the action of two justices rather than one to overturn the decision, except in cases of extreme emergency.

Five years after the passage of these acts, James Ebenezer Bicheno, a pamphleteer in Berkshire, noted approvingly that select vestries had 'commenced the renovation of the system in a safe and sober way'.[38] How accurate was this assessment? When Bicheno wrote, the new system was expanding, especially in Berkshire, which was, after all, the 'Speenhamland county' and therefore emblematic of the worst abuses of the old system. A total of 46 select vestries had been formed in the county by the beginning of 1825. In the first year or two of operation, these Berkshire vestries set to work with a will. The 'idle and profligate' were turned away, workhouse tests were imposed, dietaries and other aspects of workhouse life were made more unpleasant, and fathers of bastards were pressured to pay for support. The Thatcham select vestry adopted as one of its first policies the refusal of relief to anyone who kept a dog, a horse, or a cart.[39] Ratepayers were delighted to see their assessments drop dramatically. The parish of White Waltham experienced a reduction of 33 per cent during the first year of its select vestry. The heavily pauperized parish of Bray, which had spent £2713 in 1821–22, had reduced it to £1604 in 1822–23, its first year with a select vestry; this was a reduction of 37 per cent. That same year, the total reduction for all Berkshire parishes (the majority of which did not adopt the new system) was 18 per cent from the year before; the figure for the whole of England and Wales was 9 per cent.[40]

As these figures suggest, heavily pauperized areas were apt to find select vestries a highly effective device, but certain lightly rated regions were also enthusiastic about them. Lancashire and Yorkshire were notable for their adoption of select vestries, and this is one reason that leaders in those counties later asserted they had no need of the New Poor Law.[41] On the other hand, many parishes in all parts of the country could not be persuaded to adopt the acts. The major obstacle was that the traditional open vestry, elected on a one-ratepayer, one-vote basis, had to agree to the change, and there was still a powerful attachment to 'village democracy'. Parliament had again shrunk from making an innovative policy mandatory, hoping instead that once the benefits of an optional programme were manifest, other parishes would follow suit. The desire to emulate parishes that lowered their rates substantially does seem to have been powerful through the 1820s, and ultimately 15 per cent of the parishes in England and Wales opted for select vestries. After that, there was a fall-off, however, as many parishioners grew weary of attending meetings and incurring the hostility of the poor by trimming poor relief.[42] The latter concern became pronounced after the Captain Swing riots of 1830–31 (taken up below), in which the cutbacks in the poor laws were a key grievance.

One aspect of the Select Vestries Act that did prove enduring was the appointment of salaried assistant overseers. Under the 1819 Act, any parish could avail themselves of this provision. Thus many a parish whose vestry refused to adopt the select vestry system nonetheless appointed a salaried overseer. On the eve of the New Poor Law,

3376 parishes were using them; this represented more than 20 per cent of the parishes in England and Wales.[43] The duties typical of the office are suggested by an advertisement placed by a Kent parish in 1832. In addition to the routine administration of poor relief, the assistant overseer was to represent the parish at petty and quarter sessions, prepare the parochial returns, and inspect each pauper's house as well as the parish poorhouse once a week.[44] In part, the growing popularity of assistant overseers grew out of the desire of local inhabitants to save themselves the trouble of dealing with the indigent. But it also represents a growing professionalism, and an increased public awareness that paid officials were usually more effective in the post than reluctant parishioners taking the office in rotation. The relative success of the paid assistant overseers, often drawn from outside the local area, helped pave the way for the acceptance of the 'poor law civil service' (relieving officers, workhouse masters, and the like) under the New Poor Law. This was one important legacy of the Select Vestries Act. The other was the plural voting system, which was to be used in the elections of poor law guardians after 1834.

The Nottinghamshire Reformers

While the extension of the Select Vestries Acts represented an important aspect of the final decade of the Old Poor Law, there were also important innovations that proceeded entirely from local initiatives. The most important of these, in terms of their wider influence, were in Nottinghamshire. In a sense it is odd that Nottinghamshire should have been the site of ardent reform efforts, since it was a relatively prosperous county, the fifth most industrialized in the nation. Its thriving framework knitting industry provided nearby labour alternatives for the rural population, and the per capita relief expenditures of less than 11s. in 1820–23 put it well below the English average. The allowance system, introduced only recently, was unknown in some parishes, while in others it came into operation only with families of at least four children.[45] Nonetheless, by the 1820s, the county was coming to be looked on as a laboratory for poor law experimentation. There, three determined gentlemen, alarmed at rising rates and declining morals, set about reforming the poor laws through their own exertions. Two of the figures in this group, the Reverend J. T. Becher of Southwell and the Reverend Robert Lowe of Bingham, had laboured for years in relative obscurity to infuse greater rigour in the poor laws, but it was not until the arrival of George Nicholls that these efforts were expanded and widely publicized. Becher, Chairman of Quarter Sessions for the Newark Division, had been actively involved since the 1790s in trying to put the poor laws on a sounder footing. Both an earnest Malthusian and a kindly man, he sought to ameliorate the condition of the poor as well as to instil discipline and morality. He supported a variety of measures in the locality, including savings banks, dispensaries, cottage provision for the 'guiltless poor', Friendly Societies, free schools, and libraries. Yet he had also come to be a staunch advocate of a deterrent workhouse, strict classification and segregation of pauper inmates, and more careful accounting.[46] The centrepiece of what Becher called his 'Anti-Pauper System' was the establishment in 1823 of a large Gilbert Act union of 49 parishes, and the erection of two large new workhouses at Upton and Southwell. While deterrence was the most important aspect of these institutions, a workhouse school was also established, and was even made available to children of able-bodied labourers outside the workhouse who had four or more children. In Becher's book, *The Anti-Pauper System*, first published in 1828, the harsh, deterrent aspects of Thurgarton Incorporation policies were emphasized, giving a somewhat misleading idea of the true nature of the union's regimen. While tenderness towards the aged, infirm, and 'guiltless' is enjoined, readers were drawn to the promise of 'wholesome restraint upon the idle, the profligate, and the refractory'.[47] For the same reason, the Nottinghamshire reforms attracted poor law hardliners throughout the country.[48] But several years before Becher's book, the reforms were being publicized and exaggerated to an even greater extent by George Nicholls.

Nicholls, a retired sea captain in the service of the East India Company, moved to Farndon, Nottinghamshire in 1816. He immediately became active in parochial affairs, taking over the management of the village school and starting a savings bank. He also began to take an active interest in poor relief. It was of course a time when the poor laws were the most widely discussed social problem of the day, and Nicholls became an avid reader of everything published on the topic. He was especially impressed by the report of the House of Commons Select Committee of 1817, and subscribed wholeheartedly to its conclusion that a guaranteed subsistence and the baneful operation of the allowance system were producing demoralization and a disastrous growth of a pauperized population. Looking back in the 1850s over his long career as a poor law reformer and official, which included being one of the three

Poor Law Commissioners after 1834, Nicholls described the effect that the 1817 report had on him:

> The writer well remembers reading the report not long after it was issued, and he believed it was the means of first opening his mind to the consequences of the existing system, and awakened in him an earnest desire for remedying the evils it portrayed, of the actual existence of which he saw proofs everywhere around him.[49]

Moving to Southwell in 1819 and determined to take an active part in the management of the poor laws, Nicholls was appointed an overseer of the poor by Becher. The two men held similar views on the need for more stringent administration of relief, although Becher was to prove more flexible than the increasingly doctrinaire Nicholls. The latter's deterrent policies were much closer to those of a neighbouring magistrate, the Rev. Robert Lowe of Bingham. Both Lowe and Nicholls came to place their faith in the eradication of outdoor relief and the offer of the workhouse as a test of destitution. Lowe is credited with initiating the policy of 'less eligibility' in the county in 1818. He explained to Becher that order could be restored only by 'forcing able-bodied paupers to provide for themselves through the terror of a well-disciplined workhouse'.[50] As Nicholls, who applauded Lowe's efforts and emulated them at Southwell, put it in a letter to the *Nottingham Journal*, the key was to place the poor in a position in which the parish was 'the hardest Taskmaster, the closest Paymaster and the most harsh and unkind friend that they can apply to and whose aid they cannot receive without sacrificing a large portion of their independence and self respect'.[51] Regarding the workhouse, 'the rules observed in it should be so strict and repulsive ... that ... there ought to be nothing in the situation at all calculated to create any desire among the surrounding Population for becoming residents therein ...'.[52]

When Nicholls published this letter and others on the subject in 1822, he injected himself into the national debate on the poor laws. In his pamphlet he revealed himself to be not only an enthusiastic devotee of the workhouse test but a committed Malthusian and doctrinaire believer in classical political economy. The 'wages fund', he insisted, was in dire threat of being swallowed up by the ever-advancing tide of poor relief, resulting in economic ruin if unchecked. While he mentioned the importance of basic schooling, religion, and savings banks as devices for reforming the character of the lower orders, the emphasis throughout was on managing the poor through deterrent relief policies. Nicholls denounced the destructive force of the allowance system, though in fact it had been but recently introduced into Nottinghamshire, and was responsible for relatively modest claims on the poor rates. Nevertheless, he claimed that major reductions in poor relief had been achieved during his tenure as overseer, crediting it to the ending of outdoor relief and the establishment of a well-regulated workhouse. His work impressed the 1824 House of Commons Select Committee on Labourers' Wages, which praised his application of the principle of 'less eligibility'. Thus Nicholls, who had far less to do with the establishment and day-to-day operation of stricter poor law administration in the county than Becher, became its most potent advocate. His writings, especially his *Eight Letters on the Management of the Poor* (1822), did more than anything else to drive home the point with the public that the Nottinghamshire reformers had crafted an austere, rigorous system that was turning back the tide of pauperism. Furthermore, Nicholls's high visibility, enhanced by his testimony before the select committee in 1824, paved the way for his appointment as one of the three Poor Law Commissioners in 1834.

Poor Relief in the Final Years of the Old Poor Law

While focusing on Nottinghamshire gives the impression that the country was moving inexorably towards the New Poor Law, caution is needed. It is true that elsewhere in the country, other resolute magistrates and local leaders were determined to duplicate the successes of Becher, Lowe, and Nicholls. Here and there throughout the country, local leaders applied the Nottinghamshire model. At Lowe's urging, a Gloucestershire JP, J. H. Lloyd Baker, undertook in 1830 the reform of poor law administration at Uley. A community of 2641 inhabitants, mostly employed in the failing local woollen industry, Uley had a full-blown allowance system and an annual relief bill of £3185. Turning the workhouse into a place of terror was the secret. Baker's formula was simple: 'Make the house so disagreeable that no will stay who can work elsewhere'. Within two years, the number of paupers on outdoor relief fell from 977 to 125. Similar policies were adopted at Penzance and Redruth in Cornwall and St Werburgh in Derbyshire.[53] In other places, while the workhouse test was not put into operation, an outdoor labour test on the 'less eligibility' principle was. The Reverend Thomas Whately of Cookham in Berkshire adopted a new policy regarding able-bodied applicants, 'giving them hard work at a lower price than is paid for any other labour in the parish'. Sixty-three long-term recipients of outdoor relief are said to have left the parish as a result. Other places adopted similar policies, including parishes in cities like London, Bristol, Nottingham, and Norwich.[54]

Elsewhere in the 1820s and early 1830s, however, the movement was often in the opposite direction: retreating from a formerly strict regimen, or adopting seemingly more efficient and less demoralizing forms of outdoor relief. Even in places where there were workhouses capable of some classification and rigour, it required the determination of local leaders over a period of years to turn them into effective deterrents against pauperism. Few places had figures as dedicated to the task as Becher and Lowe. Moreover, it must be remembered that many magistrates were unreconstructed paternalists, still operating within the framework of a traditional ethos of caring for the poor. In this light, it was clearly impossible that the deterrent workhouse system would become widespread until Parliament summoned the will to make it mandatory. Given the legislature's manifest unwillingness to pass anything other than permissive acts, parishes throughout the country did what they could to render relief less objectionable and burdensome. In many areas, using the workhouse to discipline the able-bodied was given up altogether, vestries preferring to put their faith in the outdoor labour tests described above.[55] But even this required supervision by parish officials. What was needed was a method of ensuring that the able-bodied performed some sort of regular labour for their parochial pension without placing undue burdens on the time and energy of the overseers. For a time at least, the answer seemed to be two administrative practices, the roundsman system and the labour rate.

The roundsman system began some time in the eighteenth century and was a way of ensuring, in those numerous rural parishes with a surplus population and underemployment, at least minimal compliance with the work requirement of the Elizabethan Poor Law. It involved sending the settled labourers in rotation to each of the farmers, who would then assign whatever work might be needed or invented to the roundsmen, whose wages were paid partly by the farmers and partly out of the poor rate. This system was found useful throughout much of the cereal-growing South and East, especially with the disappearance of rural industry and the spread of threshing machines, both of which reduced employment opportunities. By the 1820s, however, the roundsman system was coming in for increased criticism as further stripping the labourers of all initiative and respect. As a witness before the 1824 House of Commons Select Committee on Labourers' Wages observed, the roundsmen, already work-shy, 'become still worse, by the indolent habits they thus acquire'.[56] It was also an affront to those who believed in the efficacy of free markets, confounding as it did public monies and private wages. Not surprisingly, there was a notable tendency for the portion of the worker's income received in wages to shrink as the amount paid out of the rates grew. In 1822, in one Sussex parish, 'the surplus labourers were put up to auction, and hired as low as two pence and three pence per day, the rest of their maintenance being made up by the parish'.[57]

By the late 1820s developments such as this were causing the roundsman system to fall into disfavour. But it was replaced by an extra-legal expedient known as the labour rate. This involved voluntary agreements among the parishioners to establish a labour rate in addition to the poor rate. The total labour bill of the settled labourers was computed according to what were assumed to be market wages, and each employer was assessed a percentage, in some places on the basis of rateable value and in others on acreage. Any employer not paying the assessment in wages was required to pay the shortfall to the poor rate. This avoided one of the evils of the roundsman system; the tendency for wages to become nominal and most of the workers' income to be paid out the poor rate. With the labour rate, farmers had every incentive to offer employment, and were constrained by the parish agreement to give the 'market' rate of pay (in practice there was usually a small discount off the market wage). Farmers reported improved habits on the part of their labourers, and there was a move to facilitate the adoption of the practice. An 1831 statute provided that any vestry, voting according to the Sturges-Bourne plural voting system, could adopt a legally binding labour rate. The act was valid for three years, terminating in March 1834. By that time, however, the Royal Commission on the Poor Laws, appointed in 1832, had turned its fire on the labour rate and the law was not renewed. The practice was denounced both for its unfairness to ratepayers who employed little or no labour, and for its tendency to promote hiring only settled labourers.[58] In a larger sense, it was past time for such fine tuning of the Old Poor Law. A sea change had occurred in public opinion, especially within the landed interest, in favour of a major overhaul of the system. The chief reason for this dramatic shift was the impact of the Captain Swing riots.

Captain Swing and the Poor Laws

From the summer of 1830 to the winter of 1831, starting in Kent and spreading to other southern, eastern, and Midland counties, a great rising of the labourers took place. Two generations of major social and economic change in the countryside, including the enclosure movement, the disappearance of cottage industry, and the ending by farmers of the practice of providing board for their unmarried labourers, had wrought havoc on the social fabric. These changes, long perceived by workers as detrimental to their interest and dignity, finally caused an eruption of concerted activities ranging from petitioning and mass assemblies to machine breaking, extortion, and arson. Demands for higher wages, the elimination of threshing machines, and less demeaning poor relief testify to the crisis in social relations in the English countryside in 1830. The disturbances also revealed deep fissures within the rural middle and upper classes. Many magistrates and some farmers responded sympathetically to the demands of the poor, others were intimidated into at least outward compliance, while others were determined to restore order at all costs and mete out savage punishments to rioters. The crisis caught the rural social order in a confused, transitional stage between the deeply localized, paternalist certainties of an earlier age and the brave new world of abstractions and automatic market forces offered by the political economists.[59]

Although the early phases of the Swing riots were taken up overwhelmingly by demands for higher wages and the elimination of machinery, grievances over the poor law soon began to surface. As rioting spread into Sussex in October 1830, there were repeated arson attacks against the homes and property of overseers of the poor. Special hatred was held for some of the professional assistant overseers for their tight-fisted policies. In the village of Brede, an assembly of 50 paupers demanded higher allowances and the firing of the assistant overseer, to which the frightened local gentry agreed. Indeed the rioters insisted on subjecting the overseer to the indignity of being ousted from the village in the demeaning parish cart which he had used to convey paupers. This form of intimidation was rapidly copied in adjoining villages.[60] Near Lewes, Lord Gage, the major landowner in the district, had to agree to demands by a large assembly not only to raise wages but 'that the permanent overseers of the neighboring parishes may be directly discharged, particularly Finch, the governor of the Ringmer poorhouse and overseer of the parish'.[61] In Hampshire, the workhouses at Headley and at Selborne were destroyed by mobs at the end of November.[62]

The labourers believed they were operating within the terms of traditional 'moral economy'. Where magistrates and farmers accepted the premises of this traditional ethos, or at least expressed some sympathy for the workers, the atmosphere of the protest could be genial, even festive. When there was strong opposition, intimidation and violence often resulted. The poor were of course aware of those among their betters who had been well disposed on relief questions and those who sought cutbacks and discipline. In the Wiltshire parish of Tisbury, the major landowner, John Benett, MP, who had drawn up the parish's harshly reduced allowance scale in 1817, was particularly hated. Benett responded in kind, leading an aggressive troop of local yeomanry against rioters, yet also found himself at odds with the major farmers in the vestry, who invited the paupers to a vestry meeting to present their grievances. Ironically, while Benett might seem to be a prototypical member of the 'new gentry' and presumably desirous of eliminating the last vestiges of paternalist poor relief, he was to be numbered among that small minority in the House of Commons who voted against the New Poor Law.[63] The Swing riots, while revealing a powerful pent-up set of grievances against a changing agrarian system and harsh poor relief policies, do not demonstrate revolutionary intent or even radicalism on the part of the rioters. Neither do they show a necessarily antagonistic relationship between social classes, but often 'a reciprocal one in which plebeian independence and paternal power coexisted in a complex and mutually sustaining manner'.[64]

In spite of the complexity of reaction in the countryside, however, the Swing riots did create a political climate, especially in Parliament, that made possible the wholesale reform of the poor laws. For one thing, Swing was not an isolated series of events, but rather coincided with the major political upheavals of 1830–32. The death of King George IV as well as the second and final overthrow of the Bourbon dynasty in France, generated enormous political excitement. Anticipations of sweeping reforms in the British electoral system were encouraged by the return of the Whigs to government after decades in the political wilderness. The new ministry's adoption of a major parliamentary reform measure in 1831 stirred political passions even further, and when the House of Lords' initial rejection of the bill led to widespread rioting in cities and countryside, the nation seemed poised on the brink of revolution. Even with the peaceful passage of the Great Reform Act in 1832, there was a profound sense of the precariousness of the established system. Radical forces had been deeply stirred and no one could be confident they would lapse into quiescence just because Parliament had passed one rather limited measure of reform. The Whig leaders, men of great property and aristocratic lineage, were as worried about social stability as the

Tories. This explains their deep concern over Captain Swing, and the savageness of the punishments meted out to the rioters by the government. Nineteen men were executed, and nearly 500 were transported to Australia, a judicial toll greater than that exacted on the Luddites or, later, on the Chartists.[65] Government ministers and many MPs were determined that the anarchy of 1830–31 should never recur. The labourers may have been partially chastened by the courts, but there was further disciplinary work to be done. And that required major reform of the poor laws.

4

THE NEW POOR LAW TAKES SHAPE, 1832–1847

The Reform Ministry and Poor Relief

The leading item on the agenda in Earl Grey's ministry was the reform of Parliament, but was poor law reform also a high priority? Some Whig leaders were deeply involved in the issue both as major landowners and as men with a compelling interest in political economy. The same can be said of those liberal Tories who were also part of the ministry, for it must be remembered that Grey's government was a coalition. Indeed, the reforming segment of the Tory Party had shown a more sustained interest in poor law reform during the previous decade or so than had the Whigs.[1] Furthermore, from the time the government took office it had been faced with the major crisis of the Swing riots, which were widely considered to have resulted in part from demoralizing forms of poor relief. It is also true that there were widespread expectations, especially on the part of liberals within and outside of Parliament, that the new government undertake reforms in other areas. With many of the new MPs representing freshly enfranchised towns in the industrial North and Midlands, there was a greater disposition in the House of Commons to tackle previously intractable problems like poor relief. On poor relief, however, we should not make too much of the shift of personnel in the Lower House, for the new urban members, though mostly Liberals, were not necessarily strongly committed to the issue. The national debate on the poor laws to this point had focused on the crisis in the countryside, and so far it did not appear to have a pressing urban dimension. Also, most of the new Liberal urban MPs were from the North, where in general the poor laws were viewed as less of a problem. Thus, although many of the new MPs might be ideologically disposed, and many members on both sides of the House, especially from rural constituencies, were willing to consider significant reform, it is not clear that the ministry was firmly determined to undertake it.

The government found itself committed to poor law reform in June 1831, when the Lord Chancellor, Lord Brougham, responding to a question from the Earl of Winchelsea, stated that ministers were planning a measure in the next session or two of Parliament for 'the consolidation and simplification of the existing Acts on the subject of the Poor-laws'.[2] Brougham, a Scottish-educated barrister, long-term campaigner for reform of the law, education, and charitable institutions, and founder of the Whig *Edinburgh Review*, took a deep interest in the poor laws. His interests intersected with those of Jeremy Bentham, and he was one of the conduits by which Benthamites like Edwin Chadwick were to acquire important roles in the reform process. Yet it appears likely that Brougham had not consulted his cabinet colleagues, whose hands were forced by his initiative. In February 1832, Lord Althorp, the Chancellor of the Exchequer, told the House of Commons that there would not be a government measure that session, but rather a preliminary investigation. But instead of the customary device of a select committee of the House, Althorp announced that a royal commission would be appointed to conduct an elaborate investigation of the poor laws throughout the country.[3] While not exactly a constitutional innovation (a royal commission on factory conditions for children was already under way), it was an unusual step. Placing the assessment of the problem and the framing of a solution in the hands of extra-parliamentary experts smacked of Benthamite disdain for 'amateur' legislating. However, the shock factor of employing such a device was lessened by the fact that several members of the royal commission appointed in 1832 were present or former MPs.

The Royal Commission on the Poor Laws

The suggestion for a royal commission came from Thomas Hyde Villiers, the Earl of Clarendon's brother, a friend of John Stuart Mill, and secretary of the Board of Control for India. Among Villiers's recommended commissioners were two 'theoretical' men: James Mill, a leading Philosophical Radical, and Nassau Senior, professor of political economy at Oxford. His other recommendations were 'practical' men with a long-term interest in or experience of poor law administration.

One was John Bird Sumner, Bishop of Chester, the Evangelical and moderate poor law abolitionist discussed in the last chapter. The other two on Villiers's list were men of practical administrative experience in the countryside. One was T. L. Hodges, Liberal MP for West Kent and an active magistrate in that county. The other was the Reverend Thomas Whately, a 'dispauperizer' of the parish of Cookham, Berkshire. To Whately, any pauper who was neither elderly or sick was automatically classed among 'the idle, the improvident, vicious'.[4] Lord Brougham, who accepted the wisdom of a royal commission inquiry, solicited names from Nassau Senior. The latter suggested Walter Coulson, barrister, journalist, and a former secretary to Bentham. He also recommended Henry Frankland Lewis, a translator of German works ('sufficient proofs', noted Senior, 'of his diligence') and son of the future Poor Law Commissioner Thomas Frankland Lewis. Rounding out Senior's list was the Reverend Henry Bishop of Oriel College, Oxford, who had 'much exerted himself' administering a country parish. The government appointed two of the men put forward by Villiers (Senior and Sumner) and two from Senior's list (Coulson and Bishop). In addition to William Sturges-Bourne and Henry Gawler, the government also appointed Charles James Blomfield, Bishop of London, who was to prove a tireless proponent of the New Poor Law. Sturges-Bourne was especially reassuring to those who hoped for a practicable reform, since the Select Committee of 1817 that he had chaired was looked upon as an effective inquiry, and the Select Vestries Act that he had devised as one of the most effective pieces of legislation of the post-war period.[5]

In spite of several judicious appointments by the government, the royal commission inquiry faced considerable scepticism as it set about its work. To begin with, the use of a royal commission seemed to many conservatives a dangerous innovation. This feeling was more pronounced in the politically charged atmosphere that prevailed in the aftermath of the narrowly approved and bitterly contested passage of the Great Reform Act. Widely distrusted, Whig ministers were believed to be all too willing collaborators with the reinvigorated forces of radicalism. Moreover, as a party that had spent decades in the political wilderness, their sudden accession to power in 1830 created a widespread anticipation of massive Whig patronage. Each new royal commission (with numerous paid, albeit temporary assistant commissioners) and each new law that created permanent administrative positions was looked upon with a jaundiced eye. Thus the royal commission on the poor laws had to contend with a great deal of scepticism and sometimes outright hostility, from labourers as well as from the middle and upper classes.

Twenty-six assistant commissioners were appointed, each paid a daily allowance and given charge of a particular district in which to conduct his inquiries. In addition to numerous retired military officers and barristers, there were some men from prominent landed families. The most notable of these was C. P. Villiers, a younger brother of the Earl of Clarendon and a future president of the Poor Law Board. Among the 'new men' was a humourless, hard-driving young barrister, Edwin Chadwick, who had worked for two years as secretary to Jeremy Bentham. The most productive investigator and talented report writer of the entire corps of assistant commissioners, Chadwick was promoted to the royal commission the following year, bringing another Benthamite (besides Coulson) to that body. While Senior had wished to give the assistants a free hand in conducting their own inquiries, the full commission insisted on a much more focused investigation. Precise instructions were given to the assistants, directing them to inquire about employment practices and prospects in the district, wage rates, seasonal unemployment, the effect of poor relief on family income, the amount of savings by labouring families, workhouse provision, the degree of magisterial interference, and so on.[6] One question, which suggests the influence of William Sturges-Bourne, directed assistants to examine the advisability of allowing landlords to vote for parochial vestries, on a plural voting system proportionate to the value of land.[7] Such a system, which prefigured the New Poor Law and was already partly embedded in select vestries, could make a critical difference in controlling policy in rural districts. As with the agricultural thrust of most of their labour questions, it is clear that the commission was thinking primarily of the countryside. This can also be seen in the queries that were sent directly by the royal commission to overseers and magistrates throughout the country. Although there were separate town queries, they were closely patterned on the rural queries, making assumptions about employment more appropriate to agriculture.[8]

The assistant commissioners were required to keep daily journals and submit them at the end of each week. This mass of material, together with completed queries from about 10 per cent of the 15 500 parishes in England and Wales, came flooding back upon the royal commission. Not surprisingly, given the fact that the assistants had been instructed to explore the problems growing out of the allowance system and other 'evils', the commission had ample evidence from which to construct a damning report. As John Walter, editor of *The Times*, who was to become a determined foe of the New Poor Law, put it, the questions to local authorities had been designed 'to draw out answers corresponding to the preconceived notions of the commissioners ...'.[9] The slippery wording of some of the questions, plus the ambiguous answers to many queries made it possible to construct a report that, while seemingly an objective digest of the returns, in fact obscured the true complexity of poor relief practices and present a skewed picture of the prevalence of allowances in aid of wages. This was done by a loose usage of the term 'allowance', making it appear that allowances to supplement wages (the classic Speenhamland model) were commonplace, whereas the practice had largely died out during the 1820s. What was usually meant was family allowances, but even here the commissioners obscured the fact that most parishes did not begin to pay a family an increased amount in relief until the third or fourth child. Anyone wishing to challenge the largely predetermined conclusions of the commissioners would be forced to wade through the mass of evidence contained in the appendices to the report. This material was in nine folio volumes, running to nearly 5000 pages.[10]

Knowing that much of the public awaited the results of the inquiry, in 1833 the government rushed into print a volume of extracts from the evidence. This collection of largely anecdotal material painted the alleged abuses of the system in lurid colours, paving the way for the full report in 1834. The official report of 1834, by Senior and Chadwick, while somewhat more measured in its phraseology, still relied a good deal on anecdotes of corruption and abuse. It was constructed in such a way that readers could only conclude that the existing system was grievously flawed and in need of drastic reform. Senior wrote the first part of the report, detailing the abuses of the Old Poor Law, while Chadwick was charged with setting forth the remedial measures necessary to place poor relief on a sound footing. The evils outlined by Senior were declared to be 'steadily and rapidly progressive', though here and there checked by the extraordinary diligence of individuals. The Nottinghamshire reformers were held up for praise, and their labours, along with those of other 'dispauperizers' were linked to a local decline in crime and illegitimacy.[11]

One disagreement that arose between Senior and Chadwick was over the advisability of endorsing the principle of a national mandatory poor law in the report. Senior, much more inclined to abolitionism, wanted to leave it out, but Chadwick prevailed. In the section on remedial measures is his critically important passage:

> In all extensive communities, circumstances will occur in which an
> individual, by the failure of the means of subsistence, will be exposed
> to the danger of perishing. To refuse relief, and at the same time to
> punish mendicity when it cannot be proved that the offender could
> have obtained subsistence by labour, is repugnant to the common
> sentiments of mankind; it is repugnant to them to punish even
> depredation, apparently committed as the only resource against
> want.[12]

Readers who might have considered this a significant concession to
humanitarianism were quickly disabused, however, for the remainder
of the report made clear that the reformed system, at least for the able-
bodied, would be unremittingly harsh. The object was to deter applications for assistance by making the nature of the relief and the conditions
under which it was given repugnant. The twin engines of this new
regime were to be the principle of 'less eligibility' and the workhouse
test. The former required ensuring that the situation of the pauper 'on
the whole shall not be made really or apparently so eligible as the
situation of the independent labourer of the lowest class'.[13] This could
be achieved only by making the able-bodied and their families enter the
workhouse as a test of their destitution. Within the walls of these
forbidding institutions, strict discipline, hard work, a monotonous
diet, and separation of family members would render conditions so
undesirable that labourers would undertake any course of action short
of starvation rather than submit. It was a classic Benthamite squaring of
the circle: do not abolish the poor laws, for this would give starving
workers an excuse for criminal acts. But with the properly designed
building, scheme of classification, indoor regimen, and administration,
a minimal poor law could be safely maintained while poor rates
declined and work discipline and morality were strengthened.

The 21 remedial measures recommended by the royal commission were
scattered through the second half of the report. The most important
points were: ceasing all outdoor relief to the able-bodied, creating a central board to control the administration of all the poor laws, grouping
parishes into poor law unions, authorizing unions of parishes to
create common workhouses, regulating apprenticeship, facilitating
the relocation of paupers to places where work was obtainable, and
lightening the burdens and penalties on fathers of illegitimate children.

There were also recommendations for uniform accounting and contracting systems, the hiring of officers, regular reporting, and other administrative matters that would make the new system both efficient and open to public scrutiny.[14]

Passing the New Poor Law

The main responsibility for turning the recommendations into a workable Act of Parliament was placed in the hands of Nassau Senior and William Sturges-Bourne, assisted by parliamentary solicitor John Meadows White in the drafting of the bill. However, they met frequently with the cabinet during this process, and were instructed to make important changes, including one that limited the life of the new central Poor Law Commission to five years.[15] Moreover, Chadwick was by no means excluded from the process. Even before the report was published, he had been circulating his 'Notes for the Heads of a Bill' to other commissioners and to cabinet ministers. In this document appeared an all-important item which was not in the report: the vesting of local control of poor relief in partially elective boards of guardians for the poor law unions. The final version of his bill gave plural voting rights for guardians' elections on the basis of Sturges-Bourne's Select Vestries Act. It also provided for making magistrates ex-officio guardians in the unions in which they resided. This provided a positive new role for active magistrates, who in parts of the report found themselves vilified for setting aside the decisions of parochial vestries. Now they were being slotted in for an active role in the new system, albeit at the cost of giving up most of their former capacity to control the nature and amount of relief within their districts.[16]

The bill, an amalgam of Chadwick's 'Notes for Heads of a Bill', the input of Senior and Sturges-Bourne, and changes and additions made by the cabinet, was introduced to the House of Commons on 17 April. Lord Althorp's able speech excoriated the allowance system and saluted the efforts of reformers in Nottinghamshire and elsewhere. On the bill's second reading a few weeks later there was some concern expressed about the ominous advance of centralization represented by the bill, but most MPs who spoke in the debate expressed approval, some referring to the frightening ordeal of the recent Swing riots. The bill passed by a vote of 319 to 20.[17] Out of doors, however, the response was much more mixed. While receiving the support of most Liberal papers, the bill drew

the fire of *The Times* and a number of Tory papers, resistance to centralization and jibes at Whig patronage being the main themes of opponents.[18] *The Times*, for example, complained that the proposed new
central commission would have 'the unconstitutional direction and control of the entire funds of upwards of 15 000 parishes in England and
Wales'.[19] Yet other voices began to be raised against the measure that
evoked the historic rights of the poor under the Elizabethan statute and
sought to preserve what they considered a time-honoured and humane
system of relief. In the House of Commons this sentiment was represented by William Cobbett and like-minded radicals, but also by George
Poulett Scrope, economist, geologist, and Liberal MP for Stroud.
Scrope, who had already published an impressive, well-informed critique of the commission's report in the *Quarterly Review*, asked the house
whether Parliament

> was prepared to abrogate, at a word, the legal and ancient title of the
> poor to existence – a title 300 years old, as old, as legal, as fully rec-
> ognized in Acts of Parliament, as the title of the wealthiest noble to
> his estate, and founded on still more evident principles of justice and
> truth.[20]

Such an argument carried little weight in either House of Parliament,
but it resonated powerfully with some squires and farmers, and, most
importantly, among the poor. This would become abundantly clear
when implementation of the statute began the following year.

After the bill proceeded smoothly through the Lower House, it was
sent to the House of Lords in early July. There it encountered somewhat
more resistance, at least on key elements of the measure. The Marquis
of Salisbury, whose opinion carried weight among his fellow Tory peers,
had significant reservations. The most important of these was his opposition to ending all outdoor relief the following summer. Chadwick and
Senior failed in their mission of convincing Salisbury of the importance
of this clause, and it was accordingly dropped.[21] This critical alteration
meant that the eradication of outdoor relief to the able-bodied would
have to be a piecemeal, drawn-out affair, with everything hinging on the
determination of the new central commission and its ability to convince
or compel local boards of guardians. Another critical part of the bill ran
into tremendous resistance in the Upper House: the bastardy clauses.
Negative feelings towards unmarried mothers had been building steadily
for over 30 years, fuelled by Malthusian concerns over population

growth and Evangelical fears of moral collapse. Respondents to the royal commission's queries had been especially severe on women, a typical response being that a woman was 'nine times out of ten, less the seduced than the seducer'.[22] Rural respondents took a considerably harsher view of unwed mothers than their London counterparts. The appearance in 1833 of Harriet Martineau's 'Cousin Marshall' (a story in her *Illustrations of Political Economy*) served to amplify public concern over the allegedly immoral, socially irresponsible, and even predatory sexual behaviour of working-class women.[23]

The bill reflected this vilifying of single women and their offspring by making bastard children the sole responsibility of their mothers. Affiliation proceedings were to be eliminated entirely, thus, it was claimed by supporters, ending the inducement to lewdness, lying, and blackmail. The Commons, however, baulked at the unfairness of placing the entire onus on women (the bill was, according to one detractor, a 'philanderer's charter'), and restored affiliation proceedings, though before two magistrates rather than one, making it more difficult.[24] The exchange in the Lords was even more heated. When Bishop Philpotts of Exeter launched an attack on the bastardy clauses, he was answered by Bishop Blomfield of London, a debate that was quickly dubbed the 'battle of the bishops'.[25] In the end, however, the hardliners prevailed. The Duke of Wellington successfully moved to render affiliation actions virtually impossible by requiring that they be brought before quarter sessions. Furthermore, even with a successful action, maintenance payments were to cease when the child reached the age of seven, and fathers could not be imprisoned for non-payment. When Philpotts and other opponents continued the attack in the following weeks, a compromise was rejected by the government, and the bastardy clauses were approved only by a very narrow margin. When the bill passed its third reading, Philpotts and other opponents inserted a protest in Hansard denouncing the bill's cruelty, the workhouse provisions, and the bastardy clauses.[26] The Poor Law Amendment bill was signed into law by King William IV, a staunch proponent of the measure, on 14 August 1834.

The Poor Law Commissioners Assume Authority

Among the aspirants for appointment to the three Poor Law Commissionerships (paying £2000 a year each) were the anti-slavery activist Zachary Macaulay, the London Philosophical Radical Francis

Place, the Berkshire 'dispauperizer' Thomas Whately, and of course Edwin Chadwick. While the first three merely hoped for an appointment, Chadwick expected one. When the cabinet chose others, Macaulay, Whately, and Place were disappointed; Chadwick was angry and bitter. Nassau Senior had suggested to Lord Melbourne (Prime Minister since the major reshuffle of Grey's cabinet) that Chadwick was well-nigh indispensable. The cabinet decided that Chadwick's appointment might give offence and that he was not of sufficient 'rank and station'. They chose two of the other men on Senior's list, Thomas Frankland Lewis and George Nicholls, and added J. G. Shaw Lefevre. Lewis's chief qualification was his active participation on Sturges-Bourne's select committee of 1817–18. Nicholls, a retired sea captain and Bank of England official, was one of the Nottinghamshire reformers. Thanks to his own publications and the extensive coverage of his reforms in the royal commission's report, Nicholls was already known to the public as both an expert and a practical man. Shaw Lefevre was bailiff of the Spencer estates and a friend of Lord Althorp. Although he clearly owed his selection more to traditional patronage than did his colleagues, he was also a figure of considerable intellectual attainments. He was also the only Whig among the new commissioners, as Lewis was a Tory and Nicholls's political views were unknown.[27] Chadwick, fobbed off with the £1200 a year office of secretary to the commission, was assured he would be a virtual fourth commissioner and next in line for a full appointment; both of these assurances were to prove hollow.[28]

While the Poor Law Commissioners were settling into Somerset House and the assistant commissioners were being appointed, Chadwick unleashed a dizzying array of circulars, memos, and replies to parish officials throughout the land, informing them of the principles of the new system and preparing them for what was to come. This was a heady taste of administrative authority for the ardent Benthamite official, but he was soon to find himself eclipsed as the new board took over its duties.[29] Although frustrating to Chadwick and other Benthamites, this transition to a more measured administrative style was reassuring to the great majority of Liberals and moderate Tories throughout the country who hoped that the prudent men on the Poor Law Commission would set the tone. Above all, they hoped for a respectful attitude on the part of the central agency towards the needs and wishes of the leading elements of the various localities. Of course, even the most conciliatory proceedings would not protect the commissioners from vituperation by those Tories of a passionately partisan persuasion. Nor would they be shielded from denunciation by radical defenders of the rights of the poor, or by the poor themselves. To all these opponents, the Poor Law Commissioners were the 'Tyrants of Somerset House' or sometimes simply the 'Triumvirate'.

There were also assistant commissioners, whose task was to be the eyes and ears of Somerset House in the regions which they superintended. There were nine assistants at first, but with the enormous labours required in setting up the poor law unions and boards of guardians, the Treasury was appealed to repeatedly to sanction additional appointments. This was done reluctantly, but by 1836 there were 21 assistant commissioners. The commissioners were given the direct power of appointing these £700 per year officials. The variety of backgrounds of the corps ranged from barristers and country gentlemen to retired military officers, often with aristocratic relations. The most colourful was the restless Major Francis Bond Head, a Napoleonic War veteran whose lively accounts of his adventures in South America had earned him the sobriquet 'Galloping Head'. The most talented was clearly James Kay (later Sir James Kay-Shuttleworth), whose later career as a major educational reformer under the 1839 Education Act was prefigured in his work as an assistant commissioner.[30]

Creating Poor Law Unions and Boards of Guardians

The most pressing task assigned to the assistant commissioners was the forming of poor law unions and the establishment of boards of guardians. Wearisome travel through the extensive districts assigned to them, often on appalling roads, was required in order to acquire the information and local preferences on which to base these decisions. Encounters with cool and sometimes hostile locals was an everyday reality, though frequently offset by generous hospitality. The Poor Law Commissioners' official criteria for creating poor law unions made the task sound simple: 'The limits of unions which we have found most convenient are those of a circle, taking a market town as a centre, and comprehending those surrounding parishes whose inhabitants are accustomed to resort to the same market'.[31] However, the process was seldom that straightforward, and there were wholesale departures from the market town principle, usually to satisfy the wishes of local elites. This was especially true in gentry-rich agricultural counties like Northamptonshire. Even before newly appointed assistant commissioner Richard Earle set foot in the county in

1835, he had received a written request from the Duke of Grafton's steward requesting that the parishes comprising the estate be formed into a
poor law union. Although this would make an unusually small union,
oddly shaped and without a market town, the request was acceded to and
the Potterspury Union declared. Most of the other 11 unions formed in
the county also departed from the official principle of union formations,
though none quite so egregiously as at Potterspury. Nonetheless, important interests such as the Spencers (the Brixworth Union), the
Cartwrights (the Brackley Union), the Knightleys (the Daventry Union),
and the Fitzwilliams (the Peterborough Union) were accommodated.[32]

In a few other counties where leading local interests took an active part
in the process, there were similar results.[33] In many other parts of the
country, catering to special interests in the formation of poor law unions
was far less marked. It usually required a resident landed magnate
determined to keep his parishes within one union or at least to ensure
that the resulting confederation was politically harmonious. A leading
example is the Duke of Richmond's influence in Sussex. A cabinet
minister as well as the leading landowner in the district, he was determined to have his way in the creation of poor law unions. Matters were
complicated by the presence of several Gilbert Act incorporations, which
the commissioners lacked the authority to dissolve. Elsewhere, Gilbert
unions proved tough nuts to crack, but in the area where the Richmond
estate was centred, it proved effortless. The duke simply requested that
the guardians (many were his tenants; the chairman was his steward)
dissolve the incorporation. It was replaced by the new Westhampnett
Union, which became a model of strict poor relief from the outset. The
Richmond interest on the board was overwhelming. His agent and solicitor was appointed clerk of the new union, and many of the guardians
were Richmond tenants. William Cobbett, a staunch opponent of the
policies pursued by the Westhampnett board, lamented that most of the
guardians were 'tenants of the Duke and of Lord George Lennox [one
of Richmond's brothers], except for one or two, who are tenants of an
old mother Dorien, I think it is, who is a sort of relation of some kind to
this family of Lennox – this endless swarm of everlasting pensioners'.[34]

In the absence of this sort of active influence, assistant commissioners
were relatively free to form poor law unions with administrative efficiency and the convenience of the general inhabitants in mind.
Ordinary magistrates and most members of the gentry lacked the kind
of clout wielded by an Earl Spencer or a Duke of Richmond. While
most proved receptive to the new law, some were apprehensive that the

drastic change in relief might touch off another labourers' revolt. A recent study of union formation in Oxfordshire shows what happened when no resident magnate was concerned to exert himself. With no preponderating landed influence brought to bear (the anti-New Poor Law Duke of Marlborough, a Whig, largely ignored the process), decisions were made chiefly on the basis of general convenience, with the exception of the Thame Union. However, the mostly Tory magistrates in the county, some of whom were middling landowners, did favour the law and tended to take an active part on the boards as ex-officio guardians, at least during the first year or so. An obvious concern to coordinate their roles as magistrates and guardians can be seen in their determination after 1834 to have petty sessional division boundaries redrawn so that they conformed to those of the poor law unions.[35] Thus, whether or not union boundaries were constructed to accommodate landed estates, many magistrates believed that they had a vital role to play as poor law guardians. It helped that the majority of them accepted the wisdom, or at least the necessity, of the new system. For these reasons, the act's implementation proceeded relatively smoothly, especially in the rural South-east and Midlands, through 1835 and 1836. The word 'relatively' needs to be underscored, for, as we shall see in the section on labourers' resistance, all was not quiet, not even in the seemingly well-ordered areas.

In London, and in quite a few Midlands and northern industrial towns, the middle and upper classes were less receptive to the act than most of their rural counterparts. The long tradition of proud self-government in the capital was evident in the voting in the House of Commons, where a number of metropolitan MPs had opposed the bill. Sir Samuel Whalley had rhapsodized about his parish, St Marylebone, being 'a little kingdom – aye, a little kingdom'.[36] The desire of some of these 'little kingdoms' to remain free of central government interference was played out in the law courts. When ordered to conduct elections according to the system provided in the statute, the parish of St Pancras, constituted under an 1819 Act, contested the commissioners' authority, winning an important battle in the Court of King's Bench in 1837. This victory encouraged other London parishes to offer similar defiance, though few were as successful as St Pancras.[37] In much of the rural North, the creation of poor law unions and boards of guardians proceeded smoothly enough through 1836 and 1837, but many urban leaders proved resistant, especially in middling size industrial towns. Large cities such as Manchester, on the other hand, witnessed a relatively quiet implementation. In the North, the commissioners soon came to realize that the smaller the town, the more likely they were to encounter resistance.[38] Opponents of the law were often elected guardians, and, when in a majority, were able to thwart the implementation of the statute by refusing to build a workhouse or even to appoint a clerk. In some cases, new workhouses were not built for another 20 years and there was considerable footdragging on major policy matters.[39] This resistance was sometimes evident even before town labourers had shown their own intense hatred of the new law.

Workers' Resistance to the New Poor Law

There was determined resistance by the labourers to the New Poor Law in both rural and urban areas, and in both South and North. Since the implementation of the act began in the Midlands and South, the first outbreaks occurred there. Not surprisingly, many of the disturbances took place in areas marked by the Swing riots a few years earlier. Kent proved an especially difficult southern county to bring under the law. The Milton Union, near Rochester, witnessed a number of outbreaks when it was announced that henceforth most outdoor relief would be paid in kind instead of in cash. Relieving officers were mobbed and their papers destroyed. In one instance the entire board of guardians, pursued and showered with stones and other missiles, was saved by the timely arrival of a detachment of troops.[40] In another part of the county, when magistrates tried to quell an anti-poor law riot, they told the crowd they were only carrying out the law. The workers retorted that 'they knew better, the justices had made the law themselves'.[41] Considering the overlapping of the magistracy with that reforming part of the gentry that had been of major importance over several decades in promoting a drastic overhaul of the poor laws, this was a shrewd observation. Buckinghamshire witnessed major demonstrations as well. A large crowd of women booed and hurled stones at officials transferring paupers from small parish workhouses to the large centralized one at Amersham. A separate crowd rescued paupers being conveyed in a cart to Amersham, ignoring the accompanying magistrate's reading of the Riot Act and pelting him with stones for good measure.[42] Through the autumn of 1834 and the winter of 1835, rural Wiltshire witnessed large demonstrations of workers, punctuated by incidents of incendiarism and threats against local officials deemed responsible for harsher policies.[43] Labourers in Wales also showed a marked repugnance for the new system. When the Llanfyllin guardians voted to discontinue paying pauper rents, hundreds of workers surrounded the meeting, a red flag was waved, and the guardians had to flee under a bombardment of eggs and other objects. Smouldering resentment of the New Poor Law continued for years in Wales, and was an important factor in the Rebecca Riots of 1842–43.[44] There were also major anti-poor law riots in Suffolk, Devon, and Cornwall. By 1837, however, the Poor Law Commissioners and local magistrates had restored order, using London police detachments as well as military units.[45] But that same year, the North erupted in opposition.

Throughout most of the rural North, the act was implemented relatively quietly, though usually without much enthusiasm. Certain northern towns saw the most concentrated and determined resistance to the new system. Popular radicalism was a critical factor in the region. Inspiring other towns in its defiance of the New Poor Law was Oldham, a Lancashire textile town whose MPs were none other than William Cobbett and John Fielden, both active opponents of the law. Most other middle-class leaders in the vicinity were also either unfriendly to the measure or intimidated from showing support for it. Large crowds of workers and their families were mobilized to prevent the process of electing guardians from going forward in the central townships of the union. With few willing to risk incurring the wrath of the community and possibly even suffering physical injury, there was a total boycott of the first poor law elections, a severe embarrassment to the Poor Law Commission.[46] Oldham was unique, however, in carrying this off. Elsewhere the boycott strategy was only partially successful, with outlying townships in many unions proceeding to elect guardians. A split developed over the best strategy for confounding the new law between advocates of election boycotts and those arguing for the election of anti-poor law guardians. The Poor Law Commissioners did ultimately have the power to compel compliance by northern boards of guardians, but with the intense popular agitation, much of it backed and even encouraged by middle-class leaders, they often temporized. This became especially true after 1837, when Parliament took a more critical view of the New Poor Law, and especially the workhouse test.

The Workhouse and the Strategy of Deterrence

As originally envisaged by the royal commissioners, the new measure would have eliminated all outdoor relief to the able-bodied and their

families, who henceforth would be confronted by an offer of the
workhouse. If truly indigent, they might avail themselves of it rather
than starve, but after experiencing the rigours of the institution would
surely discharge themselves and go to any lengths to find the necessary
employment for sustenance. As the repellent nature of the workhouse
regimen became widely known among the poor, applications from the
able-bodied were expected to fall off sharply, leaving the workhouse as
chiefly a recourse for the aged, the infirm, and unattached children.
The original poor law bill in 1834 reflected this policy, calling for an end
to all outdoor relief to the able-bodied by July 1835. However, this
clause had been struck from the bill in the House of Lords, and the
workhouse test moved from being a mandated policy to one that was
provisional in character. Certainly the Poor Law Commission had the
authority to issue orders abolishing able-bodied outrelief, but because
Parliament had refused to make the policy statutory, the commissioners
were obliged to proceed with caution. In practice, the workhouse test
often became a matter to be negotiated between the central authority,
the guardians, and, because of fear of mass insurrections, the poor
themselves.

Another aspect of the official thinking of 1834 that underwent a drastic overhaul as the law was implemented was the nature of the workhouse itself. The royal commission seemed to have envisaged a set of
smaller workhouses, each designated for a different class of pauper. The
1834 report described different types of institution which should,
ideally, be provided in each locality, serving the able-bodied males, able-
bodied females, aged and infirm males, aged and infirm females, and
children. The report even spoke of 'indulgences' for the aged, along
with education for the children. Both would be severely compromised by
an indiscriminate mixing of paupers under the same roof.[47] As boards
of guardians took up their duties in late 1834 and 1835, the policy of
several smaller workhouses in each poor law union proved unpopular
with most boards. It was originally thought that the policy would appeal
on economic grounds, for having several establishments would permit
the use of existing parish workhouses, thus avoiding major expenditures
on new construction. This was an argument pushed by Assistant
Commissioner William Day to his boards of guardians as well as to his
superiors at Somerset House, who were at first disposed to approve of
it. But Day's colleague, Sir Francis Bond Head, argued for the benefits
of a single new workhouse in each union, and this proved much more
popular with boards of guardians. While the cheese-paring mindset of

poor law guardians predisposed them to avoid major outlays, other factors encouraged the creation of a large new central workhouse. It offered considerable savings on staff, since four separate establishments in each union would have required more personnel. Furthermore, guardians were apt to see a large new workhouse as a potent symbol of the new order, one that would serve to underscore the futility of labourers' resistance.[48] Combined with this show of authority was the desire to inculcate pride in an important new organ of local government. As Sir Francis Bond Head explained:

> The very sight of a well-built efficient establishment would give confidence to the Poor Law Guardians; the sight and weekly assemblage of all the servants of the Union would make them feel proud of their office; the appointment of a chaplain would give dignity to the whole arrangement, while the pauper would feel it was utterly impossible to contend against it.[49]

The Poor Law Commission engaged a young architect named Sampson Kempthorne to provide ready-made plans that poor law unions could adopt. His designs, which were circulated to boards of guardians and printed in the first annual report of the commissioners, offered a choice of two basic plans, one cruciform, the other hexagonal, accommodating 200–500 paupers. Both featured the workhouse master's quarters at a point of convergence of the accommodation blocks, thus symbolically reinforcing the impression of constant surveillance, though it was but a faint echo of the invasive visual monitoring integral to Bentham's Panopticon. Both designs provided for classification by gender, as well as separate wards for children and special provision for the infirm. Kempthorne's cruciform design was to prove the more popular, though usually with considerable local variation: an extra storey here, an extension of a wing there.[50] If the different wards and the classification scheme would make the new workhouse 'well regulated', the regimen within would provide the all-important element of deterrence. But even the façade was designed to strike terror into the hearts of prospective relief applicants, and one commentator, otherwise well disposed to the reform, noted that Kempthorne's 'unhappy designs ... suggested the ideas of Bastiles'.[51] This was indeed the term that had been applied by the poor and their defenders from the very outset. There were, of course, a number of larger workhouses from earlier periods that were deemed suitable, such as the Southwell workhouse, which had been such a powerful instrument for the Nottinghamshire reformers. Though constructed a decade before the New Poor Law, its design and operation were very much like those built after 1834. Similarly, the Richmond workhouse, though erected in 1786, was praised as well designed and well run by the royal commission of 1832–4, and continued to operate as a workhouse until the early twentieth century. It is now a block of luxury flats.[52]

The forbidding nature of the new establishments was underscored by the nature of the personnel recruited to staff them. There was a marked preference, on the part of Somerset House and the local boards, for men with military experience for the particularly sensitive posts of workhouse master and relieving officer. A Poor Law Commission directive expressed it well: 'The habits of firmness, self-control, and coolness, combined with attention and exactitude, imparted by military services, have been found peculiarly to fit them for the performance of the duties of relieving officers of workhouses, or of masters, with instructions'.[53] Nothing better conveys the harsh disciplinary character of the new regimen than the thousands of former non-commissioned officers who were engaged to superintend and regulate the lives of those unfortunate enough to fall under their sway. While there were certainly competent and even humane officials among them, workhouse masters on the whole demonstrated little sympathy for the inmates, even for the children, aged, and infirm who were supposed to be treated kindly. The worst were corrupt, sadistic tyrants.

The Somerset House establishment was divided on the wisdom of trying to enforce the workhouse test when there was significant local opposition, either from guardians or from paupers. As befit a former Nottinghamshire reformer, George Nicholls was the commission's hardliner. He argued for working to eliminate outdoor relief to the able-bodied as quickly as possible, and was strongly supported by the secretary, Edwin Chadwick. But Frankland Lewis and Shaw Lefevre, the other two commissioners, were more moderate and cautious. They were much more inclined to accommodate 'respectable' public opinion about the use of workhouses. Although they were willing to issue prohibitory orders against outdoor relief, these carried a critically important exception for 'cases of sudden and urgent necessity'.[54] The decisions of boards of guardians about whether particular applicants fell under this provision were generally accepted by Somerset House. Within a decade, as we shall see, a separate stream of orders specifically sanctioning an outdoor labour test for the able-bodied was also in place. Yet, in spite of there not being an unequivocal mandate from central government, many local boards enthusiastically proceeded to use the workhouse test on the large number of outdoor paupers who were accustomed to receiving weekly pensions. Rapturous anecdotes about the effectiveness of the system began to pour into Somerset House. The clerk of the Bicester Union in Oxfordshire reported that a tailor who had been receiving outdoor relief for years, when offered a ticket of admission to the workhouse, said that he would 'rather be tied to the top of the highest tree in the parish than go there and has never applied for relief since'.[55]

Other boards of guardians were less aggressive in their use of the workhouse test, reserving it for those deemed recalcitrant, shiftless, or immoral. Certain boards, especially in the North and Wales, refused either on ideological or financial grounds to use the workhouse (some even refused to build one) in this fashion.[56] It is also true that the allowance system was by no means eliminated by the New Poor Law. Many boards found it cheaper to maintain a pauper and his family outside the workhouse, especially if this was seen as a temporary expedient to get them through a bad patch occasioned by sickness, injury, or seasonal unemployment.[57] The continuation of allowances and the considerable local and regional variation should not, however, obscure the fact that the workhouse was used in a deterrent fashion to a far greater extent than had been the case prior to 1834, and that such outdoor relief as was given to families under the New Poor Law was generally less than it had been before. The results were dramatic. The total poor relief expenditure in England and Wales, £6 310 000 in 1834, had declined to £4 045 000 by 1837, and would not reach Old Poor Law levels again until the 1860s, in spite of a rapidly growing population. More tellingly, relief expenditures per head of total population declined from 8s. 10d. in 1834 to 5s. 5d. in 1837, and remained in the 5s. to 7s. per head range for the remainder of the nineteenth century.[58] Moralists, ideologues, and ratepayers had fashioned a powerful weapon indeed against the importuning of the poor. As Assistant Commissioner E. C. Tufnell observed approvingly of the new workhouses, 'their prison-like appearance, and the notion that they are intended to torment the poor, inspires a salutary dread of them'.[59]

The workhouse was a place of dread for several reasons. The loss of personal freedom, accompanied by a sense of shame and failure, operated as a powerful psychological deterrent quite apart from the conditions encountered within. Then a host of visually repellent impressions assailed the pauper as he or she entered the house: the grim, prison-like exterior, the rough reception by the porter, the joyless aspect of the interior, the demeaning nature of the workhouse garb. Family members entering together were split up and assigned to the appropriate wards: able-bodied men, able-bodied women, the aged and infirm of each sex, and children. The only exception was that, after 1840, in response to public outcries, any married couple over the age of 60 had a right to their own room in the workhouse.[60] Dormitory sleeping and repellent privies added to the pauper's woes. Even a privy could be a luxury. One 18-year-old woman, confined to a workroom with others who had not laboured satisfactorily, described it as 'very close and offensive, owing to a pail in which we all did the calls of nature, and the place being constantly locked'.[61] The activities of each day were regulated with an irksome and unvarying precision. Rising at dawn, bathing hurriedly and communally, the pauper dressed and went to the dining hall for a breakfast of thin gruel and bread, always in the precise and insufficient portions spelled out in one of the Poor Law Commission's approved dietaries. Dinner was the only meal to show any variation, small quantities of meat, bacon, and vegetables being added to the bread and cheese a few days of the week. Supper was bread and cheese. Smaller portions were allotted to women and children. Persons over 60 were often allowed a bit of tea and sugar, an inducement for paupers to claim a more advanced age when they were admitted to the workhouse.[62] The sick were generally dieted at the discretion of the medical officer.[63] Such 'indulgences', as well as the roast beef dinners provided on Christmas Day and a few special occasions such as the coronation of Queen Victoria, did little to counter the dismal dining experience of indoor paupers. The quality of the food was often appalling, and the cooking designed to make it as unpalatable as possible.

In between meals, of course, came the major activity of the day, that which gave the institution its name: work. Like the meals and every other aspect of workhouse life, it was designed to be as monotonous and irksome as possible. Able-bodied men were generally put to the heaviest tasks, which, depending on the workhouse in question, might be breaking stones for use in road repair, pulverizing bones for fertilizer (introduced at Southwell by George Nicholls in the 1820s[64]), or picking oakum. The last of these involved the untangling of strands of hemp from pieces of old, tarred rope, a task very hard on the hands. Then there was 'the crank', a multi-handled corn mill turned with great exertion by several paupers to produce flour.[65] Able-bodied women were usually assigned to long hours of domestic work: cleaning, scrubbing, preparing food, laundry, and infant tending. Not infrequently, women, especially those considered recalcitrant by the master or matron of the house, were assigned to oakum picking or other tasks ordinarily reserved for men.[66]

The aged, while exempt from most work requirements, had a particular reason to fear becoming indoor paupers: the very real possibility that if they died in the workhouse, their bodies would be turned over to medical schools for dissection. Workhouse masters were empowered to do this under the terms of the Anatomy Act of 1832. As the study of anatomy and surgery expanded in the eighteenth and nineteenth centuries, the number of hanged felons (the traditional source of supply) proved inadequate. With the market price of cadavers on the rise, there was a growing incentive to grave robbing (often connived at by the anatomy professors) and even murder (or 'burking', named after a notorious Glasgow supplier, who, with his partner Hare, suffocated his victims). The Anatomy Act, while undermining the incentives for body-snatching and burking, substituted poverty for criminality as the legal qualification for dissection. The intense anxiety among the poor about their looming post-mortem desecration (endangering or preventing, many believed, their resurrection in the afterlife), is expressed in an 1834 broadsheet titled 'The Christian's Appeal against the Poor Law Amendment Act by a Working Man.' Part of the poem reads:

> Driven before the wind and pelting storm
> Of Bastile fury – lo! The bending form
> Of the old man, his anxious care-worn brow,
> He smites in anguish, solitary now:
> No rural cot, no lovely daughter's smile,
> No sons, to soothe him in the dreaded Bastile –
> No tender partner of his sorrows near.
> To cool his bosom with a falling tear;
> At thoughts of by-gone days he inly mourns,
> And vainly on his wretched pallet turns;
> No help is nigh, a dread and fearful gloom
> Surrounds him with the horrors of his doom.
> A worse than felon's doom! For when his life
> Returns to God! Then, then, the bloody knife
> Must do its work – the body that was starved,
> By puppy doctors must be cut and carved:[67]

And this was written before the New Poor Law had begun to be fully implemented.

Anti-Poor Law Politics and Chartism

In spite of the lopsided majority by which the New Poor Law had passed
and in spite of the strong support given by Sir Robert Peel and other
Tory Party leaders,[68] the measure was politically vulnerable, especially
after 1837. Throughout the countryside and in many towns, there continued to be a great deal of scepticism and some outright hostility. Many
provincial newspapers had struck a critical note early on. Political passions, often more intense in the counties than at Westminster, found a
natural outlet in anti-poor law politicking. This was especially true since
the Poor Law Commission had been granted only a five-year term, and the
renewal legislation would offer a tempting target. For several years, the
intensity of resistance to the law in the North gave shape and focus to
this opposition, yet the combination of political forces in this opposition
quickly proved untenable. An important part had been taken by
key Conservative figures in the region, such as the Anglican parson
G. S. Bull, the Methodist leader Joseph Rayner Stephens, and the land
agent Richard Oastler.[69] Such men, also active in factory reform, articulated an especially combative brand of Tory paternalism based on ideals
of organic social relationships inherited from an earlier age. As such,
while they could join in common cause with radicals and Chartists
against the New Poor Law, their basic political creed diverged sharply
from their allies. Conservative opponents of the law embraced a well-
ordered hierarchy in which a powerful sense of duty to care for the poor
was to be reciprocated by deference and respect. Radical middle- and
working-class opponents, on the other hand, espoused an essentially
secular and egalitarian ethos. In their eyes, the New Poor Law was a
symptom of class rule. Once the electoral system was democratized, the
people would quickly put an end to the New Poor Law and all other
oppressive acts. The conservative–radical alliance scarcely survived the
1830s, at which point militant working-class opposition to the poor law,
by now thoroughly enmeshed in the Chartist movement, was discountenanced by all but a handful in the upper and middle classes.

A broader and more diffuse opposition to the law was also in evidence
among the 'respectable' classes. It was apt to be expressed in print
rather than in the streets, lacked a sharp political focus, and was not necessarily paternalistic or Christian. The chief articulator of this largely
middle-class distaste for the law's harshness was Charles Dickens. *Oliver
Twist* was presented to the public in serialized form from 1837 to 1839.
Whatever its inaccuracies as to the details of workhouse life, the novel

portrayed powerfully the essential inhumanity of the new law. The outrage felt by Dickens's readers over the brutal treatment of a hapless foundling derived from their sense that there should be a fundamental decency to public life. Oliver's close brush with a life of crime made an additional point. The new institutions were not only morally repugnant but apt to produce the very conditions they claimed to combat: poverty and crime. In *A Christmas Carol* (1843), Dickens again attacked the work-house system, this time by having Scrooge invoke it to justify refusing all charitable assistance to the poor. Moreover, Dickens made the link between the New Poor Law and Malthusianism explicit by having Scrooge express satisfaction when told that many of the poor would rather die than enter the workhouse: 'If they would rather die, they had better do it, and decrease the surplus population.' The Malthusian link had certainly been played up by others, most notably in the scurrilous *Marcus on Populousness*, allegedly written by one of the Poor Law Commissioners, instructing poor law officials to limit the population by all means necessary. This publication and its offshoots came to be accepted by many in the labouring class as official 'murder manuals' for exterminating paupers,[70] though few among the educated accepted this attribution. For his part, Chadwick considered the charge of heartless Malthusianism especially unfair, as he had consistently denied that there was any surplus population.[71] A compendium of alleged workhouse abuses, G. Wythen Baxter's *Book of the Bastiles* was published in 1841, the same year that A. W. Pugin, in *Contrasts*, depicted a prison-like Panopticon workhouse dominating a town in 1840, juxtaposed to a pic-ture of the same town in 1440 graced by a welcoming almshouse.[72]

While apocalyptic fear and intense hatred of the New Poor Law were working-class phenomena, there was at least some uneasiness among all classes. This did not translate into a movement for repeal, and most members of the troubled middle and upper classes continued to support the law but salved their consciences through greater philanthropic efforts. What it did translate into, however, was Parliament's willingness to undertake an inquiry into the act's operation and to attempt to secure some protection against the worst abuses. In 1837 and 1838, a House of Commons select committee probed the law's defects. The committee's reports, while favourable on the whole, called for greater vigilance to prevent cruelties and more discretion by boards of guardians in grant-ing relief.[73] There was also a general election in 1837, in which the Whig government lost 23 seats. Here and there, ardent Tories made poor law opposition a rallying cry, but most of the government's losses were due to other issues.[74] The ministry and the commissioners took satisfaction at the crushing defeat of John Fielden's motion to repeal the New Poor Law. However, they were forced to accept a loosening of central government authority as the price of favourable select committee reports in 1837 and 1838 and the renewal of the Poor Law Commission's powers for an additional five years in 1839.[75]

Poor Relief in the Hungry Forties

Somerset House was afflicted by considerable disarray and not a little demoralization by the end of the 1830s. The chorus of criticism had increased, particularly when the law began to be implemented in the industrial North. The New Poor Law survived handily, when judged by the lopsided parliamentary majorities against repeal and in favour of the continuation bill of 1839, yet a considerable abatement of the commission's power had taken place. Even favourably disposed districts insisted on operating with a far greater degree of autonomy than Chadwick and other centralizing zealots had envisaged. And although the great majority of boards of guardians found the workhouse test a useful device for disciplining their poor, there was considerable scepticism about using it in a rigidly doctrinaire manner. Moreover, Chadwick's stalwart ally, George Nicholls, was no longer on hand, having been ordered to Ireland to implement the 1838 Irish Poor Law, the first in that country's history. The problem of destitute Irish labourers in England and Wales, without any statutory provision for poor relief in Ireland, had long been complained of by local poor law authorities. The Home Secretary, Lord John Russell, who wanted a particularly strict version of the English Poor Law for Ireland, set aside an earlier, more progressive set of recommendations, directing Nicholls to conduct his own inquiry. After a whirlwind tour of 12 counties over 6 weeks, Nicholls issued his report. Asserting that the Irish were a work-shy, reckless race who needed the strong medicine of a deterrent workhouse system, Nicholls called for an extension of the English New Poor Law to Ireland. An Irish Poor Law bill modelled on his recommendations was passed in 1838, and he was ordered to Ireland to bring it into operation. In contrast to the English Poor Law, where powerful local interests had to be consulted and sometimes deferred to, Nicholls was given a free hand in Ireland. The country was quickly formed into 130 poor law unions, each with its own central workhouse. In stark contrast to the system in

England and Wales, the Irish Poor Law prohibited all outdoor relief to the able-bodied, a provision that Nicholls had insisted upon. Returning to London in November 1842 after wielding supreme authority for four years, Nicholls found the resumption of his official duties at Somerset House an ordeal. He failed to influence his new colleagues, Sir Edmund Head and George Cornewall Lewis, who followed their predecessors J. G. Shaw Lefevre and Sir Thomas Frankland Lewis in steering a cautious, conciliatory course in poor law administration. In his absence, the two had succeeded in marginalizing Chadwick, whose interests had turned decidedly towards public health, even though he continued in his post as secretary to the Poor Law Commission.

Apart from the pragmatic predilections of two of the three Poor Law Commissioners, there was another key factor that militated against doctrinaire policies. A trade depression that began in 1837 had, by the early 1840s, caused a major downturn in key industrial sectors, including textiles. For the first time since the passing of the New Poor Law, the country was hit with massive urban unemployment. If many workers had proved hostile to the law in the still relatively good times of the New Poor Law's first two years, what would be their reaction if officials compelled the use of the workhouse in a time of economic crisis? Moreover, if more than a small portion of the unemployed were actually to accept the offer of the house, the workhouses would quickly be overwhelmed. Thus in terms of both political expediency and the lack of indoor accommodation, a sanctioning of outdoor relief in some form was a necessity. This had indeed been done from the outset, in the form of the 'sudden and urgent necessity' clause of the commissioners' orders. The 1834 law had provided that any 'general order' issued by the commissioners had to be laid before Parliament and would not come into effect for 40 days, during which time Parliament might decline to sanction it. 'Special orders', on the other hand – those addressed to a single poor law union – were subject to no such delay and parliamentary review. Quite naturally, Somerset House chose to issue all its directives as special orders, at least until 1841. Hundreds of these special orders were sent at the same time, identical except for the name of the poor law union. These orders covered such topics as management of workhouses, the duties of officials, medical relief, education, and of course relief to the able-bodied.[76] In addition to the 'sudden and urgent necessity' exception embedded in all the relief orders, clause 52 of the New Poor Law allowed boards of guardians considerable discretion, especially when outdoor relief took the form of food, temporary lodging, or medicine.[77]

From 1841, Somerset House altered its policy in regard to relying on special orders, and began issuing a stream of general orders, even though this meant submitting to parliamentary scrutiny and accepting a 40-day delay. The change is possibly linked to the coming to power of Sir Robert Peel's Conservative government that year. Although Peel and the new Home Secretary, Sir James Graham, were friends of the New Poor Law, they might have considered parliamentary oversight a useful check on any future administrative high-handedness. The most important order issued during these years was the Outdoor Relief Prohibitory Order of 1844. In its original form, this order stipulated that no outdoor relief was to be given to the able-bodied without some sort of approved task work being exacted in return. Moreover, at least one-third of such relief was to be paid in kind (usually bread or food tickets), and was to be disbursed only from week to week. However, the outcry from boards of guardians at this seeming curtailment of their discretionary powers led the House of Commons to insist on loosening the order.[78] Thus, even had Chadwick and Nicholls been able to promulgate draconian outdoor relief orders, the political system in which their administrative authority was enmeshed would have ensured that it was moderated.

On the other hand, we should not be misled by these manoeuvrings into thinking that there was a struggle between central government and the localities regarding the fundamental nature and quality of poor relief. Most guardians throughout the country considered the curtailment of poor relief necessary to both the moral health and the fiscal integrity of their communities. This could only be achieved by stigmatizing relief, especially to the able-bodied. To be sure, they sharply contested doctrinaire directives from London, believing that, as local leaders, they were in the position to discriminate between the deserving and undeserving (a distinction not recognized by official doctrine). Yet, from the all-important vantage point of the poor, there was no meaningful distinction between central and local policies. Workers and their families were acutely aware that when hard times struck, they would be thrown on the tender mercies of a tight-fisted board of guardians, harsh treatment by poor law officials, and the all-too-real possibility of having to enter the workhouse. Even those granted outdoor relief were made to feel the shame of their situation, and of course generally received less than they would have under the Old Poor Law. This is why unemployed workers, like those in Manchester in the mid-1840s, chose on average to wait six weeks after losing their jobs before applying for relief. They preferred exhausting every other means of support and communal credit before submitting to the brutal indignities of the poor law.[79] Such feelings of repugnance were gratifying to both local and central officials, and were precisely what had been intended by the architects of the New Poor Law.

The Andover Scandal and the End of the Poor Law Commission

Not surprisingly, in an atmosphere of intense hostility to the law by the working classes, as well as considerable uneasiness about it on the part of many others, any abuses were quickly made public. Throughout the 1840s, a series of workhouse cruelties, involving violations of Poor Law Commission guidelines, were reported by *The Times*, various provincial papers, and of course the Chartist press. Most of these were found upon examination to have involved at least some degree of exaggeration. *The Times* routinely published stories of inmates being confined, whipped, and receiving inadequate diets, some of them allegedly dying as a result of such cruelties.[80] Boards of guardians were quick to deny these allegations, and most incidents were investigated, usually by the Assistant Poor Law Commissioner assigned to the district. A whitewash was the usual result, or at least a claim that the abuses were relatively minor. A close study of 21 reports carried in *The Times* suggests that 12 were largely false, 5 were true, while the other 4 were never investigated.[81] Chartists were behind some of the charges, and in at least one instance in 1844 – in the Basford Union in Nottinghamshire – a radical guardian colluded with workhouse inmates, Chartists, and a local paper to bring false charges of vermin-infested bedding and clothing.[82] The absolving of the workhouse master and guardians of blame in the matter in the ensuing investigation, typical of most cases, helped convince the public that conditions were not nearly as bad as portrayed in the pages of *The Times* and other papers. However, in 1845, a workhouse scandal of major proportions triggered a public outcry and parliamentary investigation, which in turn led to the first major overhaul of the administrative structure of the New Poor Law.

The Andover Union in Hampshire had been a model of strict poor law administration from its creation in 1835. Its determination to stop all outdoor relief to the able-bodied and its 'well-ordered' workhouse (using the lowest of all the officially sanctioned dietaries) had won official recognition from the Poor Law Commissioners in their annual reports. In 1837, the board appointed as workhouse master Colin M'Dougal, a former sergeant major who had fought at Waterloo and had a reputation as a strict disciplinarian. His grim-faced wife Mary Ann was hired as workhouse matron, the guardians approving the appointments by a large majority and with every expression of satisfaction.[83] Over the next years, the M'Dougals were given a remarkably free hand, the guardians carrying out only the most cursory inspections, and invariably accepting the master's assurances that all was well. In 1845, there was the first public revelation that all was not well. A report that famished pauper inmates assigned to bone-crushing had resorted to gnawing the rotten bones to extract the marrow and gristle led to a question in the House of Commons by Thomas Wakley (Finsbury), a medical doctor and avowed opponent of the New Poor Law. The ensuing investigation by the overworked assistant commissioner, Henry Parker, found that not only was the original report true, but that all the inmates were served less food than even the inadequate dietary specified.[84]

The Poor Law Commission tried to protect itself by issuing a general order prohibiting bone-crushing in workhouses and by securing the workhouse master's resignation. Furthermore, they blamed their own assistant commissioner, Parker, for failing to uncover these abuses in his regular inspections, ignoring the fact that the corps of assistants had been pared back from a high of 21 to a mere 9, making meaningful inspections impossible. Forced to resign, Parker struck back with an ably argued pamphlet. His cause was taken up not only by the law's opponents within and outside Parliament, but eventually by Edwin Chadwick, who championed Parker in order to attack his superiors, especially George Cornewall Lewis and Sir Edmund Head.[85] By the time Chadwick weighed in, the matter had been referred to a House of Commons select committee which contained three outright opponents of the law: Thomas Wakley, John Fielden, and Benjamin Disraeli. In the course of the inquiry, a host of other iniquities was brought to light, including M'Dougal's drunkenness, sexual abuse of female inmates, and gruesome irregularities in pauper burials. The committee was highly critical of the Poor Law Commission's oversight, their failure to prohibit labour of a 'penal or disgusting' nature, and their treatment of Parker.[86] It was clear that a major shake-up was in the works, though the government decided to wait until the five-year term of the Poor Law Commission expired in 1847.

The reorganization bill introduced in 1847 under the recently reinstalled Liberal government headed by Lord John Russell created a major change in the central agency. The Poor Law Commission was swept away, replaced by a Poor Law Board consisting of four senior ministers: the Home Secretary, the Chancellor of the Exchequer, the Lord President of the Council, and the Lord Privy Seal. This body was never really intended to meet; real authority was vested in the president of the Poor Law Board, who was to sit in Parliament, and his two secretaries, one of whom was also to be in Parliament. It was anticipated that the president would be in the House of Lords while the parliamentary secretary would be an MP, but in practice both officials were in the Commons throughout the life of the Poor Law Board, which was terminated in 1871. This administrative change seemingly made the central agency less autonomous; at least it reassured those who felt more comfortable having Somerset House under closer scrutiny and subject to direct questioning in the legislature. The Poor Law Board was certainly to prove far less controversial than its predecessor, and the New Poor Law itself became less contentious under the new structure.

5

MID-VICTORIAN POOR RELIEF, 1847–1870

The Poor Law Board

When central authority over poor relief was transferred from the Poor Law Commission to the Poor Law Board in December 1847, George Nicholls was appointed permanent secretary, which under the new arrangements was the executive in charge of day-to-day operations. His two parliamentary colleagues, the president of the board, Charles Buller and the parliamentary secretary, Lord Ebrington, were both in the House of Commons. While Nicholls kept them informed of important issues and problems, the real guidance of the agency fell to him. Given the connection between the Andover scandal and the fall of the Poor Law Commission, it might seem odd that Nicholls was the only hold-over, for not only had he been the most avid supporter of bone-crushing, but he had blamed the gruesome occurrences in the Andover work-house on the 'depraved appetite' of the paupers.[1] On the other hand, the appointment carried an implied rebuke, for Nicholls's salary was reduced from £2000 to £1500. Moreover, his erstwhile colleagues from the Poor Law Commission, arguably less efficient and committed to the service than he, moved into prestigious posts in imperial administration. Sir Edmund Head was appointed Governor-General of New Brunswick, while George Cornewall Lewis became secretary to the Board of Control for India. Chadwick, whose relations with Nicholls had cooled, was appointed a member of the General Board of Health, though the controversial nature of this new agency, coupled with his own abrasive personality, were to prove his undoing within a few years.[2]

Also retained were the assistant commissioners, renamed poor law inspectors. Although their number was augmented somewhat, from

9 to 13, each was still expected to superintend a dauntingly large population, which was rapidly increasing at mid-century. There were few fresh initiatives from Gwydyr House (where the new agency moved from Somerset House), and the crusading fervour of the 1830s was no longer in evidence. Nicholls, who might have been expected to push for stricter regulation of outdoor relief, no longer seemed to have the will or energy. He was aware that Parliament was unlikely to tolerate bold and unpopular initiatives by the central agency. Moreover, he was in his late sixties when he assumed control of the Poor Law Board, and not in the best of health. A mild stroke forced his retirement in 1851, and, with a knighthood and pension, he devoted the next few years to writing his self-justifying histories of the English, Irish, and Scottish Poor Laws. His departure removed the last of the 'men of 1834' from positions of authority, though several of the inspectors had begun their service then and were to continue for a number of years. Some of them, displeased at the sense of drift that had taken hold, urged a more forward and vigorous policy from London. They were momentarily heartened when, in 1852, the Poor Law Board devised a new general order that would have tightened restrictions on outdoor relief to all paupers. However, the outcry from boards of guardians and their parliamentary supporters caused the central board to back away, issuing instead a revised Outdoor Labour Test Order that applied only to able-bodied males.[3] The work to be required of able-bodied paupers on outdoor relief was to be as unpleasant and monotonous as possible, stone breaking and oakum picking being the leading examples of such drudgery. Thus, it was thought, the 'less eligibility' principle could be honoured without compelling a worker and his family to enter the workhouse.

While the 1852 order seemed to create greater uniformity by bringing in areas, especially the North and London, that were previously exempt from much regulation, the pattern that emerged was quite different. Maps of the incidence of the ratio of outdoor to indoor pauperism showed marked variations, even in adjacent districts sharing the same socio-economic profile.[4] In spite of fresh initiatives from the central agency in subsequent decades, this pattern was to endure throughout the history of the New Poor Law, and testifies to a determination by local authorities to maintain a fair measure of autonomy. The prevalence of outdoor relief is also testament to its relative cheapness. The weekly cost to maintain an indoor pauper was about 6s. One on outdoor relief cost only about 2s., as boards of guardians assumed that paupers had unreported resources, or expected relations and friends to make up the difference.[5] The Poor Law Board lapsed into relative quiescence, revived only at the end of the 1860s by a new campaign against outdoor relief. Most workers continued to dislike the law, but it was largely accepted as an established part of the political landscape. Poor law scandals ceased to attract the same level of press coverage that they had in the 1830s and 1840s, though there was a flurry of scandals connected with poor law medical care in 1865–6.[6] In short, the poor law system at mid-century was considered routine and rather dull by the public. All parts of the United Kingdom were now covered by three separate laws, the English law of 1834 and Irish law of 1838 being joined by a measure for Scotland in 1845. In spite of important differences among the three, they all shared, at both the central and local level, a harsh view of pauperism and a dedication to deterrent policies. These policies would be sharply contested with the rise of democracy and socialism later in the century, but in the 1850s they seemed an ingrained and even natural part of the Victorian ethos. Yet, despite the seeming dormancy of poor law administration in this period, there were important changes under way. Many of them were initiated at the local level, some in response to new social legislation that looked to boards of guardians for its implementation.

Expanding Poor Law Services: Education

The schooling of children was not usually a part of poor relief under the Old Poor Law. Few parish workhouses had done much more than provide limited instruction, often by an adult pauper inmate, for the small number of children lodged there. In a few places, notably Leeds, Birmingham, and parts of London, schools of industry taught the three Rs and emphasized job training. Orphaned children were almost invariably apprenticed or sent into domestic service. The royal commission of 1832–4 sought to eliminate the system of apprenticing, substituting schooling in reading, writing, and religion. The object was both to prepare youngsters for useful labour, and to moralize them, thus, it was hoped, breaking the cycle of dependent poverty. The commissioners envisioned educational establishments separate from the workhouses, and of such a size as to permit aggregating pupils by age and ability.[7] These hopes were dashed by the decided preference shown by boards of guardians for the 'general mixed workhouse', which the Poor Law Commission accepted. Many boards, disliking the bother and expense of establishing separate institutions, and sceptical of any kind of pauper education, made only the most niggardly allowance. Absurdly low teacher salaries, plus the necessity of boarding in the workhouse and often being obliged to perform additional duties, made the quality of teaching as bad as can be imagined. Being subject to the authority of the workhouse chaplain could be an additional disincentive for many teachers.[8] The chaplain was better educated and often more humane than the workhouse master, though there were of course numerous exceptions like the neglectful City of London Union chaplain, whom the guardians and central authority laboured for years to remove from his post.[9] Whatever the quality of the master or the chaplain, the daily interaction between the children and adult paupers in most workhouses resulted in the demoralizing of the young, and their acquiring of bad habits, precisely what the reformers had hoped to prevent.

Two of the original corps of assistant commissioners attempted to counteract this woeful state of affairs and were supported by Chadwick. James Kay and E. C. Tufnell, recognizing that the small population of most poor law unions made efficient schooling impossible, urged the combining of unions for educational purposes. The enlarged poor law district schools they envisaged, each with at least 500 children, would be able to offer much more professional schooling, conducted away from the evil influences of workhouse life. Their scheme was embraced by the Poor Law Commissioners, who held up the example of the Norwood School as the model for poor law unions to adopt. This exemplary private establishment, with about 1000 students, operated on a contractual basis with London poor law authorities, and a few other poor law unions. Liverpool and Manchester adopted this approach in the early 1840s, building large poor law district schools. In fact, the Norwood model became important in the general field of elementary education, which was undergoing expansion, especially after 1839, with the first government grants to schools by the newly established Education Committee of the Privy Council. Kay himself, soon to be Sir James Kay-Shuttleworth, was chosen to head the new agency. The poor law service thus seemed well placed to be the hatchery of educational reform, and the commissioners urged the government to facilitate the creation of poor law district schools nationwide. Poor law schooling was a very low priority for the Tory government of the 1840s, and little was done beyond an 1844 Act so loaded with restrictions that little use could be made of it. Under Russell's Liberal government, the central agency (now the Poor Law Board), was finally able to secure a District Schools Act in 1848.[10]

There was a promising flurry of district school creation during the first year. Six new districts, in and around London, where it seemed easiest to procure the consent of boards of guardians, were created. By 1849, however, the movement's force had been spent, and only three more districts were created throughout the remainder of the century. The problem, especially in the rural areas, was the parsimony and scepticism of guardians. Many farmer and village tradesman-guardians, usually wretchedly educated themselves, were worried that decent schools might cause their pauper charges to set their sights higher than farm labour and domestic service. If pauper children could be better educated than the sons and daughters of independent labourers, it might even be an inducement for parents to throw themselves on the ratepayer – a perverse inversion of the 'less eligibility' principle. The rural Martley Union in Worcestershire persisted for many years in refusing to teach the children to write, thinking such an attainment above their callings as labourers and servants.[11] For guardians in sparsely settled areas, an additional problem with district schools was that districts would have to be enormous in size in order for the requisite classification to be viable. For example, there could be only two districts for the whole of Wales if the 500 workhouse children per school rule were to be observed. To economy-minded guardians, who would not even consider alternatives like boarding schools, such distances made the scheme unworkable.[12]

Thus the poor law educational system settled into one based chiefly on workhouse schools with often poorly trained teachers, small numbers of children, and the baneful influences of adult paupers. However, there were a number of bright spots, and some progress. The low quality of teachers was addressed with some success in 1846, when Parliament passed an act providing £30 000 to augment salaries. The grant for any particular teacher usually did not exceed £30, and there were of course strings attached. Workhouse schools were subject to inspection by the Committee of Council on Education, teachers were to be better housed and exempted from menial service, the guardians were to provide books, and a school attendance register was to be kept.[13] In spite of this state aid, many workhouse schools continued to be abysmal. When, in December 1853, the school inspector visited the just-opened Merthyr Tydfil workhouse (the guardians had refused to build a workhouse for years), he found the school so deplorable that he refused the grant and secured the schoolmistress's dismissal. Returning in August 1854, he was chagrined to find that, out of 44 children (27 boys and 17 girls), only 13 could read at all.[14] A few unions had even continued into the 1840s the practice of using pauper inmates to instruct the children.[15] There were also many cases of abuse, some of them involving savage corporal punishment, others sexual in nature. The schoolmistress at Droitwich was dismissed in 1864 for improper relations with the porter; the schoolmaster at Kidderminster resigned in 1869 after admitting that he had impregnated a pauper inmate.[16] The books used in the classroom were often little more than bibles and tracts supplied by the Society for the Promotion of Christian Knowledge, an inevitable result of giving the chaplain a major role in directing the school. On the other hand, in many unions there was substantial improvement, at least as measured by the percentage of workhouse teachers earning one of the higher certificates ('efficiency' or 'competency', as opposed to 'probation' or 'permission') from the education inspectors. In 1849, only 137 male workhouse teachers received one of the higher certificates, while 236 received the lower. By 1857, the proportion was reversed: 234 higher and 134 lower. Only 7 received the lowest certificate of 'permission' in 1857, a striking reduction from the 45 so graded in 1849.[17]

Furthermore, the advocates of large district schools had to face opposing expert opinion that smaller schools in workhouses were superior to what they dubbed 'barracks schools'. The Newcastle Commission on elementary education, heavily influenced by the pro-district schools view of the Education Department, issued a report in 1861, severely criticizing workhouse schools and recommending the compulsory extension of district schools. The Poor Law Board fought back with several ably argued reports, pointing out that many workhouse schools were quite effective in preparing children for gainful employment and useful lives. Workhouse schools like Atcham near Shrewsbury and Quatt in Staffordshire were said to be superior to any district school.[18] Furthermore, they emphasized the success of a number of unions in keeping workhouse schools completely separated from the rest of the institution. They also pointed out the greater attention to individual student needs that was possible in smaller schools. In this inter-agency dispute, the Poor Law Board seemed to get the better of the argument, when, in 1863, Parliament transferred inspection of poor law schools to the board.[19] Of course, whatever the merits of the two type of schools, both were confronted with the intractable problem of the 'ins' and 'outs'. Most pauper children did not reside continuously in the workhouse; they would enter with one or both parents, stay perhaps a few weeks, and then be released when parents found employment or some other form of support. With discharge from the workhouse came an end to their schooling, at least for a while. With such stop-and-go education, progress was bound to be modest. An additional channel that began to be used by poor law authorities from the late 1850s was the array of certified denominational and philanthropic schools that were willing to take workhouse children on payment of from 3s. to 10s. per week. Large numbers of Catholic children in particular were accommodated in this fashion.[20] Further gains would not come until after Forster's Education Act of 1870, when the ability to send workhouse children to schools run by local boards of education, as well as poor law innovations like the cottage home movement, offered a more promising educational environment.

Expanding Poor Law Services: Medical Care

Medical care had been an important component of the Old Poor Law, and by the early nineteenth century it had evolved to the point that many parishes contracted with medical doctors to provide care for the indigent. In 1834, however, it was unclear just how much provision would be made for it under the new system. The topic received little attention in the royal commission's report, and the New Poor Law itself said little about it other than giving JPs the authority to order medical relief in cases of sudden illness.[21] There was no medical advisor to the central authority, and in their first instructional letter regarding medical relief, the Poor Law Commissioners stipulated that it was to be for workhouse residents only. However, boards of guardians throughout the country, accustomed to parochial systems of contract management, operated on the belief that timely medical care could restore a person to the workforce and keep him out of the workhouse, thereby saving money. Thus, haltingly and unofficially, something like a poor law medical service began to take form. In spite of their own earlier restrictive leanings, the commissioners did begin to take a more positive view following the influenza epidemic of 1837–38. Ordered by the Home Secretary, Lord John Russell, to undertake a study of the relationship between illness and poverty, they turned the project over to Chadwick. This inquiry led ultimately to his famous *Sanitary Report* of 1842, the classic text of the early public health movement. Making a solid case for the connection between environmental degradation and illness, and between illness and poverty, the report was a clarion call for government action. Vast new water supply and sewer projects, he claimed, would restore the health of town dwellers and bring about a further decline in pauperism. In making this argument, Chadwick believed, he had catapulted himself into the forefront of the sanitary movement, and distanced himself from the charge of being the chief architect of a repressive system.[22]

Undoubtedly, sewering and cleansing of towns, together with the supplying of fresh drinking water, began to pay important health dividends later in the century, and much of the impetus had been provided by poor law officials. But the mundane medical needs of an often exhausted, ill-nourished population had to be met day in and day out by overworked, underpaid medical practitioners of the poor law service. With their customary parsimony, boards of guardians secured the services of local doctors willing to make the lowest bid. A fee of £50 per annum or even less was not uncommon, for which the doctor had to attend the workhouse inmates as well as those outdoor paupers granted medical relief, though in time unions were divided into districts, each with its own doctor. This system was amended by the General Medical Order of 1842, which called for local boards to adopt salaried remuneration in place of the contract system.[23] There were frequent complaints by guardians about 'extravagant' extras ordered for certain patients, including medicines, wine or brandy, and an enhanced dietary. In order to better serve their patients doctors frequently had to battle against the inertia and ignorance of guardians and workhouse staff, and sometimes against Somerset House (Gwydyr House after 1847), for the central authority saw no reason to appoint a medical expert until 1865. As John Simon, a leading doctor and civil servant put it, the guiding official philosophy seemed to be that, 'for the ordinary medical business of the Board, the common sense of secretaries and secretarial inspectors did not require to be helped by doctors'.[24] There were of course ill-qualified, incompetent, and even corrupt practitioners, but by and large the record of the poor law medical officers is impressive, especially when considered in relation to the obstacles against which they struggled. On the other hand, the quality of workhouse nursing was extraordinarily bad, most boards being quite content with using pauper inmates for the task, a practice not prohibited by the central authority until 1897. In 1864, the Liverpool philanthropist William Rathbone paid out of his own pocket for a staff of well-trained nurses for the Brownlow Street workhouse. Superintended by Agnes Jones, the so-called 'Florence Nightingale of the Poor Law' (who later died of typhus contracted there), this dedicated corps achieved major improvements in the health of their charges.[25] In spite of this impressive demonstration project, most boards of guardians remained unmoved; the same tight-fisted attitude that promoted outdoor medical relief to keep able-bodied paupers out of the workhouse counselled doing nothing to prevent the early demise of the mostly elderly indoor paupers who required nursing. Major improvements in workhouse nursing would not come till later in the century.

The 1860s saw the beginnings of reform in the unwieldy, complacent, and often ineffective poor law medical service, following public outcries over publicized abuses. The press played a key part in this campaign, as did dedicated individuals like Joseph Rogers and Louisa Twining. In 1856, Rogers was appointed medical officer of the Strand Union workhouse in London at an annual salary of £50, out of which he was expected to buy any medicines he might prescribe. He immediately encountered and tried to correct a number of glaring abuses, including the practice in the lying-in ward of keeping unmarried mothers on a starvation diet for nine days after confinement, and the employing of paupers to beat carpets (at a profit to the union of £400 per year), the noise and dust from which caused severe health problems.[26] Frequently at odds with the guardians, Rogers fought for poor law medical reform, not only in the Strand Union but throughout the country. *The Lancet* used him as a major resource when it undertook a series of articles on workhouse medicine in 1865. These exposés helped secure the passage through Parliament of the Metropolitan Poor Act in 1867, by which new infirmaries were created in London separate from workhouses. Following his dismissal by the Strand guardians in 1867, Rogers helped found the Poor Law Medical Officers' Association, the most important pressure group working for further reform of the poor law medical service.[27]

Another major force in bringing to light the glaring abuses in workhouse medicine and nursing were the women social activists who were organizing themselves into visiting societies. Their aim was not just to bring comfort to workhouse inmates, but to carry out first-hand investigations that could lead to improvements. The most determined of these activists was Louisa Twining, who began visiting in 1854, and later declared that 'in matters connected with the poor, the sick, and the aged, it would seem to be especially the mission of women to work a reformation'.[28] She quickly became an active, well-informed publicist of workhouse abuses, and a paper she read on the condition of workhouses before the National Association for the Promotion of Social Science in 1857 led to the creation of the Workhouse Visiting Society. With Twining as secretary and a host of social notables, bishops, and doctors, the society set about reforming many aspects of workhouse life, including nursing. Other women reformers, like Frances Power Cobbe and Angela Burdett Coutts, also played key roles. The *Journal of the Workhouse Visiting Society*, launched in 1859, was an important source of information to the public about the horrors and iniquities of workhouse life. Further evidence was provided when Twining appeared as a witness about workhouse conditions before an 1862 select committee of the House of Commons.[29] Another important reform body was the Association for Improving Workhouse Infirmaries, established in 1866 by Joseph Rogers, and including such luminaries as Charles Dickens and John Stuart Mill. The work of these organizations began to pay important dividends by the end of the decade, with significant improvement in several of the larger poor law unions.[30]

Treatment of the Insane

A relatively hidden aspect of medical relief that began to be brought to the public's attention after mid-century was treatment of the insane. Little had been said on the subject by the royal commission and the 1834 Act merely stipulated that no 'dangerous lunatic' was to be kept in a workhouse. This left the matter largely to the discretion of boards of guardians, and they generally saw little need to make elaborate provisions for those of unsound mind. Local boards generally sought to avoid the additional expense of removing their 'lunatic' paupers to county and other specialist asylums. Neither the Poor Law Commission nor the Poor Law Board saw fit to require special workhouse wards for the insane.[31] A gradual reform in the treatment of the mentally ill began in the 1840s, after the authority of the Metropolitan Commissioners in Lunacy was extended to the whole country by Lord Ashley's 1842 Act.[32] As county asylums began to be built under the mandatory provisions of an 1845 Act, and the Lunacy Commission's inspectors began to take note of the often primitive treatment of the insane in workhouses, quite a few were transferred out of the workhouses to the asylums. The number of workhouse lunatics began to decline from a high of 6000 in 1847.[33] By the 1850s, however, with the filling up of many asylums, a reverse flow began. The process gave rise to jurisdictional disputes between the Poor Law Board and the Commissioners in Lunacy, not unlike that going on in education. There was also greater publicity given to abuses in treatment of the insane, with *The Lancet* taking the lead. The Lunacy Acts of 1862 and 1863 facilitated the removal of paupers from workhouses to asylums, but also helped bring about improved conditions in workhouse lunatic wards.[34] The Metropolitan Poor Act of 1867 improved conditions for pauper lunatics in London and led to the creation of new poor law asylums for the insane. By the end of its tenure in 1871, the Poor Law Board had come to accept the need for more humane and specialized treatment of the mentally ill.

Migration, Emigration, and Vagrancy

When the New Poor Law was passed, the only provision made in regard to emigration was to empower local authorities to pay the transportation expenses of those settled paupers who wished to emigrate, subject to the approval of the Poor Law Commission.[35] This was seen as supplementing the assisted emigration schemes of Edward Gibbon Wakefield and others, by which a stronger empire could be forged, colonial labour needs met, and markets for British goods enlarged. Little use was made of the poor law emigration provision at first, and the commissioners were at first reluctant to sanction emigration schemes. In part this was due to Chadwick, who insisted, contrary to the Malthusians, that there was no surplus population. Instead, he argued, there were stagnant pools of unused labour locked away in rural districts because of the baneful effects of outdoor relief and the settlement laws. It was therefore internal migration, from rural to urban areas, that government needed to facilitate. Chadwick took the initiative, verifying through correspondence with northern manufacturers and with Assistant Commissioner James Kay that there was indeed a substantial need for factory labour. Accordingly, Chadwick established a Migration Agency attached to the Poor Law Commission to bring employment opportunities to the attention of rural guardians and paupers. However reasonable in concept, the scheme, hatched in the excited political atmosphere of the late 1830s, was attacked by conservatives and radicals alike. The former accused Chadwick of destroying 'Old England' by draining the countryside of its residents, while to radicals he was the strike-breaker-in-chief, bringing in low-cost labour from the countryside to take over the jobs of skilled, unionized operatives. The Migration Agency was allowed to expire in 1838.[36]

Assisted emigration was very uneven in the 1830s, with the high number of 5241 emigrants in 1835–36 falling off rapidly. Only those cases that seemed perfectly suited to the needs of the programme were sanctioned. For example, the commissioners refused absolutely to approve requests by several boards of guardians to finance the sending out to Australia of the families of men already transported there for criminal offences, even though this would clearly have relieved the localities of numerous dependants.[37] By the 1840s the programme showed modest growth, partly because of the sound information and advice provided to poor law authorities by the Colonial Land and Emigration Commission, established in 1840.[38] By the end of the century, 12 000 men, women, and children had received assistance from the poor rates to emigrate, mostly to British colonies.[39] This is, of course, an insignificant fraction of the millions of emigrants leaving the country in the nineteenth century. Amounting on average to less than two persons per parish and township, it shows that poor law-assisted emigration was a quite minor programme. In 1843, Charles Buller, an MP and later president of the Poor Law Board, sourly characterized the policy of assisted emigration as 'shovelling out paupers'. A recent study challenges this picture of the dumping overseas of a passive population, suggesting a much more enterprising and positive role on the part of pauper emigrants.[40] While this does seem to have been the case for many adult paupers, the assisting of juvenile paupers to emigrate was more problematic. Since most boards of guardians could only be induced to pay passage money when colonial authorities contributed as well, problems arose when those on the receiving end insisted on having juvenile emigrants sign on as indentured servants. The Poor Law Board was concerned about saddling juveniles with obligations in a distant land which they could not well grasp, and the process went very slowly. Indeed it came to a near standstill in 1869, when only 47 people emigrated with the assistance of poor law authorities.[41] The various emigration lobbies tried hard to interest the Poor Law Board and the metropolitan guardians in cooperative schemes to send out paupers to the colonies, but with little success.[42]

If the problem of those who insisted on remaining rooted in one spot produced policies to facilitate migration and emigration, the opposite problem – those constantly on the move – called forth different solutions. The threat to social order posed by 'idle' and 'dissolute' wanderers had perplexed lawmakers since Tudor times. While savage penalties for vagabondage had abated by the nineteenth century, authorities, convinced that most vagrants were immoral and predatory, were still concerned. The problem was not highlighted by the royal commission of 1832–34 and the New Poor Law was silent on it. For Chadwick, the assumption was that the strict application of the workhouse test would deter vagrants along with everyone else; the new police he envisaged would deal with the disorderliness and crime associated with vagrancy. As this expectation proved largely illusory, the Poor Law Commission had to develop policy guidelines for boards of guardians. These included requiring some form of labour in response for a night's lodging, and also encouraging the building of separate vagrant (or casual) wards in workhouses. For London, the commissioners divided the whole metropolitan area into districts corresponding 'to the great lines of roads along which mendicants and vagrants' entered the city. They tried to compel London unions and parishes to build special vagrant institutions, but were largely unsuccessful.[43] Nevertheless, driven by their own needs and the prodding of the commissioners, most guardians were providing special casual accommodation. This was made as unpleasant as possible – the less eligibility principle writ large – including worse diets and sleeping arrangements than that given to ordinary inmates, as well as increasingly long and arduous work required for a night's stay. The system was further formalized by an 1843 Act of Parliament,[44] by which any board of guardians could detain a vagrant for four hours on the morning after his admission. In spite of such harshness, the numbers of vagrants tended to increase.[45] There were major surges associated with calamities like the Irish Potato Famine, though, on the whole, the Irish seemed to have been strikingly underrepresented among relief applicants.[46] Vagrants were the one group whose treatment became ever more punitive during the century following the enactment of the New Poor Law.

Changes in Settlement and Rating

The New Poor Law had kept the parish as the unit of rating and settlement. This was clearly advantageous to major landowners in the countryside, whose sparsely populated close parishes kept the relatively low poor rates they had enjoyed under the Old Poor Law. Thus, after 1834 there continued to be large disparities in the burden of poor rates among parishes within the same union. The only common charges in a union were those connected with the poor law establishment: the cost of building and maintaining the workhouse, paying salaries, and so on. Otherwise, each parish was assessed on the number of its settled paupers receiving either outdoor or indoor relief, and this was naturally a much heavier burden on more heavily populated parishes. Nor had disputes over settlement ceased with the 1834 Act. Each guardian still jealously safeguarded the interests of his own parish, even as he tried to keep some of the wider interests of the union in mind as member of the board. Another hold-over from the Old Poor Law was the practice of rural parishes paying non-resident relief to their settled labourers who had taken employment in a town and lost their jobs, either because of sickness or trade depression. It was usually cheaper to do this than to pay the removal cost of the labourer and his family to his parish of settlement. Remittances were constantly being posted from one parish to another to pay the cost of the more than 82 000 settled poor residing elsewhere.[47]

By the 1840s, there was considerable unhappiness with this system on the part of the landed interest. While individual magnates might have sparsely populated and hence lowly rated parishes, they often also held land in larger, more populous parishes, whose farmers were saddled with higher rates. Since the amount of poor rates in a parish was an important factor in determining rentals, most landowners and farmers were affected to some degree. The long-standing practice of paying relief to settled paupers in distant towns exacerbated the situation. Many landowners and rural ratepayers came to resent a system whereby someone born in their parish might move at an early age to a manufacturing town and perhaps live the rest of his life there, working and raising a family. Yet with sickness, unemployment, or old age, the applicant's rural parish of settlement became liable. It seemed unfair that towns profited from the labour of former country dwellers, yet could compel rural areas to support them in adversity. The Poor Law Commission denounced the practice of non-resident relief in their ninth annual report, realizing that legislation would be required to alter the power of parishes to remove paupers settled elsewhere. Accordingly, Parliament passed an act in 1846 by which anyone resident in a parish for five years was rendered permanently 'irremoveable' to their parish of settlement. Widows, who otherwise took their husband's parish of settlement, were made irremoveable in the first 12 months of their widowhood. At one stroke, large numbers of urban labourers and their dependants were able to demand relief from the towns where they lived, and rural parishes ceased providing non-resident relief. The sudden skyrocketing of urban poor relief led to an outcry from the towns, and in 1847 a partial corrective was enacted. Henceforth, those rendered irremoveable by the previous year's statute were to be supported out of the common poor law union fund, not chargeable entirely to the parish of residence.[48]

The corrective legislation of 1847 ushered in a de facto form of union settlement, at least for a particular category of paupers. The expansion of the area of settlement for everyone had been sought by many reformers since the eighteenth century. Chadwick and others had tried in vain to enlarge the area, but their efforts had always foundered on the rock of parochial self-interest. Now that this 'sacred' principle of local government had been breached, however, the voices calling for a more comprehensive reform grew louder. A House of Commons select committee called for union settlement in 1847.[49] A number of heavily burdened boards of guardians in industrial areas, including Manchester, called for a national poor rate.[50] Disraeli's motion for shifting all poor law establishment charges and the maintenance of vagrants from local rates to a national fund narrowly failed in 1850. Pressure groups to equalize the burden of poor rates were organized in the 1850s.[51] There was a growing recognition that without union settlement or perhaps something even wider, it would be impossible to induce most boards of guardians to undertake the expenditures necessary for improved facilities and services. As Frances Power Cobbe put it in an 1864 article: 'If these wants cannot be supplied by other citizens a mile off, they must be supplied by those 100 or 500 miles off.'[52] Legislation of 1861 and 1862 helped to prepare the way for further change by reducing the period required for irremoveability from five years to three, and by making rateable value the sole basis for assessing contributions to the common union fund.[53] In 1865, Parliament finally passed the Union Chargeability Act, by which all poor law charges in each union were imposed uniformly on the landed property within the union, irrespective of the number of relief recipients in each parish. A remarkably durable feature of the old system that had survived 30 years into the New Poor Law era was transformed into a wider and more efficient system. On the other hand, the principle of settlement had survived. While the settlement area was henceforth to the union rather than parish, the 650 separate poor law unions were to maintain the principle of local attachment and control through the remaining 65 years of the poor law.[54]

The Increasingly Urban Character of Poor Relief

When the New Poor Law was passed, the concern of reformers and Parliament had been overwhelmingly with the crisis in the countryside. Pauperism was thought of primarily as a rural problem, and the bulk of the royal commission's inquiry had been concerned with a pauperized agricultural labour force residing in villages. Since most of the salient pathologies of the Old Poor Law, especially the allowance system, were either absent or attenuated in towns, urban poverty received secondary attention. The Poor Law Commission had begun implementing the statute in the rural South and Midlands for this reason, and when they did get around to London and the industrial areas in 1836–37, many urban leaders argued for being left alone partly on the grounds that they had no need of a system designed for rural conditions. With the onset of a major and protracted trade depression in 1837, however, Poor Law Commissioners and local leaders were forced to make urban poor relief much more central. Moreover, by the end of the 1840s, it was becoming clear to some that a poor law built around deterrence had little relevance to sudden mass unemployment brought about by unforeseeable swings in the trade cycle. From the outset, radicals had considered the New Poor Law the most abominable piece of legislation to issue from the 'reformed' Parliament, and it was the thing that had driven many of them into the Chartist movement. For most people, the susceptibility of the industrial economy to sudden swings simply pointed up the need for greater flexibility. This in turn led to the various kinds of labour tests for the able-bodied outside the workhouse, as represented by the Outdoor Labour Test Order of 1852.

The next great crisis of the urban poor law came early in the next decade, with the onset of the Lancashire Cotton Famine during the American Civil War. The US Navy's effectiveness in choking off the supply of cotton from the Confederate states to the mills of Lancashire brought cotton spinning to a standstill, and in a relatively short time hundreds of thousands of men, women, and children were unemployed, or placed on short time. The ripple effects of the sudden cutting off of pay affected a great many more among the area's shopkeepers and artisans. At the height of the crisis, in December 1862, there were nearly a half million people (one-quarter of the county's population) receiving aid from poor law authorities or from the relief committees that had been set up. Not until 1865 did the number on relief drop below 100 000.[55] The Poor Law Board insisted, not always successfully, that local authorities exact some kind of labour test in return for outdoor relief, consistent with their general order of 1852. More imaginatively, they dispatched a special commissioner, H. B. Farnall, to Lancashire to coordinate relief efforts among boards of guardians and with private charities.[56] The board followed up on this by sending its chief engineer, Robert Rawlinson, to the area in 1863 to plan public works projects that could both meet the labour requirement for outdoor relief and improve roads and other components of the local infrastructure. Rawlinson's efforts, like those of Farnall, prompted Parliament to facilitate borrowing by local authorities and to spread the cost most evenly across the parishes in poor law unions.[57] Lancashire's Cotton Famine, the most severe urban crisis of the era, played a major role in moving poor law policy in a direction less in conformity with the principles of 1834, and more attuned to the complexities of modern industrial society. It also provided a close working relationship between poor law officials and leaders of organized charity, a topic that will be taken up in the next chapter. Nevertheless, there was much official worrying about the abandonment of strict relief principles, even during a temporary crisis, and this contributed later in the decade to a backlash aimed at undoing the 'mischief'.

This backlash might not have developed if Lancashire had been the only site of a major urban poor relief crisis in the 1860s; unfortunately, there was also rapidly increasing pauperism in the metropolis. It was clear that the cotton famine was an emergency situation that would cease with the end of hostilities in America. No one could have foreseen it, and no amount of 'prudence' on the part of factory operatives could have saved them from severe distress. There was also a generally more favourable public image of the northern industrial worker than there had been at the height of the Chartist agitation. In spite of continued radicalism and the growth of trade unions, the northern worker was more frequently imagined now as a steady, industrious sort, the very sinews of Britain's industrial might – a revised view that made possible the conferring of the franchise on urban male workers in 1867. These favourable attitudes made it somewhat easier to accept the relaxing of harsh and deterrent policies during a protracted emergency. The image of London pauperism was considerably different. In Henry Mayhew's *London Labour and the London Poor*, first published in serial form in the *Morning Chronicle* in the early 1850s, the face of the metropolitan poor was not necessarily an industrious one. Among the classifications he developed, the central one of 'those that will not work' certainly made the most compelling, not to say titillating, reading. Mayhew's odd and colorful array of petty thieves, prostitutes, swindlers, street performers, and the like, conditioned the public to regard London's poor as undisciplined, immoral, and parasitic.[58] While there had been some sympathy for the plight of dockworkers unemployed by the extraordinary frost in the winter of 1860–61, on the whole, the plight of London's industrious labour force tended to be overshadowed by repellent images of freeloading slackers. Thus the greatest anxieties about relaxing the workhouse test derived from middle-class loathing of the dense nest of paupers in the heart of the nation's capital. Furthermore, it was the increase in metropolitan outdoor relief that was most evident in the late 1860s. By 1866, after the end of the Cotton Famine, the percentage of the total population in receipt of outdoor relief had dropped to 3.7; by 1869 it had grown to 4.[59] The abandonment of sound relief principles in London was also tied to the proliferation of charities there, and the profligate ways of local authorities like the City of London poor law union.[60]

The Growing Alarm over Outdoor Relief

Many poor law inspectors and some officials had long bemoaned the erosion of rigour in dispensing poor relief. They castigated lax boards of guardians and fumed about the abandonment of the 'principles of 1834'. It was not that guardians were being generous, but rather that it was easier, and, in the short run, cheaper, to keep families out of the workhouse by granting niggardly outrelief. Opponents of this laxness saw the consequences to be the same as those that allegedly afflicted the lower orders in the last decades of the Old Poor Law: loss of virtue and the work ethic. They held to the view that one of the principal aims of the poor law was to develop character. The conflict between such moralists and a typical metropolitan board of guardians is evident in an anonymous 1859 pamphlet by a 'Late Relieving Officer' (the poor law union is also not specified). This man, by his own admission a 'failed tradesman', took the post at a salary of £100 a year. He soon discovered some glaring 'abuses' on the outdoor pauper list, including a 'sickly man, with a wife and five children' who were receiving 7s. 6d. per week; they were 'evidently gypsies' and the wife was a fortune teller. The indignant relieving officer saw to it that the pension was stopped, and a ticket of admission to the workhouse given instead. When the family promptly turned up to be admitted to the workhouse, the guardians berated their relieving officer, saying: 'See what an expense *you* have put the parish to; here, instead of paying 7s. 6d. a week, we are called upon to pay 17s. 6d., besides, what have we to do with character?' Lest this relieving officer seem a caricature of the local official wishing to grind the faces of the poor, his pamphlet also highlighted instances of unwarranted harshness, and cases of paupers dying from medical neglect.[61] His seemingly contrasting views reflect something of the bifurcated legacy of poor law attitudes and policies in the 1860s. It is a pivotal decade both for the exposure of glaring abuses which demanded new policies and institutional innovations, and also for powerful efforts to recommit the country to the workhouse test.

It was not only poor law officials who sounded the alarm about lax relief policies. Many philanthropists believed that the unprecedented amount of charitable giving, which accelerated during the Cotton Famine, was prone to the same abuses. The close partnership in the early 1860s between poor law and philanthropy helped pave the way for coordinated efforts between the private and public spheres to curtail what were seen as demoralizing types of relief: outdoor relief by the poor law, undiscriminating and profuse giving by charities. Another factor was that the Union Chargeability Act of 1865 had unwittingly produced two kinds of attitudinal changes regarding poor relief. On the one hand, within many boards of guardians it encouraged more profuse relief, since the charges were now spread evenly on the rateable value of the entire union. On the other hand, it brought into play the hitherto relatively disengaged wealthy ratepayers. They had been largely unconcerned before, because their own parishes had been lightly rated. With their own financial interests now on the line, they were stirred to action. They might not be able to affect the actions of their own boards of guardians, but they could deploy their considerable political and social power to help bring about a further shift in Poor Law Board policy.[62]

With the appointment of G. J. Goschen as president of the Poor Law Board in Gladstone's government in 1868, poor law policy came under the direction of one who fully shared the reformers' anxieties about the increasing burden of poor relief and its lax administration. An MP for the City of London and former director of the Bank of England, Goschen was determined to put a stop to the practice of supplementing insufficient income out of the poor rates, insisting that only the truly destitute were the proper target of public relief. All others must appeal to the discretionary powers of private charity. Accordingly, in November 1869, he issued a document of great importance – the Goschen Minute – which was to be frequently cited by those seeking to curtail outdoor relief. A clear division and cooperation between the statutory and public sectors were henceforth to be official policy. As he concluded his minute:

> It would seem to follow that charitable organizations, whose alms could in no case be claimed as a right, would find their most appropriate

sphere in assisting those who have some, but insufficient means, and who, though on the verge of pauperism, are not actual paupers, leaving to the operation of the general law the provision for the totally destitute.[63]

Considerable effort would be devoted over succeeding years to make this austere and tidy vision a reality. From the outset, a number of metropolitan parishes expressed scepticism about the possibility of clearly distinguishing destitution from mere poverty.[64] Full implementation of the policy, however, would not be attempted until the Poor Law Board was transmuted into a more comprehensive agency in 1871.

6

THE REVIVAL OF DETERRENCE AND THE EXPANSION OF SERVICES, 1870–1900

The Local Government Board and Poor Relief

The Poor Law Commission had been dismantled in 1847, as a direct result of the Andover Scandal, and an urgent sense that the head of the central agency needed to be a MP. In the decision in 1871 to terminate the Poor Law Board and replace it with the Local Government Board, the workhouse medical scandals of the mid-1860s played a key, though somewhat less direct, role. In the ensuing public and parliamentary outcry, it was felt that the central authority needed a permanent and expert medical component. Accordingly, the 1871 Act amalgamated the Poor Law Board, the General Register Office, the Local Government Act Office, and the Medical Department of the Privy Council into the new agency. The latter two bodies had, since the demise of the General Board of Health in 1858, administered a wide array of public health and medical laws. Ever since the 1840s, the Poor Law Board itself had been responsible for certain medical and sanitary functions, such as vaccination and the supervision of poor law dispensaries. The transfer of the General Register Office to the new board derived both from the important mortality data in the vital statistics, and the fact that, under the Registration Act of 1836, boards of guardians were the authorities keeping track of all births, deaths, and marriages. While there was a clear logic to the 1871 amalgamation based on combining agencies with overlapping functions, a struggle for the nature of direction of central policy provided the dynamic.

The role of the British Medical Association, and especially its publication, *The Lancet*, in revealing earlier workhouse medical abuses, has already been recounted. As a follow-up to these revelations, the BMA, in conjunction with the Social Science Association, undertook intense lobbying for a comprehensive health authority. When a Royal Sanitary Commission began its investigations in 1869, it was widely anticipated in the medical community that the result would be a Ministry of Health under the control of medical experts. The Medical Officer of the Privy Council, Dr John Simon, an ardent centralizer, was expected to be appointed to head the new agency.[1] Instead, officials of the Poor Law Board, as well as those local officials worried about being placed under a 'medical dictatorship', lobbied to keep poor law officials in the ascendant. Fears about creating a medically oriented central agency, even under such able hands as Simon's, derived partly from entrusting 'experts' with too much authority. Even the poor law medical officers within the poor law establishment were looked upon as men all too likely to dictate visionary and costly schemes if given a chance. The longest serving Poor Law inspector, Robert Weale, who had begun his service in 1834, was an outspoken advocate of keeping control in the hands of generalist administrators. Such men, often of superior social rank, would, he believed, hold to the well-proven course of careful negotiations and the establishment of a bond of trust with local boards. His views were widely shared, both by parliamentarians and by members of the Royal Sanitary Commission. By 1871, it was clear that the government would opt for what has been called the 'political-diplomatic' approach to central–local relations, rather than the 'technical-bureaucratic'.[2] Under the 1871 Act, the Medical and Poor Law Departments were both answerable to the president and secretary of the Local Government Board. John Simon, who was appointed medical officer of the new agency, found himself in a circumscribed position, with policy formulation largely in the hands of poor law officials. Simon later noted drily that under the 1871 Act, the poor law 'came to be of overruling consequence',[3] and he retired in 1876. More forthrightly, Dr Joseph Rogers, whose Poor Law Medical Officers' Association had lobbied hard for the creation of an autonomous medical agency, called the act a 'disastrous and ludicrous failure'.[4]

Due largely to the rejection of bold administrative or policy initiatives in the 1871 legislation, the Local Government Board ultimately became 'a byword for compromise, pragmatism and conservatism induced by its sensitivity to the conventional rights of traditional and partial interests'.[5] However, it was by no means clear in 1871 that this would be the case. The transition had been overseen by the energetic president of the Poor Law Board, G. J. Goschen, and he no doubt would have continued to head the new agency, but instead Gladstone appointed him First Lord of the Admiralty. James Stansfeld, who became president of the Local Government Board, promised to be equally energetic, and was as committed to curtailing outdoor relief as his predecessor. He built a stronger *esprit de corps* by inaugurating a system of dinners and periodic week-long conferences at which he and the inspectors discussed policy and implementation.[6] The permanent secretary to the board, John Lambert, was also a man of extraordinary talent and diligence.[7]

Under such leadership, the 'crusade' against outdoor relief as well as the increased auditing powers of the central agency offered the promise of renewed vigour. One of the major shortcomings of the 1834 law had been placing the appointment of auditors in the hands of boards of guardians. A move away from this extreme localism came in 1844, when the Poor Law Commission was empowered to create audit districts, each comprising a much wider area than a poor law union. The appointment of auditors, however, was given to a committee of the chairmen and vice-chairmen of the constituent unions. In 1868, driven by Treasury insistence on tighter fiscal monitoring, the Poor Law Board gained the all-important power to appoint district auditors. In 1879 the district audit became a full-time salaried department of the Local Government Board. The total effect of these changes was considerable. On the whole, much more vigilance was exercised by auditors in the 1870s and 1880s, though it tended to decline thereafter. Yet, despite the rising volume of disallowances by auditors, they were often for relatively minor expenditures such as bats and balls for poor law school playgrounds, or seaside outings for workhouse children and the elderly. And the Local Government Board, to whom many disallowances were appealed, not infrequently overruled their own auditors, sanctioning, for example, expenditures on handicraft teachers for the blind, newspapers in workhouses, and snuff and tobacco in the workhouse on Christmas Day.[8] Since the Local Government Board declined to use its audit powers systematically to curtail outdoor relief, the 'crusade' had to be conducted largely within the parameters of the departmental culture of persuasion and negotiation.

Organized Charity, the Poor Law, and the Crusade against Outdoor Relief

Since the eighteenth century, poor law reformers had frequently considered the closely related problem of charitable giving. They tended to see profuse and undiscriminating philanthropy in very much the same light as the poor law allowance system and other 'abuses' of the statutory sphere. Yet, the royal commission of 1832–34 made only passing reference to the topic, and poor law and charity continued to operate on parallel tracks.[9] Although at the official level, early Victorian poor relief and charity tended to be separate spheres, they were intertwined in the minds of many of those who administered the poor laws at the local level. Leading poor law guardians involved in local charities frequently found themselves operating at cross purposes with their official duties. In Nottinghamshire in the 1840s, Assistant Commissioner Gulson had tried to get the boards to stop outdoor relief altogether. Not only did they refuse, but a separate private relief fund was raised to offset the effects of trade depression, to which the chairman of the Basford Union Board of Guardians personally contributed £100. Unable to prevent this repudiation of official doctrine, Gulson exclaimed futilely: 'Charity and compulsory maintenance of the destitute ought never to be mixed together – each stands upon a different principle...'[10] Close cooperation between local poor law authorities and charitable organizations was also a hallmark of the early Victorian period. It became an increasingly common practice for boards of guardians to place certain categories of pauper in specialist institutions run by private charities. The mentally ill and other classes of the indigent were thus being maintained at public expense in private facilities, with guardians periodically conducting inspection tours to ensure adequate treatment.[11] Representatives of charities, most notably the Workhouse Visiting Society, also had access to poor law institutions. The women visitors of this organization donated money and time to improve the internal arrangements and comforts of workhouses; their activities ranged from decorating to distributing toys to establishing libraries. Visitors also assisted in training workhouse girls for domestic service and finding employment for them.[12]

As much as private charity might be seen to compromise proper poor law administration in certain districts, it was the phenomenal growth of charitable giving that created a sense of crisis by 1860. This was especially true in the metropolitan area, where 279 new charities were established in the first half of the nineteenth century; an additional 144 were added just in the 1850s.[13] The East End of London, with its demoralized and poverty-stricken masses, was the obvious target of choice for charities. East End boards of guardians, mainly from the class of small shopkeepers, lacked vigorous leadership, while large charitable funds originating in the West End were squandered without any thought of the consequences.[14] The combination of lax poor law administration and lavish, indiscriminate private giving seemed to many a formula for social and economic disaster. In an 1866 article, Florence Nightingale praised the earlier efforts by Thomas Chalmers to withhold relief to the undeserving. She also pointed out the dilemma of having both a private and public sphere, quoting with approval an unidentified French 'administrateur':

> We cannot understand your English laws – you have a Poor Law – you pay rates for your child paupers to be educated – for your sick paupers to be housed and doctored in places called workhouses, etc. etc. And then you subscribe to private charities to take your paupers out of the power of the Poor Law. If you do the one, why do you do the other? Would it not be cheaper to see that the two work in the same direction?[15]

Such outcries clearly pointed the way to a new era of partnership between poor law authorities and charitable organizations to avoid working at cross purposes. The coordination of private and public relief during the Lancashire Cotton Famine has already been described. Similar coordination was achieved by the Edinburgh Society for Improving the Condition of the Poor (1867). In Carlisle, the board of guardians worked closely with the private relief committees during times of distress.[16] The London Association for the Prevention of Pauperism and Crime (1868) reflected most accurately in its name the intense anxiety about the relationship between lax poor relief and social pathology.[17]

The Goschen Minute issued by the president of the Poor Law Board at the end of 1869 brought many of these matters to a head. Seeking to restart the campaign against outdoor relief, he called for close cooperation with organized charity, initially in metropolitan poor law unions. The initial response was heartening. Three East End Unions – St George's in the East, Whitechapel, and Stepney – agreed to stop all outdoor relief immediately, with charitable agencies relieving only those applicants considered 'redeemable'.[18] That Goschen and the three boards of guardians were able to act so decisively is due to the fact that a major organizational breakthrough had been achieved earlier in 1869: the formation of the Charity Organisation Society. The COS had already lobbied the Poor Law Board for such action and some of its members had secured election as poor law guardians. To underscore the new spirit of cooperation, Goschen himself became a vice-president of the COS.[19]

The ideas and methods of Thomas Chalmers provided the most important model for leaders of the crusade against outdoor relief. C. S. Loch, who became secretary of the COS in 1875, frequently invoked Chalmers's doctrine that social distress was caused by individual character flaws. To ensure that only the 'deserving' poor would receive any relief outside the workhouse, the COS instituted the casework method, an important step towards the professionalizing of social work.[20] By coordinating the efforts of boards of guardians and the COS, the workhouse could be offered only to the undeserving. A test of character would thus be provided by the case study, a minute investigation into every aspect of the applicant's character and circumstances.[21] Not only was COS casework much more thorough and intrusive than the investigations of earlier visiting societies, their definition of what constituted good character was much stricter.[22] Overworked poor law relieving officers, on the other hand, could spare little time for such efforts,[23] and thus the rigorous casework on which the discrimination between deserving and undeserving turned became largely a COS preserve. Moreover, it was not merely a question of weeding out the obviously dissolute or work-shy. The 1876 annual report of the COS specified those contingencies for which it was the obligation of the individual to make prudent provision: temporary sickness, unemployment, early marriage, a large family, and old age.[24] Failure to make such provision was evidence of character deficiencies, thus, in theory at least, consigning the applicant to the 'undeserving' category and the tender mercies of the poor law.

In practice, the collaboration between poor law guardians and the COS was very uneven. It was quite close in Stepney, Whitechapel, Camberwell, and Marylebone; a number of Marylebone guardians were COS members. Outside London, too, certain unions were, in the eyes of the COS, models of strict administration and close cooperation: Newcastle, Darlington, Durham, and West Hartlepool. Unions in which there was little or no cooperation were, however, much more common.[25] The most striking characteristic to emerge from a study of poor law–COS relations in the North-east is the extreme variability, even in adjoining unions, and the modest achievements in some of the most 'advanced' unions.[26] A recent survey of COS activities outside London finds that provincial COSs were often ineffective in the campaign against outdoor relief, and that, contrary to the claims of COS propaganda, they signally failed to assist the 'deserving' poor.[27] In the end, the crusade against outdoor relief did prove strikingly effective in

London and a number of Midlands and north-western cities. Most London poor law unions managed to cut back the proportion of out-door paupers to less than 30 per cent of the total.[28] While most smaller towns and rural districts seem to have gone on much as before, the national figures are impressive. Between 1871 and 1876, the number of outdoor paupers declined from 843 000 to 567 000. Women – mostly wives of able-bodied men, single women without children, wives of men in prison or the military, and even widows – were also hit very hard by the crusade. Female recipients of outdoor relief declined from 166 407 in 1871 to 53 271 in 1892.[29] Overall, for both men and women, outdoor paupers as a percentage of the total population were reduced from 3.8 to 2.4 per cent.[30] Still, we must place these figures alongside those show-ing that, even at the height of the crusade in the late 1870s, nationwide 73 per cent of those in receipt of relief were outdoor paupers.[31] Thereafter, the crusade lost some of its fervour, partly due to the recog-nition by some caseworkers that urban poverty was more complex and intractable than was allowed for in the deserving/undeserving character model. As we have seen, the Local Government Board was unwilling to use to the full its audit powers against lax poor law unions, a policy that would have secured much greater compliance, but one that would have exposed it to severe political repercussions.

Another factor attenuating the success of the crusade against outdoor relief is that most charities refused to submit to COS leadership and doctrine. Even at the height of its influence, the COS was never the dominant force in the world of philanthropy. Enormous sums continued to be raised and dispensed in a far looser fashion by a variety of orga-nizations, drawing upon the generosity of the public in hard times. The Mansion House Fund, started up in response to the exceptional distress of 1886, had no difficulty in raising (and squandering, according to the COS) £79 000 in short order.[32] The great majority of those contributing to charity (and this included many of the working class) had little use for the close, suspicious scrutiny of COS casework. Cardinal Manning no doubt spoke for many when he exclaimed, 'As to the waste and wisdom [of donations], I am content that many unworthy should share rather than one worthy case be without help.'[33] Moreover, the late Victorian period was a golden age of voluntary bodies, such as Friendly Societies, cooperative societies, burial clubs, and saving banks, a vast network of voluntary associations catering to the working class. They provided alternative sources of support for the working poor in time of crisis. These organizations, whose aggregate resources were far greater than those provided by the poor law, were based on the principle of self-help within a cooperative framework, rather than the dispensing of charity, It is also true to say that their great importance testifies to the success of the New Poor Law in stigmatizing poverty.[34]

Official support for the crusade began to wane by the 1880s. In 1886, the president of the Local Government Board, Joseph Chamberlain, adopted a policy that COS leaders considered grievously flawed: public works projects for the unemployed. His poor law minute of 1886 and subsequent years called on municipal councils to provide employment for those out of work.[35] Despite this heresy, however, many long-term officials remained wedded to the cause of strict administration. This included a number of poor law inspectors as well as Edwin Chadwick, now an elder statesman of the sanitary movement but one who had never relinquished a keen interest in 'sound' principles of poor relief. An important forum for their views was provided by the annual Poor Law Conferences, national and regional gatherings starting in 1876 that brought together officials and guardians. Not that most of those who attended were committed to the crusade against outdoor relief. One of the most devoted hardliners, Albert Pell, a Tory MP for South Leicestershire who had transformed his own poor law union (Brixworth) into a model of strict administration, characterized as 'pearls before swine' two papers against outrelief delivered at the South Midlands Poor Law Conference of 1876.[36] Still, the well-publicized efforts of such devoted men constitute a counterpoint to a quite different campaign during these decades, one to liberalize relief and extend the range of services. Though more amorphous and diffuse than the campaign against outdoor relief, the movement to extend benefits, which will be taken up later, ultimately had greater success.

The War on Vagrants

The original view of the reformers of 1834, that vagrants required no special provision other than improved policing, and would be deterred from public relief along with the rest of the able-bodied, had long proved erroneous. A diverse, highly mobile population roaming the country in search of work, adventure, or whatever legal or illegal opportunity might turn up, was a marked feature of the Victorian era, as it had been earlier. The itinerant worker component of this preponderantly male population consisted chiefly of agricultural labourers, navvies, and sailors. The rest were not necessarily 'tramps', however, for there was an indeterminate group consisting of those such as demobilized soldiers without a peacetime occupation and casual labourers working sporadically in various parts of the country.[37] A certain number of the homeless were, then as now, mentally ill. In the public imagination, itinerant labourers were increasingly overshadowed by the image of the tramp: slovenly, drunken, wily, unwilling to work but ready to engage freely in whatever criminal opportunity might present itself. Even those who kept within the letter of the law were often feared as an unhygienic and corrupting element. These attitudes hardened in the late Victorian period. The intense moralizing of the COS and the campaign against outdoor relief made the vagrant particularly repugnant, and a threat to Christian civilization. C. J. Ribton Turner of the London COS published *A History of Vagrants and Vagrancy, and Beggars and Begging*[38] in 1887, which served up to the public a colourful and appalling array of vagrant types, each more cunning than the last. Because their dissolute and uprooted way of life could not be accommodated within the framework of a well-ordered society, vagrants did not participate in that transition to more positive imagery of the poor in middle-class minds that characterizes the period.[39]

In 1843, Parliament had tried to restrict the number of vagrants receiving relief by requiring them to be detained at hard labour before discharge. But this was difficult to enforce, and some unions with lax policies or light work requirements tended to attract vagrants. The City of London Union, with its enormous rateable value and low number of resident paupers, was especially notable in this regard. Between 1842 and 1845, 170 000 vagrants had been assisted by the union at a cost of £17 000.[40] A more stringent procedure was adopted in 1848, including the searching of applicants and criminal prosecution of impostors, which moved the union closer to the policies of other metropolitan unions.[41] Policemen were often employed as supplemental relieving officers, and vagrants were required to apply to them for workhouse admission tickets.[42] Nonetheless there remained disparities in the treatment meted out to vagrants, both in London and throughout the country. Vagrants were adept at spreading the word among the homeless confraternity about the regimen in each workhouse, or 'spike', as they preferred to call it. Relatively generous establishments naturally drew larger numbers of applicants, and became regular stops on many a vagrant's itinerary. Andrew Doyle, a poor law inspector for the West Midlands, copied and later published some of the graffiti from various workhouse walls in the 1860s. In addition to personal notices of vagrants' plans and whereabouts ('Saucy Harry and his moll will be at Chester to eat their Christmas dinner, when they hope Saucer and the fraternity will meet them at the union'), there were also assessments of various workhouses, some in verse. One, in praise of the Seisdon Union at Trysull, reads in part:

> Dry bread in the morning, ditto at night,
> Keep up your pecker and make it all right.
> Certainly the meals are paltry and mean,
> But the beds are nice and clean;
> For men there are neither lice, fleas, or bugs
> At this little clean union of Trysull.[43]

A tramp's list of 'easy' workhouses had to be frequently updated as various unions adopted more stringent procedures. When the Bromsgrove Union in Worcestershire adopted a ticket system in 1867 in which vagrants had to prove they were in search of work and had travelled at least 20 miles that day, it led to a reduction of 607 applications and a saving of more than £34.[44] As word of this change spread, vagrants simply turned up at other workhouses. Clearly, such 'competition' between unions tended to drive vagrant policy in an ever harsher direction.

By the 1870s, 572 of the 643 poor law unions had established separate vagrant or casual wards. A stream of directives from the central authority sought to impose a common regimen, including the precise width of a vagrant's sleeping partitions (2 feet 3 inches) and an injunction that the dietary 'not be such as would tend to increase the number of applicants'. The board also got Parliament to pass an act requiring that a vagrant could not discharge himself earlier than 11 a.m. on the day following his admission, thus allowing time for stone-breaking or oakum-picking. The Local Government Board secured the passage of the Casual Poor Act in 1882, by which the vagrant was required to stay until 9 a.m. on the second day after admission, and the fourth day if it was his second application within one month to the same union. Yet, while compliance seems to have been reasonably high immediately after its passage, a poor law inspector complained in 1886 that only half the unions observed the requirements of detention for an extra day.[45] Mitigating the severity of this provision was the simple calculation by guardians of immediate cost; it was cheaper to turn a vagrant loose the next morning than incur the expense of one or two night's additional lodging. Another thing that perhaps gave some boards of guardians pause in their treatment of vagrants was the periodic press revelations of brutal and unhygienic conditions in casual wards, sometimes written by undercover reporters representing themselves as itinerant workers.[46]

Parliament and the Local Government Board were not always consistent in their demands for harsher treatment of vagrants, especially after the 1880s. In 1886, the central authority began recommending early discharge of casuals, on the grounds that if they were detained until 11 or even 9 a.m., any work for the day in the vicinity of the workhouse would have already been taken by others. In 1888, a House of Commons select committee on poor relief heard evidence that oakum-picking was a demoralizing practice for honest wayfarers. A desire to discriminate between them and the host of immoral, hardcore tramps led to the spread, in the 1880s and 1890s, of the use of wayfarers' tickets. This development was the result of local initiatives. Under this system, a wayfarer presented himself at a workhouse, indicating where he planned to look for work. He was issued a ticket specifying the prospective place of employment and the casual wards along the way.[47] Poor law officers supplied employment information to sojourners and encouraged local employers to notify them of openings. The itinerary was worked out by local poor law officials so that it required a minimum of 20 miles walking per day, thought sufficient to deter all but the most determined work-seekers. Provided the sojourner adhered to the prescribed route and timetable, he was provided dinner, a comfortable lodging each night, breakfast, and a midday meal of bread along the way.[48] At the same time that support was growing for this system of treating the honest wayfarer, there was also increasing demand that tramps be subject to protracted committals to so-called 'labour colonies', patterned after those in use in Switzerland. There they would have to submit to a harsh regimen of agricultural labour ('from rosy dawn to dewy eve',[49] as one poor law inspector noted approvingly) for months on end. This idea was to gain ground in the early years of the twentieth century, even among progressive poor law reformers.

The Changing Nature and Uses of the Workhouse

By the 1860s, especially in larger towns and cities, the size, design, and functioning of workhouses had begun to undergo significant change. In the countryside, the hundreds of grim workhouses built in the 1830s and 1840s continued to operate, many of them virtually unchanged since 1834. In larger communities, however, workhouse accommodation was responding to changing policies, greater professionalization, and new ideas of specialized treatment for a variety of conditions found among the nation's paupers. Initially, as new functions (such as schooling) or new classes of pauper had to be provided for, the tendency was simply to add another wing, or to subdivide an existing ward. By the 1860s, however, the trend was away from the 'general mixed workhouse' of the 1830s to separate facilities for various functions and classes of pauper. As far as expenditures are concerned, the most important item was for separate sick wards or workhouse infirmaries, 155 of which were constructed between 1867 and 1883. This conforms to what we have seen was the primacy of medical concerns in the poor law controversies of the 1860s. In the same period, 175 vagrant wards, 14 lunatic wards, and 57 children's wards, homes, or schools were also authorized.[50] Children's institutions were especially important in London, where between 1867 and 1883 each union spent an average of £35 185, indicating large-scale projects.[51]

As we have seen, an earlier trend towards aggregating workhouse children from several unions in district schools was challenged in the 1860s for their barrack-like, impersonal character. Louisa Twining, founder of the Workhouse Visiting Society, called instead for a 'family system' in which children could receive individual attention. The concept of individual development of the child, however, was not necessarily foremost among the reformers' concerns. For Mary Carpenter, one of the great deficiencies of district schools was in the training for domestic service; girls emerged from them, she claimed, 'quite unacquainted with the way to boil a potato or make a family pudding'.[52] Carpenter, along with Twining and others promoting the 'family system' for poor law children, were also active in the reformatory movement. They considered juvenile pauperism to be closely linked to juvenile crime; both pointed to the need for state-sponsored moral training. These views conformed closely to those held by central agency officials, who were also concerned to head off the growth of radical ideas among working-class males. Advising the guardians of the Merthyr Tydfil Union, the Inspector of Workhouse Schools wrote that in an industrial district like theirs, 'it is particularly necessary to train the children of the working class in habits of self-denial and providence and, wherever possible, to check the development of a communistic spirit'.[53] In 1873 the Local Government Board asked a leading reformer, Jane Senior (daughter-in-law of the economist) for a 'woman's view' of the treatment of girls in workhouse schools. Her report, which endorsed 'cottage homes' rather than large facilities, provided a major impetus to the formation of smaller, more domestic arrangements for accommodating pauper children. The Local Government Board gave this approach its official blessing in 1878. Between 1870 and 1914, nearly 200 cottage homes were authorized for construction by boards of guardians.[54]

If cottage homes represented the new kind of facilities designed to be completely removed from the vicinity of the workhouse, there were also substantial changes under way within the grounds of the workhouse itself. There was a decided preference for separate buildings for various classes of pauper. A Poor Law Board order of 1847 had specified a sevenfold classification scheme for indoor paupers (aged or infirm men, aged or infirm women, able-bodied males over 13, able-bodied females over 16, boys aged 7–13, girls aged 7–16, and all children under 7). By the 1860s, this scheme had become obsolete, with the rise of new categories and forms of specialized forms of treatment. A Poor Law Board memorandum of 1868 called for further classification, including imbecile wards, schools, sick wards, and isolation wards, Further subdivision of classes of paupers was also encouraged where numbers were large. The 1868 memorandum stressed that 'care must be taken to avoid aggregating large numbers of inmates in a single block'. The result was to make many a large urban workhouse a complex of separate buildings or 'pavilions' by the end of the century, providing more specialized treatment within each and avoiding some of the demoralizing aspects of the 'general mixed workhouse'.[55] The construction and maintenance costs attendant upon this new policy are the chief reason that overall poor relief costs did not decline after 1870, in spite of major reductions in outdoor relief.

Family Maintenance on Poor Relief

Even during the most intense phase of the campaign against outdoor relief, those paupers most likely to be affected were single men and women. In many parts of the country, even 'lax' poor law unions eliminated or severely curtailed outrelief to this group. Married couples as well as single women with several children were far less likely to be forced into the workhouse, even in 'strict' unions. Central government directives discouraged relief to single women with only one child, and, if there were more children, recommended sending some of them into the workhouse, leaving the mother to support herself and one child on her own earnings.[56] Generally, boards of guardians continued to hold to their traditional and not irrational view that it was cheaper to keep families out of the workhouse. Only the most doctrinaire boards accepted the central authority's argument that all outdoor relief was morally and economically destructive. Ongoing doles to families were thus maintained for long periods. These were inadequate in themselves for maintenance, since guardians always assumed that unreported resources or the help of family and friends would make up the difference. Obviously, such calculations by local poor law authorities were only a guess. While there might be sufficient resources in some cases to maintain the family at a reasonable level, in many cases there was not.

While most local boards were reluctant to compel families to enter the workhouse, they usually did impose a test of character. In some cases, this could be the exclusion of men or women of 'immoral habits' or even 'known to be in the habit of frequenting public houses'. Some even adopted a sliding scale, in which a calculus of character was applied to determine the appropriate amount of relief. At Sheffield, the most respectable class of recipient was granted 5s. a week, while those deemed to be less worthy were given 4s., 3s., or 2s. 6d. At Bradford, a detailed list of specifications for widows with children to be eligible for outrelief included sobriety, cleanliness, not allowing their children to beg or sell in the street, and not having any male lodgers. If everything was judged satisfactory by the guardians or their visitors, these widows were granted outdoor relief. Keeping a dog or other animal operated as a disqualification in many unions. In spite of the central authority's fulminating against relief in aid of wages, this was commonly given to 'respectable' women with children. There was invariably a cap on such earnings, in some places as low as 2s. a week.[57]

If a highly moralized form of the allowance system was one element that survived from the Old Poor Law, non-resident relief was another. The Local Government Board had to admit in 1874 that, in spite of its repeated strictures, non-resident relief was given in most unions.[58] Chief among the motives of guardians was parsimony. In the Axminster Union in Devon in 1878, a policeman's widow with five children, legally settled in that union but resident in the Bedminster Union, was receiving non-resident relief. When there was an attempt to move the family into the Axminster workhouse, she appealed on the grounds that her children were 'in a way of earning something' and that she could maintain the family in Bedminster on a small allowance. The guardians relented, recognizing that the pittance they paid, 3s. a week, was far less than indoor maintenance costs for the entire family.[59]

The Devon widow's successful appeal illustrates some marked features of relief under the New Poor Law: applicants' knowledge of the law, plus a willingness to use it to maintain a family, often without a feeling of being stigmatized. Wider kin networks were often brought into play in the complex process of negotiation with poor law officials, such as requests in behalf of one's elderly parents. The wide array of services available in London was well known to the poor, and most showed little hesitancy in applying for them in time of need. This was especially true for the various kinds of medical assistance available from poor law infirmaries. In London in 1870, a third of those getting outdoor relief received it in the form of medical treatment. Applications to relieving officers for medical care, often for a relative, were commonplace. Poor law doctors sometimes brought food as well as medicine.[60] The poor were also actively involved, and frequently took the initiative, in prompting the medical officer and guardians to commit mentally ill family members to asylums. Usually, this came as a result of prolonged destructive or threatening behaviour by the disturbed person.[61] Medical care, including the use of the insane asylum, was the form of assistance most effectively destigmatized in the minds of the poor. Other kinds of relief still carried some shame but were nonetheless readily resorted to in times of need. Burials of infants and mothers in a family were often provided by the poor law guardians, even in families in which the father's elaborate funeral was paid for by a Friendly Society benefit. Even the workhouse itself could be used, perhaps for one or more of the children, as a temporary expedient until the family could get on its feet.[62] Such temporary use of the dreaded workhouse did not, in the eyes of many of the poor, constitute a serious loss of status or respectability. Beyond a tendency to the destigmatizing of relief in the minds of the poor during the latter part of the nineteenth century, something more assertive was at work: a sense of entitlement. This became increasingly important as the poor law was at last caught up in the current of democratization.

Democratizing the Boards of Guardians

The poor law franchise established in 1834, which heavily favoured well-to-do ratepayers by giving them plural votes based on their rateable property, and assigned additional votes to those who owned the property, remained largely unchanged until the end of the nineteenth century. It was compounded by making active resident magistrates, who were often major landowners, ex-officio guardians of the poor. This system had the greatest impact on rural parishes, where the total number of ratepayers was small, and the plural votes given to the property-holding elite ensured their major influence if not complete control. Such control or influence was of course dependent upon the elite's taking an active interest in poor law electoral matters. In many cases, they did not exert themselves much in these matters, and consequently the office of guardian often went by rotation through the farmers and tradesmen. The system also favoured smaller parishes over large, since the central authority invariably assigned fewer guardians to larger parishes than the size of their populations would seem to warrant. This favoured close parishes over open parishes, and rural over urban in those unions where towns were combined with part of the surrounding countryside. In 1868, the Poor Law Board was empowered to combine small parishes for electoral purposes, but made relatively little use of it. In 10 years, they had combined only 580 small parishes, out of a total of 6111 parishes with a population of less than 300.[63]

While only a handful of parliamentary radicals had raised their voices against the plural voting system in 1834, criticism grew from the 1860s. The extension of the parliamentary franchise to urban workers in 1867 and to agricultural labourers in 1884, the adoption of the secret ballot in 1872, and the passing of the County Councils Act in 1888, all highlighted the poor law electoral system's oligarchic character. Radicals achieved a small success in 1885 with the passage of the Medical Relief (Disqualification Removal) Act. This statute amended that part of the 1884 Parliamentary Reform Act stripping anyone who received poor relief of his parliamentary franchise for one year. By exempting poor law medical relief, the 1885 measure recognized that it was so commonly used by respectable employed labourers that it should not be considered an electoral disqualification; in Southampton just during one year (1874–75), over one-third of the population received some form of poor law medical relief.[64] Defenders of strict administration had of course always opposed indiscriminate medical relief. One alarmed central poor law official lamented the lack of stigma attached to the use of poor law infirmaries;[65] another later described the 1885 act as the 'first nail in the coffin' of the New Poor Law.[66]

Full democratization of the boards took longer. In 1878, a House of Commons select committee on poor law elections disappointed radicals by failing to recommend a one-ratepayer/one vote system and the use of the ballot. Local Government Board officials who testified before the board favoured the maintenance of the status quo on the grounds that it secured the return of more 'respectable' guardians.[67] Albert Pell, who had been the key figure in 'dispauperizing' the Brixworth Union by eliminating outdoor relief, was extremely active on the committee in his defence of plural voting, fearing that democratizing boards of guardians would open the floodgates of profuse relief. Yet, like many other crusaders against outdoor relief, Pell had an equivocal view of ex-officio guardians. On the one hand, they were the most 'respectable' component of local boards; on the other, they were apt to be more sympathetic to the poor and often opposed to any drastic curtailment of outdoor relief. In his own poor law union, Brixworth, Pell had to carry the abolition of outdoor relief in the face of the opposition of Earl Spencer, the leading ex-officio guardian.[68]

Advocates of outdoor relief won a major victory when the Liberals were swept back into office in 1892. Split asunder by the defection of Joseph Chamberlain and other opponents of Irish Home Rule in 1885, the Liberal Party in opposition had fashioned a more radical electoral strategy. Part of its Newcastle Programme in 1891 was democratization of poor law elections and the abolition of ex-officio guardians. After the Liberals took office, a Local Government (District and Parish Councils) bill was introduced in 1893. Although it was commonly called the Parish Councils bill, its main purpose, as a junior cabinet minister admitted in the House, was to democratize poor law elections.[69] The government began to take steps even before the bill was passed. Henry H. Fowler, the new president of the Local Government Board, issued a circular in November 1892 lowering the minimum qualification for guardian to an annual rateable value of £5 (from a previous £15 to £40, depending on the part of the country). This allowed workers, for the first time, to stand for election. In the Brixworth Union, an Outdoor Relief Association, with the blessing of the Spencer interest, succeeded in winning several seats in the 1893 guardian elections, even with the plural voting system still in place.[70] After the hard-fought passage of the Parish Councils bill in 1894, poor law elections throughout the country were held under the new democratic ratepayer franchise. The overall results were less dramatic than might have been expected. Most guardians were re-elected, and most ex-officio were either returned as elected guardians or else chosen as 'additional guardians' by their local boards, as provided for in the act. However, in those unions where a bitter struggle had taken place over the abolition of outdoor relief, fierce contests and the repudiation of the old guard were common. This was nowhere more true than at Brixworth, where the newly elected board restored the policy of outdoor relief at its first meeting. As Pell lamented in a 1907 letter to the *Charity Organisation Review*: 'The policy of strict administration of the poor law, after being in force for many years in the Brixworth Union, was reversed about twelve years ago.'[71]

A change of regimes and policies was also occurring in far more heavily populated urban unions, some of which, like Poplar, would become synonymous with the struggle against the 'principles of 1834'. The metropolitan poor law unions, in addition to those in cities like Manchester and Liverpool, had been quite effective in pruning outdoor paupers from their relief lists during the crusade against outdoor relief. Of the 41 boards of guardians that managed to reduce their outdoor paupers to less than 30 per cent of their total between 1872 and 1893, 24 were in London.[72] The results of democratic poor elections in many of these parishes and unions after 1894 are striking. As a conservative critic of the 1894 act pointed out to a Poor Law Conference in 1901, in 1890, the total outdoor relief bill for St Olave's, St Saviour's, Poplar, and Whitechapel was £26 505. By 1900, after several years of a fairly robust economy, it had increased to £49 104. The indoor relief bill had also gone up substantially, from £121 854 to £179 309, reflecting more liberal treatment as well as the important spatial transformations still under way in large urban workhouses. Nationwide, the differences were less dramatic, since most unions had never enrolled under the banner of the crusade against outdoor relief. Nevertheless, the ratio of pauperism to population ceased to decline, rising from 25.6 per 1000 in 1892 to 26.2 in 1898.[73]

Women Guardians and Poor Law Officials

For roughly the first 50 years of the New Poor Law, administration was completely controlled by men. Central authority officials, as well as members of boards of guardians, were entirely male. In the 'local civil service', there were women in subordinate posts, such as workhouse matrons, teachers, and nurses. Women had of course from an early date taken an active part in charities that worked closely with local boards; the Workhouse Visiting Society was particularly notable in this regard. The relatively few women who were ratepayers in their own right could vote in poor law elections. This did not seem to create any uneasiness, especially since voting for guardians took place in the privacy of one's home; voting papers were delivered to the residence of each ratepayer and collected later. However, the prospect of women guardians was another matter. One of the first times the issue was raised was in 1850, when the clerk of the Ludlow Union wrote to the Poor Law Board inquiring whether a woman could be elected guardian, if fully qualified by residence and rateable value. The board's reply was that since the statute and the courts were silent on the issue, it was an open question. However, their reply went on:

> The objections to the appointment of a female to an office of this nature, upon grounds of public policy and convenience, are so manifest, that the Board cannot readily suppose that the question will become one of practical importance in the administration of the Poor Laws.[74]

Only a handful of women guardians were elected over the next few decades. It would not be until the democratization of poor law elections in 1894 that women began to serve on boards of guardians in significant numbers. The first woman was elected guardian in 1875; by 1909, there were 1289 women guardians in 500 poor law unions.[75]

How did the entry of women into boards of guardians affect poor law administration? Not necessarily in the direction of greater liberalization, as a number of COS women were elected to local boards from the 1880s on, and exerted themselves to reduce outdoor relief. One thing that most women guardians believed was that, as women, they brought special qualities to a local board: compassion, attention to the details of workhouse life, and a close knowledge and understanding of the needs of children and young women. In 1887, at a time when there were still only 50 women guardians in England and Wales, Caroline Biggs, writing for the Society for Promoting the Return of Women as Poor Law Guardians, urged greater participation and detailed the special duties of women guardians:

> ... the old people to be visited and cheered by a few kindly words, or by the attention to some inexpensive comforts for them; the infants' wards to be made healthier and more lively; the school children to receive the individual approbation and counsel without which a child's life becomes warped and stunted; the growing girls to be instructed in house duties, encouraged to bear the trials of their first service, or helped to do better after a first failure. Then there are girls of an older growth to be helped to retrieve some miserable downward

step; and women who have been tossed about as waifs on the social sea, who need the advice and help of a religious and cultivated lady.[76]

While these activities suggest women were urged to enter upon their public duties within the parameters of the doctrine of 'separate spheres', and to be the 'angel in the [work]house', they certainly took their duties seriously and did not shrink from challenging their male colleagues on policy matters. The first women to be elected had frequently taken an active part in the philanthropic world or other endeavours. Many had studied the issues very carefully. Moreover, they were of superior social rank and accustomed to taking leadership roles. The pattern for a certain kind of upper-class woman guardian was Louisa Twining, who had founded the Workhouse Visiting Society in the 1850s. In the 1880s, she was elected to the Kensington Board of Guardians, and later to that in Tunbridge Wells. A strong advocate of the campaign against outdoor relief as well as a temperance reformer, Twining was a formidable figure. An early attempt of hers at Kensington to prohibit the serving of porter to workhouse inmates on the occasion of the Queen's Jubilee in 1887 failed, but she continued to cajole her male colleagues on the issue. Two years later she had convinced a majority to discontinue the long-established practice of serving beer to the inmates on Christmas Day ('a glorious victory against beer', as she later recalled).[77] Yet, while Twining and like-minded women guardians tended to reinforce the hardline factions on most boards in respect to outdoor relief, they also frequently pressed for improved workhouse conditions. Twining, for example, was a strong supporter of Dr Joseph Rogers's programme of expanding and improving poor law medical services.[78]

A growing number of female guardians held more progressive views in regard to outdoor relief. This was true especially after 1900, but even before the formal organization of the Labour Party, there were a few socialist women guardians, though they were as apt as more conservative women to stress the special role of women as nurturers. Gertrude Green, a Fabian candidate for one of the seats on the Greenwich board in 1893, declared that 'the [poor law] union is a large household, and those who are already experienced in domestic matters are surely best qualified to deal with them'.[79] An important inducement for women to enter upon elective poor law office was the chance to display their fitness for the parliamentary office and franchise. Thus Emmeline Pankhurst, who was a guardian of the Chorlton Union in Lancashire in the 1890s, stressed the connection between poor law service and wider political rights.[80]

A woman guardian speaking before the West Bristol Women's Liberal Association in 1894 made a similar point.[81] The campaign to bring more women on to poor law boards bore significant fruit. From only a handful in 1880, by 1907 there were 1141, out of a total of 24 613 guardians in England and Wales. The distribution was quite uneven, however: 254 of the 644 poor law unions had no women guardians at all, and urban and suburban parishes were far more likely than rural parishes to elect a woman.[82]

In contrast to the significant increase in the number of women on boards of guardians, only a handful of women served as officials of the central agency in the nineteenth century. It had been an exclusively male preserve until the 1870s, when Jane Senior, daughter-in-law of Nassau Senior the economist, was asked to draw up a special report on workhouse education. Her 1874 report condemning district schools and recommending cottage homes and other smaller facilities was instrumental in bringing about the decline of large, barrack-like institutions for children.[83] As with female guardians, women officials were expected to confine their attention to those matters within the province of 'women's work'. Thus, in 1885 the Local Government Board appointed Miss M. H. Mason as an assistant inspector specifically to supervise those workhouse children who were being boarded out.[84] Not until 1910 was the first woman appointed to the general inspectorate.[85] With the growth of the concept and profession of 'social worker' in the twentieth century, more opportunities opened for women to become officials, but they continued to be excluded from policy-setting executive posts throughout the remaining history of the poor law.

New Definitions of Poverty

In addition to the advance of democracy, another factor promoting higher relief standards and the replacement of deterrence by treatment was the emergence of new definitions of and attitudes towards poverty. When the New Poor Law was passed in 1834, Malthusian population theory and classical economics held sway. If public relief there must be, and most accepted its necessity, it would result in economic devastation unless administered with the utmost stringency and severity. Few questioned these verities through the 1870s, but the last two decades of the century saw considerable ferment in economic thought. The economic disruption wrought by trade cycles on a workforce much more urban than it had been a half-century earlier called into question both the effectiveness and the justice of relying on a policy of deterrence. In the work of economists like Henry Sidgwick, James Thorold Rogers, and Alfred Marshall, there was a new willingness to question the efficacy of markets alone to bring about the optimal production and dispersal of goods and services. Marshall, professor of political economy at Cambridge whose *Principles of Economics* (1890) decisively shaped the emerging profession of economics, was also active in public life, offering expert testimony to a number of government inquiries. Appearing before the Royal Commission on the Aged Poor in 1893, he criticized the callousness of the poor law and denounced the workhouse test, though admitting the necessity of some kind of character test for recipients.[86] Taking their cue from Marshall, the royal commissioners did condemn the inadequacy of outrelief to the aged and the repellent nature of the workhouse, though they shrunk from what many were coming to believe was the solution: state-supported old-age pensions.[87] The 'New Liberalism' that emerged before 1900 reflected these changing values by moving away from individualism and towards a more corporatist, communitarian philosophy.[88] Related to this was the settlement house movement, starting with Toynbee Hall in 1880, in which upper-class idealists living among the poor sought to raise their moral standards and establish a new cooperative ethos without recourse to the punitive strategies of the poor law.[89]

Finally, there were the major statistical investigations of urban poverty by Charles Booth and Seebohm Rowntree in the 1880s and 1890s. Booth, a wealthy shipowner, investigated conditions first-hand in order to refute a Socialist pamphlet's claim that one-quarter of Londoners lived in poverty. Between 1889 and 1902 he published his 17-volume *Life and Labour of the People in London*. Establishing a poverty line at a minimum of 18s. a week for a family of five, he discovered that in fact 30 per cent of Londoners lived in poverty. Low wages, unemployment, and old age, rather than character flaws, were shown to be the principal causes of destitution. Similarly, Rowntree, of the wealthy chocolate manufacturing family, showed, in his *Poverty: A Study of Town Life* (1901), that 28 per cent of the population in York in 1899 lived below the poverty line.[90] With their statistical depth and scientific air, both studies served to enhance the belief that modern indigence was an economic condition, not a flawed moral state. While there were numerous challenges to their findings, many were coming to view harshness and deterrence as inappropriate and inhumane. Reformers at the end of the century were prone to see poverty not as a single monolith, but as an array of particular problems related to the life cycle of individuals and to the ups and downs of the economy. Each kind of problem could be addressed through a particular policy, such as pensions for the elderly. At the turn of the twentieth century, a democratic society confronted these challenges. The debates over how far the state should go in solving social problems, and whether in fact the poor law had outlived its usefulness, would be long and rancorous.

7

THE ECLIPSING
AND TRANSFORMING OF
THE POOR LAW, 1900–1930

Labour and Poor Relief: the First Phase of Poplarism

By the early years of the twentieth century, the English poor law system was operating in an environment substantially changed since 1834. The country, its population doubled, had evolved from predominantly rural to highly urbanized. Poverty was now thought of primarily as afflicting towns and cities rather than the countryside. Malthusian pessimism, used to justify the paring if not elimination of poor relief at the time the New Poor Law was passed, had receded. It is true that neo-Malthusian concerns about overpopulation and 'race degeneration' were coming into vogue by 1900, but they were as likely to promote as to inhibit new social programmes. Other aspects of economic belief, such as the wages-fund doctrine, deployed earlier to curtail relief, were giving way to underconsumptionist theory, which pointed to some kind of income redistribution to alleviate poverty. The rigorous individualism of 1834 was being eclipsed by collectivist and communitarian values, some of them associated with 'New Liberalism'. Advances in the social sciences encouraged the tendency to look at the manifold problems formerly covered by the concept of 'poverty' as discrete entities, each properly addressed by specialist services. Poor law schools and infirmaries were often of a decent standard, while the doctrine of 'less eligibility' had been all but abandoned. Aggregate poor relief expenditure and the amount spent per pauper had doubled between 1870–1 and 1905–6.[1] This is not to say that the 'principles of 1834' were still not considered sound doctrine in many quarters of society as well as in official circles, or that the notion that poverty resulted from character flaws still did not have its adherents. A deeply ingrained, morally charged individualism, characteristic of the Victorian era, was by no means insignificant in Edwardian Britain. A clash of values over poor relief would characterize the new century's first three decades, which were also the final three decades of the poor law.

The beginning of the century coincided with the advent of the Labour Party. In conjunction with the extension of the poor law franchise to all householders and the elimination of plural voting in 1894, this meant there would be a number of sharply contested elections to boards of guardians. Candidates of progressive and socialist views, some of them from the working class, had been contesting seats since the drastic lowering of qualifications by the Local Government Board in 1892. As we have seen, they achieved considerable success in a few poor law unions, notably in east London. Poplar became the most famous of these radical boards, though in fact the radicals never succeeded in capturing a majority of the seats there. The leading players in the radicalization of the Poplar board were Will Crooks and George Lansbury, both to become important figures in the Labour Party. Crooks was one of the first workhouse children to become a guardian. Born by the docks in Poplar in 1852, Crooks entered the workhouse in 1860 after his father had lost an arm in an accident. His experience of the stigmatizing treatment meted out to indoor paupers, together with the ghastly food and dismal conditions, led him to resolve to set things right. He was elected to the board in 1892 along with Lansbury and five years later became chairman.[2] Working with labour groups, the Social Democratic Federation, and other societies with an 'advanced' view on relief questions, the two were able to convince the majority of the board to liberalize relief.

The major breakthrough on outdoor relief came in 1903; in just two years, the ratio of outdoor paupers (excluding vagrants and imbeciles) to population in the Poplar Union had nearly doubled, from 19.2 to 35.9.[3] Not surprisingly, the free-spending ways of the Poplar guardians and those of a handful of other boards evoked spirited opposition on the grounds of expense, policy, and ideology. In 1905, the newly formed Municipal Alliance, an all-party organization of ratepayers, called for a return to plural voting,[4] and began petitioning the central authority to intercede. Accordingly, an official inquiry was held in the Poplar boardroom in 1906, conducted by J. S. Davy, an assistant secretary to the Local Government Board known for his orthodox views on poor relief.[5] The proceedings, enlivened by revelations of an affair between the workhouse master and one of the nurses, was well attended.[6] The severe unemployment accompanying the downward swing in the economy in

1904, and the near disappearance of shipbuilding and dockwork in Poplar, were brought forward to justify the guardians' policies. With casual employment the only resort, Lansbury pointed out that supplementing inadequate wages was essential. This was, of course, rank heresy to the pure of principle, as was Lansbury's later admission that the guardians granted outrelief to those over 60 'as a means of giving old-age pensions'.[7] Davy, perhaps influenced by testimony that the guardians' liberal policies had destroyed 'revolutionary anarchism' in Poplar, was fairly even-handed in his report. Still, he was highly critical of the Labour guardians' political motivations and extravagance, and the wide circulation of his report further mobilized ratepayer resistance, in Poplar and elsewhere. Over the next few years the Municipal Alliance won more seats on the board; by 1912, few of the able-bodied in Poplar were receiving outdoor relief.[8] Poplarism, in spite of the fact that it was confined to relatively few boards, served to politicize the poor law and lead to the staking out of sharp ideological positions just as the greatest official inquiry since 1834 was set in motion. Nor was opposition to Poplarism confined to Liberals and Conservatives, as the internal debate within the Labour Party was to show.

The Royal Commission on the Poor Laws, 1905–1909

The investigation of 1905–9 was not prompted by as pressing a sense of urgency as that of 1832–4, though there was a widespread sense that poor law services were often unable to meet the demands placed on them. While the incidence of poverty was lower than it had been 75 years earlier, it had begun creeping upward again from the 1890s, and unemployment rates, especially in the winter, were troubling. Unlike the 1830s, there was a broad consensus in favour of more specialist services and a gradual evolution of ameliorative approaches that had taken place. Indeed, Conservative ministers had often made important initiatives in this regard. Joseph Chamberlain's 1886 minute on unemployment, which brought municipal councils into the picture to provide public works projects, was augmented by Walter Long, president of the Local Government Board from 1900 to 1904. Long created joint relief committees of boards of guardians and the county council in the metropolis, an idea which spawned the Unemployed Workmen Act of 1905. However flawed in implementation, these measures were widely regarded as progressive.[9] Why did A. J. Balfour's government make a commitment to such a major inquiry on the eve of resigning in 1905 (and losing to the Liberals in the ensuing general election)? The initiative appears to have come from the central authority, which was headed by the Prime Minister's brother Gerald. Beatrice Webb, who was to be a central figure on the commission, noted in her diary that doctrinaire Local Government Board officials, such as J. S. Davy (newly appointed head of the Poor Law Division) sought to use the inquiry to undo the mischief of recent reforms and return the country to the sound principles of 1834. By packing the witness list and carefully crafting queries to selected boards of guardians and inspectors, the plan was, according to Webb, to discredit dubious relief policies at both the local and national level.[10]

It may seem surprising that Davy, knowing that both Beatrice and Sidney Webb sought nothing less than 'the break-up of the poor law', would make such a frank revelation to Beatrice only a few days before she took her seat on the commission. Most likely he considered her an ally on the question of profuse relief, in spite of their very different views of any desirable reform. Although the Webbs were Fabian Socialists and figures of importance in the fledgling Labour Party, they had major reservations about Poplarism. They considered the indiscriminate relief pursued by Poplar and other Labour-controlled boards to reflect the 'proletarianization' of local poor law boards, as objectionable in its way as the allowance system under the Old Poor Law. Their ideal was an array of specialist services provided by professionals under the aegis of a highly centralized and vigorous state. They viewed boards of guardians with the same jaundiced eye that Chadwick and other reformers of the 1830s had looked upon parochial vestries: as bastions of narrow self-interest, corruption, and localism. Democratic electorates, together with working-class guardians, compounded the problem, injecting demagoguery into the policy-making process.

The Royal Commission on the Poor Laws and the Relief of Distress, as it was officially named, began its labours in December 1905. Of the 20 members appointed to the commission, six were prominent members of the Charity Organisation Society, including Octavia Hill (one of its founders), general secretary C. S. Loch, and historian Helen Bosanquet. Among the five poor law guardians (two of them Labour), the most important was George Lansbury of Poplar. Since any prospective reform might embrace the whole of the UK, the permanent heads of the Local Government Boards of Scotland and Ireland were included, in addition to the Local Government Board permanent head for

England and Wales. Two political economists, one from the University of Glasgow, the other from Oxford, representatives of the Church of England and the Roman Catholic Church in Ireland, the well-known surveyor of poverty Charles Booth, and of course, Beatrice Webb, rounded out the commission. The chairmanship was vested in a Conservative ex-cabinet minister, Lord George Hamilton, an 'experienced politician and attractive *grand seigneur*', as Beatrice Webb described him.[11]

There quickly emerged some fundamental differences of philosophy between the six COS members and the four Fabian-Labour members. Under the spirited and sometimes high-handed leadership of Beatrice Webb, the latter were committed from the outset to breaking up the poor law and substituting an array of specialist services, with such local control as was to remain being placed in the hands of county and borough councils. The COS members, while not altogether opposed to this programme, were concerned to preserve some deterrent character to public relief. They were also committed to a major role for voluntary agencies under any reform. They secured J. S. Davy as one of the first witnesses. True to his reputation as a stickler for the principles of 1834, Davy advocated a return to rigorous use of the workhouse test and less eligibility, and was particularly critical of the 1894 Act that had democratized poor law elections. The 14 general inspectors of the Local Government Board who testified echoed their chief's sentiments. A number of poor law guardians, local officials, and medical officers were also examined. In addition, Beatrice Webb, C. S. Loch, Charles Booth, and other individual commissioners undertook specialized investigations of various topics or localities.[12] In addition to her tireless and dedicated husband Sidney, Beatrice had at her disposal an entire Fabian research team, which, among other things, produced an exhaustive report on central government policy since 1834. This was printed as part of the royal commission's report in 1909 (and published separately as *English Poor Law Policy* in 1910), although the results of the Fabian research team's investigations into local policies were not accepted by the commission.[13]

By the completion of the investigation a large majority of the commission had come to accept the views of the COS leaders, but their philosophy had undergone considerable changes since 1870. Deterrence was no longer central to their thinking, nor was the stigmatizing of those in receipt of public relief. The majority report of the royal commission, written by Helen Bosanquet and the Glasgow economist, William Smart, displayed a dramatic change from the spirit of the 1834 report as well as from the early doctrines of the COS itself. The revised nomenclature of poverty suggested in the report shows the concern to destigmatize. The indigent were henceforth to be the 'necessitous', while the poor law was to be renamed the 'Public Assistance Authority'. Boards of guardians were to be replaced by public assistance committees of county and county borough councils. Workhouses were to be turned to more positive purposes.[14] Overall, the underlying philosophy of the majority report was that of T. H. Green's philosophical idealism, not Herbert Spencer's atomistic individualism. The new watchwords were to be 'help, prevention, cure, and instruction'.[15]

The minority report, written largely by the 'other one', as Beatrice Webb referred to Sidney, left Victorian notions of pauperism even further behind. They argued for eliminating destitution altogether as a category requiring treatment, substituting in its place a variety of conditions attached to the life cycle, so that from birth to old age, an appropriate government bureau would provide the necessary help. Old-age pensions were to be universal, while unemployment would be dealt with by National Labour Exchanges and a Ministry of Labour. In its comprehensiveness, intrusiveness, and provision for a vastly expanded civil service, it went considerably beyond what public opinion was prepared to accept, though it met with approval among socialists and leading Labourites.[16] While many of the elements of the minority programme might seem simply an extension and amplification of what the majority recommended, there were several important differences. One was the central role in the majority report for voluntary agencies, in keeping with COS doctrine. In effect, a new kind of 'less eligibility' principle was urged, with the respectable receiving a higher standard of care from private agencies, while the less worthy received a diminished level of treatment from public authorities. Another key difference was that the majority kept a destitution authority, though with a name change, while the minority dropped such a concept altogether. The majority also had major misgivings about the minority's insistence on universal state-funded old-age pensions.

Not that the minority called for a 'free ride' or were any less determined than the majority to bring reprobates into line. Under the Webbs' plan, those who were work-shy or otherwise resistant to whatever officials decided was necessary to improve them could be sentenced to penal labour colonies for a matter of months. What was required in such cases, Beatrice wrote, was compulsory training and 'no nonsense about democracy'.[17] The Webbs' newly formed National Committee to Promote the Break-up of the Poor Law issued a charter, the final point of which was that the enumerated specialized and preventive authorities would enforce 'the obligation of all able-bodied persons to maintain themselves and their families in due health and efficiency'.[18] The Webbs were not simply rationalizing, efficiency-inspired proponents of government growth. In their way, as a recent study makes clear, they were every bit as much concerned with the effect of reform on character as the COS.[19]

Although the two competing reports were widely discussed following their publication, the government chose to ignore both sets of recommendations. The reasons for this inaction are not far to seek. Since, unlike the 1834 commission, this one failed to reach unanimity, the results were far less compelling. Moreover, after 1909 the government was engulfed by the battle over David Lloyd George's 'People's Budget', and the ensuing struggle over the constitutional role of the House of Lords. Since both reports had recommended the elimination of boards of guardians, there loomed the prospect of spirited resistance, not only from conservative boards but from those of a 'Poplarist' persuasion as well. For it was by no means clear that the minority report reflected Labour sentiment generally. Beatrice Webb had been able to persuade her commission colleague George Lansbury of the wisdom of abolishing boards of guardians, partly because Lansbury was now a member of the London County Council, which would assume the relief functions of the Poplar and other metropolitan boards under the proposed reform.

Many Labour guardians in Poplar and on other progressive boards, however, were unwilling to abandon their bastions of local control of poor relief. To do so would be to submit to the uncertainties of much larger and more conservative electorates in most counties and county boroughs. It would also mean submitting to a more comprehensive, intrusive state, wielding enhanced coercive powers, a prospect not at all to the liking of many in the working class. Democratic socialist opposition to the minority report was evident at a public debate at Holborn Hall in 1910 between Lansbury and Harry Quelch, editor of *Justice*, the weekly Social Democratic Federation newspaper. Before an audience of Labourites, Marxists, Fabians, and members of the Church Socialist League, Quelch, while accepting that there were some good points in the report, declared his firm opposition to the elimination of local boards: 'The Guardians were the most democratically-elected body in the kingdom, and if they had not been so good as they should have been, that was the fault of the people, and their business was to educate the people to elect proper Guardians.'[20]

This left-wing defence of the guardians was echoed on the right. A newly formed National Committee for Poor Law Reform represented the entrenched opposition of conservative boards of guardians throughout the country. Chaired by Sir William Chance, a guardian of the Hamdledon Union in Surrey, this organization lobbied to defeat the main thrust of both reports of the royal commission.[21] Boards of guardians were also defended by the conservative British Constitution Society, which took as its motto, 'To resist Socialism: to uphold the fundamental principles of the British Constitution – personal liberty and personal responsibility – and to limit the functions of governing bodies accordingly.'[22] Many on the democratic left and the elite-dominated right, poles apart on poor relief policy prescriptions, were united in their defence of local control.

The Liberal Government's New Array of Social Services

Besides shrinking from a fight to uproot the boards of guardians, the Liberal government's attachment to the Gladstonian legacy was still strong enough to make them uneasy about undermining local democratic bodies. On the other hand, the 'New Liberal' philosophy that had been steadily gaining ground since the 1870s pointed to a more activist, interventionist state. The result of this tension in government thinking was a selective fostering of new social reforms, while at the same time leaving the Victorian poor law apparatus much as it was. Cabinet ministers were also influenced to some extent by the 'National Efficiency' movement that had many adherents in the Edwardian era, both on the left and the right. Concerns over the physical deterioration of the 'race', coupled with the threat posed by vigorous new powers like the German Empire, seemed to require government programmes to enhance vitality. The poor showing of the British military in the South African War of 1899–1902, and the very high army rejection rate of undersized, undernourished urban recruits, underscored the need for reform. Such concerns provide one explanation for measures like that in 1906 providing free meals for schoolchildren, which had the effect of chipping away at problems broadly within the purview of the poor law. There was also the Children's Act of 1908, which allowed the state to take charge of children considered abandoned or delinquent, a measure that alarmed many working-class parents concerned about the long arm of government reaching into their families.[23] A much greater impact on the poor law, however, can be seen in the two major social reforms of the Liberal government: old-age pensions and national insurance.

Reformers had been urging the need for old-age pensions since the 1870s, but all attempts to enact them had been defeated by the COS on the one hand, ever concerned about character-corrupting giveaways, and the Friendly Societies. The latter, besides fearing government competition, championed the ideal of individual self-help. Moreover, workers were understandably reluctant to be involved in a government scheme that required contributions from them.[24] The Unionist governments of 1895–1905, pressed forward on the issue by Joseph Chamberlain, took an active interest in some form of non-contributory pension. In 1899, a committee headed by Henry Chaplin, president of the Local Government Board, recommended non-contributory pensions funded jointly out of the poor rates and Exchequer grants. However, as need and character were to be assessed by boards of guardians, the distinction between deserving and undeserving was maintained. This plan failed to satisfy progressive advocates of pensions, while most Unionist MPs refused to have anything to do with a pension scheme not tied to the poor law. A broad consensus proving elusive, the plan was dropped, only to be resurrected by the Liberals in 1906.

Had it been enacted, the 1899 recommendation on pensions would not have been greatly different, except for the Exchequer grants, from the kind of grant typically made by most boards of guardians for those considered past working age.[25] It has been estimated that, by the latter half of the nineteenth century, between one-quarter and one-half of men and from one-half to three-quarters of women over 70 were receiving a regular weekly pension from poor law authorities. The proportion was highest in the rural South and East, lowest in London and the industrial areas.[26] Conservative boards were often as involved as left-leaning boards in paying poor law pensions, but they harboured a strong opposition to nationalizing the pension system. The fear was that of losing local control over what they viewed as a potent character-shaping policy. Thus the Bradfield Board of Guardians in an 1899 pamphlet warned that any national pension would create dependency, and that 'any system tending to make such dependence attractive, and even honourable, is full of danger'.[27] Labour boards, on the other hand, were very much in favour of a national, non-contributory pension programme.

The presence in the House of Commons of a significant number of Labour MPs after 1905 helped force the Liberal government's hand on the issue. Fifty-three working men were elected in December 1905, surpassing even the boastful predictions of that former workhouse boy, Will Crooks. The government was also pressured by the publication of a new pension proposal by Charles Booth in 1907.[28] With such concerns before them, the cabinet bowed to the advocates of pensions, and a bill was passed in 1908 providing a weekly pension of 5s. for men and women over 70 within the prescribed income limits, effective 1 January 1909. Those in receipt of poor relief (except for medical relief, which was exempt) were disqualified from receiving pensions for two years. Pension payments were to be made through the Post Office, thus removing any lingering stigma associated with poor law pensions. The act was hailed as a major step forward by the aged and their political champions, though many of the aged poor, because of their infirmities, resided in workhouses and thus could not draw pensions. As predicted, the act provided some relief for boards of guardians, but the savings were modest. By the eve of the Great War, local poor law expenditure had declined by perhaps £600 000 per year, but this was dwarfed by the £11 700 000 national expenditure on pensions.[29]

The 1908 measure was a seemingly 'modern' social service with transfer payments out of a national fund to a targeted group of beneficiaries, but in practice there were lingering elements of the poor law attached to it. This can be seen in the local implementation. While the determining of eligibility was in the first instance made by an official of the Inland Revenue Board, there was a pension committee appointed by the local council to oversee his decision. The pension committees, which often included poor law guardians, were answerable to the Local Government Board. An attitude of suspicion towards claimants and a determination to weed out the morally unfit often prevailed on these bodies. Even minuscule resort to poor law services (other than medical relief) was seized upon by local committees to deny a pension. An elderly woman being cared for in an infirmary had been temporarily moved by the doctor to the workhouse to make room for more urgent cases; her workhouse admission was used to deny a pension. Another woman, who had earlier been granted two pounds of tea by a guardian, was similarly disqualified. Although prior relief ceased to operate as a disqualification after 1 January 1911, pensions were still discontinued as soon as a person entered the workhouse. The establishment of old-age pensions by no means eliminated the need to enter the workhouse upon reaching a stage of being unable to care for oneself. Thus the fear of the workhouse, and the stigma involved in entering it, survived.[30]

The National Insurance Act of 1911 grew out of David Lloyd George's determination, following his visit to Germany to study the national insurance system there, to extend the range of state-provided social services. Telling the House of Commons that 30 per cent of pauperism was attributable to sickness, he brought in a contributory scheme considerably pared down from an earlier, more comprehensive measure. Bowing to the powerful lobbying of the Friendly Societies and insurance companies, Lloyd George brought them in as partners in a measure that provided sickness benefits of 10s. a week for men and 7s. 6d. for women, for the first 13 weeks of disability, with reduced payments thereafter. The act certainly took some pressure off poor law medical services. It has been estimated that the combined effect of old-age pensions and sickness benefits was to reduce the number of paupers by nearly 20 per cent, from 916 377 in 1910 to 748 019 in 1913.[31] But poor law infirmaries, greatly improved over earlier times and resorted to freely with little remaining sense of stigma, continued to draw a majority of the poor.

The contributory unemployment provisions of the 1911 statute also had a significant impact on the poor law, though once again a majority of the poor remained outside its operation. The cumulative effect of pensions, sickness insurance, and unemployment insurance was impressive, and does represent at least a modest eclipsing of the poor law by what are usually considered modern social services. The contributory aspects of the insurance schemes, however, meant that those in the lower classes able to pay the contributions found themselves saddled with a higher effective tax burden than those in the middle class. Being enmeshed in an ever more regressive tax system seemed to be the price exacted from the poor for shielding them from the still stigmatizing features of the poor law.[32]

The Impact of the Great War on the Poor Law

In spite of the Liberals' important reforms, on the eve of the 1914–18 war the poor law was still the dominant government institution in the lives of the poorest members of society. The number of workhouse residents reached an all-time high of 280 000 in 1912, though the figures fell off thereafter, chiefly as a result of old-age pensions. The category of able-bodied had been dropped from official nomenclature in 1911. In 1913 even workhouses were renamed 'poor law institutions'. (To avoid confusion, the term 'workhouse' will continue to be used throughout the remainder of the book.) Of course, workhouses were only part of the poor law service institutional array; there were also infirmaries, cottage homes, schools, asylums, sanatoria, homes for the blind, and the like.[33] By 1914, most poor law medical facilities were of a decent standard; some were excellent. Better nurses and even nurses' aides were being recruited. For indoor paupers, medical officers lobbied for better treatment, including eyeglass prescriptions and relaxation of institutional regulations for the aged. Indeed, in 1913, MOs were given complete control over the elderly in the workhouse, a key aspect of the medicalizing of old age by the poor law, and an anticipation of the modern nursing home.[34]

With the outbreak of war in August 1914, all initiatives, medical or otherwise, in behalf of paupers, were suspended. The building of specialized institutions, as well as the improving of workhouses, came to a halt. The War Office requisitioned poor law property without compensation to boards of guardians. Hospital resources throughout the entire country were strained to the limit to minister to the wounded flooding back from France, and poor law infirmaries were pressed into service. In over 200 unions, some form of major government appropriation of property and services took place. This included using some workhouses as residences for munitions workers or Belgian refugees, necessitating the transfer of many indoor paupers to other workhouses. On the other hand, both indoor and outdoor pauperism sharply declined during the war, accelerating a trend set in motion by the Liberal reforms. Outdoor relief fell some 40 per cent between January 1910 and January 1917, while indoor pauperism declined by 25 per cent during the same period. Vagrants – seemingly the most intractable segment of the pauper population before 1914 – virtually disappeared for the duration, many of them drawn into either the military or munitions factories. Even soldiers' widows, in previous wars an ever-growing burden on the poor rates, were now relieved by a separate National Relief Fund.[35]

The determination of Lloyd George, head of the coalition government, that peace would bring more social reform, created high expectations in many quarters. Campaign slogans like 'homes for heroes' from the Prime Minister, coupled with the most serious Labour Party electoral challenge to date, upped the political ante considerably. A Ministry of Reconstruction, appointed in 1917, was charged with developing a comprehensive vision of post-war Britain. It began looking at proposals for health, housing, education, and unemployment. A subcommittee of the ministry, the so-called MacLean Committee, issued a report in January 1918 that was a virtual restatement of the minority report of the 1905–9 royal commission. This was hardly surprising, as Beatrice Webb was a member of the committee. By calling for a break-up of the poor law and expanded social services, the MacLean Committee's report was alarming to those committed to keeping the boards of guardians.[36] The proposal to reorganize all the services formerly under the Local Government Board under a new Ministry of Health antagonized an even wider circle, including the Friendly Societies and insurance companies. The Labour Party, whose election manifesto was written by the Webbs, swung behind the proposal, while the government, which had to deal with the complex negotiations over the proposed reforms, was equivocal.

Once the coalition government had won the December 1918 general election, there was little real commitment on the part of Lloyd George's Tory governing colleagues to deliver on extravagant campaign promises. In spite of the largest number of Labour MPs ever, the Conservatives were the dominant party in the House of Commons, and the Prime Minister could command the loyalty of only a portion of the Liberals. Moreover, the severe economic dislocations that followed the war made financing social reform a vexing question. One thing that was possible, however, was administrative reorganization, as it offered the appearance of a reform, while not having to provide large new financial outlays. Accordingly, the proposed Ministry of Health was created in 1919, taking over all poor relief functions formerly supervised by the Local Government Board. Medical officers of the poor law service had long sought this sort of ministerial reorganization, but the change proved more cosmetic than substantive. Long-standing fears on the part of boards of guardians that a Ministry of Health would signal the dominance of the medical interest, and that extravagant expenditures would surely follow, proved unfounded. After an initial flurry of medical activism, the new ministry quickly settled into the diplomatic, consensual style that had characterized the Local Government Board. Adroit lobbying by local boards, sheer inertia, and the continuation of a generalist Whitehall culture trumped the long-feared 'specialist takeover' of administration.[37]

Post-war Crises and the Revival of Poplarism

With the onset of post-war economic dislocations, exacerbated by the return of millions of veterans to the labour force, the wartime decline of pauperism and poor rates was dramatically reversed. Lloyd George attempted to soften the blow on the working class by making unemployment insurance universal, but those millions already rendered jobless were ineligible for the programme. By 1921, 1.5 million people, 4 per cent of the population of England and Wales, were receiving relief from boards of guardians. By 1926, the year of the General Strike, the number on poor relief had increased to 2.5 million.[38] This was in addition to the millions of unemployed relieved in some fashion by a hastily cobbled together system of doles that lay outside the poor law.

Some of the most severe, and most highly visible, economic difficulties afflicted London's working class. Labour-controlled Poplar, already targeted by conservatives for its profuse outlays before the war, freely granted outdoor relief to its mostly unemployed resident workers. As the Poplar guardians' borrowing and taxing powers reached their limits in the spring of 1921, the Poplar borough council, which included many guardians, declared they would no longer levy rates for the support of the London County Council and other metropolitan agencies, even though they were receiving substantial outlays from the Metropolitan Common Poor Fund. This fund, which aided unions like Poplar with very low rateable value, and represented a substantial transfer from the West End to the East End, failed to help in the vast post-war unemployment crisis. The problem was that the funds a union received (Poplar got about £50 000 a year) were to be used strictly for indoor paupers. Basing their refusal to pay on the fact that Poplar had overwhelming and extraordinary outrelief expenses, and that the lightly rated West End did nothing to help them out, 30 recalcitrant councillors, including 6 women, were sent to jail for contempt. There followed a comic-opera struggle between the government and the councillors, with the latter holding meetings in prison and being serenaded by the Poplar workhouse school band. The acutely embarrassed government, bested in the court of public opinion, was forced to back down. The councillors were released, and a statute hastily passed that greatly increased the contributions from the Metropolitan Common Poor Fund to the East End unions. Poplar, which saw its share increased from £50 000 to £300 000, had won a great victory, and other East End poor law unions followed its lead, making the area a haven for paupers through much of the decade.[39] The struggle with the government, however, was far from over.

Meanwhile, boards of guardians in other parts of the country, by no means all of them Labour-dominated, were doing their best to maintain their hordes of unemployed in some semblance of dignity. The South Wales coalfields, for example, faced unprecedented privation from the economic slump and labour strife of the early 1920s. The Pontypridd Union in the Rhondda Valley, the most populous in Wales (415 642 in

1921), granted outdoor relief freely to striking miners in 1921, even though the board was mostly middle class, with Labour in the minority.[40] Even more liberal relief scales were adopted by Labour-controlled boards in the Welsh coalfields and in coal-mining areas in Durham, as well as in areas with a high working-class population and high unemployment rate. For the most part, the central authority was slow to react to this violation of its orders. The Relief Regulation Order of 1911, still in effect through the 1920s, forbade outdoor relief to the able-bodied, with the usual loopholes for exceptional distress. But even when exceptions were invoked by boards of guardians, there was to be a labour test applied to outdoor paupers. This was routinely ignored by boards in the 1920s and the central authority did little to enforce it at first. This was in part a function of the rapid turnover of ministers: eight in six years. But with the appointment of Neville Chamberlain to the ministry, the resolve of the central authority began to harden.

Neville Chamberlain and the Struggle with the Guardians

Chamberlain was briefly Minister of Health in Stanley Baldwin's Conservative government in 1923, following the end of the coalition government. However, before he could fully settle in, the 1923 election brought to power the first Labour government under Ramsay MacDonald. A minority government dependent upon Liberal votes, it was ousted the next year, as the Conservatives under Baldwin swept back into office. Chamberlain, spurning what others considered a much more attractive offer to become Chancellor of the Exchequer (a post he had held briefly the year before), chose to return to the Ministry of Health. Having become increasingly disturbed over the lax ways of many boards of guardians, Chamberlain was determined to restore sound policy. It does not seem that this attitude was, on the whole, ideologically driven. Like most Conservatives, he was repelled by what he considered the ideological posturing and economic naivety of Labourites. In the climate of fear that prevailed among Conservatives following the Bolshevik revolution, there was a tendency among many Tories to view boards of guardians such as Poplar or West Ham as Red vanguards. Chamberlain may have shared to some extent in this feeling, but it is more apt to characterize his drive to stamp out Poplarism as stemming from a deeply ingrained administrative fastidiousness. He prided himself on his own attention to detail and dispassionate analysis of statistics, and insisted that those around him display similar rigour.

Far from being a reactionary, Chamberlain was an activist Minister of Health largely responsible for the Widows, Orphans, and Old Age Pensions Act of 1925, which expanded benefits and lowered the pension age to 65. He also undertook important improvements in public health, medical services, and housing.[41] Thus it was as a pragmatic, reforming minister, not unlike his father as head of the Local Government Board in the 1880s, that Chamberlain addressed the problems of poor law administration in the 1920s. There seems little doubt that his ultimate goal was to abolish the boards of guardians altogether, but he considered it necessary to proceed by degrees. The first step was to reassert the ministry's authority over relief policy, using the inspection and audit powers already in hand. No new policy enactment was required for Chamberlain to unleash a massive inspection programme to ensure compliance with the Relief Regulation Order of 1911. All available ministry personnel were assigned to assist the general inspectors in the task of examining closely into the circumstances of tens of thousands of cases in which relief had been granted under the exceptions to the 1911 order. Where irregularities were found, as they were in a majority of inquiries, guardians were ordered to desist under the threat of the ministry's coercive powers. The intimidation of guardians and relieving officers created by this inquisition began to have effect in all but the most recalcitrant unions.[42]

Another weapon at Chamberlain's disposal was the requirement for Ministry of Health authorization for any borrowing by a board of guardians. Many boards had run up considerable debts to meet the flood of post-war unemployment, and ministry approval had been routinely granted. Chamberlain inaugurated a close scrutiny of loan requests, targeting especially those Labour-controlled boards noted for dispensing generous outdoor relief. West Ham, with nearly three-quarters of a million inhabitants, had been under the control of a Labour board of guardians since 1921. By 1925, it had managed to accumulate a staggering debt of nearly 2 million pounds. The ministry refused to authorize any further loans unless the guardians agreed to a substantial reduction in relief scales. The guardians initially refused and quickly found themselves without any funds. Faced with the prospect of mass starvation in West Ham, Chamberlain moved beyond any statutory authority, announcing that the ministry would itself take over the payment to shopkeepers who supplied the indigent, except that the effective rate would be only three-fourths of what the guardians had been providing. At this juncture, the guardians capitulated, agreeing to reduce their outdoor relief scale by 25 per cent, whereupon the ministry sanctioned a loan.[43]

In taking direct control of a union whose guardians were unable or unwilling to abide by ministry directives, Chamberlain had hit upon his most effective weapon, and was able to persuade Parliament to give it sanction by passing the Board of Guardians (Default) Act of 1926. This measure, which allowed the minister to supersede any board that was 'unable to discharge all its functions', was used to great effect against the other Poplarist boards.[44] Such a powerful dose of centralization would have been a tough sell in ordinary times, because many conservative guardians would have feared the loss of local autonomy. But events played into Chamberlain's hands, because the polarizing General Strike of 1926 led frightened and angry conservatives to demand strong measures to chastise boards of guardians that were, in effect, giving strike pay in the form of outdoor relief. Since the miners were the most militant during the General Strike, and the Labour-controlled boards in mining districts the most likely to defy ministry directives, the Default Act was used primarily in the South Wales and Durham coalfields.

Colliery closures and the lingering effects of the 1921 lockout had left many Welsh miners deeply in debt and therefore in desperate straits when confronting the effects of the 1926 strike and lockout. The numbers on outdoor relief in the middle of 1926 for the most affected poor law unions were: Bedwellty, 50 000 out of a population of 140 000, Merthyr Tydfil, 67 000 out of 180 000, and Pontypridd, 94 000 out of 315 000. The boards were forced into heavy borrowing; even before the lockout began on 1 May, Bedwellty's debts had reached a staggering £700 000.[45] In May the Ministry of Health issued to the poor law unions in the coalfields Circular 703, which set out meagre new unemployment relief scales considerably lower than those in force for the pre-stoppage unemployed. And even this pittance was not to take into account the miner himself, for there was to be strict observance of the Merthyr Tydfil Judgment of 1900, which allowed relief only to the wife and other dependants of a man involved in a trade dispute; unmarried miners were also denied relief. In spite of being forced to accept Circular 703, the Bedwellty guardians could not help running their debts up to a million pounds by early 1927. At this juncture, Chamberlain, invoking the Guardians Default Act, dismissed the local board, appointing special guardians to run the union. Relief was drastically curtailed in Bedwellty as well as in other poor law unions chastened by the action.[46]

In the Durham coalfields, the Chester-le-Street board of guardians was singled out by the ministry for its defiance of directives. Specifically the guardians refused to comply with the Merthyr Tydfil Judgment, and continued outrelief to unmarried miners. By the spring of 1927, Chamberlain was determined to use the full rigour of the law against this board, drawing firm and very public ideological battle lines against Labour on the issue. At a speech in Darlington in April, he declared: 'The policy of Chester-le-Street and elsewhere is not an isolated policy; it is a deliberate, well-planned policy, thought out beforehand and adopted by the Socialist Party.'[47] *The Times* chimed in obligingly: 'The rot must be stopped, even if direct interference from Whitehall be invoked.'[48] The Default Act of 1926 was used against the guardians, and special guardians were installed by the ministry. Chamberlain had chosen his targets well. Even though only three poor law unions had been taken over by the central authority, they were at once financially precarious and militantly Labour. If the former ensured their vulnerability to a ministry takeover, the latter deprived them of the sympathy of the great majority of other boards of guardians throughout the country. To underscore the futility of resistance, Chamberlain followed up with the Audit Act of 1927, which greatly strengthened the minister's power by allowing him to recover as a civil debt surcharges against any board of guardians by a district auditor. Moreover, any guardian against whom a surcharge of more than £500 was upheld would be ineligible to serve as a guardian or as a member of any local authority for five years.[49]

As for Poplar and the other Labour-controlled London boards, their victory of 1921 in securing large increases from the Metropolitan Common Poor Fund was reversed by the Emergency Provisions Act of 1928. The act, which in effect empowered the Minister of Health to set the amount the East End poor law unions would receive, is the measure that directly put an end to Poplarism.[50] There was a dramatic drop in outdoor relief as a result of the various attacks on all the Poplarist boards. Nationwide, the proportion on outdoor relief in 1926 had been over 300 per 10 000 population; by the start of 1929, it had been cut to 160 per 10 000.[51]

The End of the Boards of Guardians

A huge growth of central authority had taken place, with only modest resistance in Parliament and throughout most of the country. There remained, however, the task of eliminating the boards of guardians altogether. This crowning piece of Chamberlain's legislative programme was delayed for a couple of years by his muted struggle with the Chancellor of the Exchequer, Winston Churchill, over the proposed derating of industry (reducing or eliminating the amount that industrial properties and railroads paid in poor rates). This was designed to make British exports more competitive, but it would render poor law reform more difficult by depriving local authorities of much of their financial support. Clearly, the money would have to be made up by block grants by the Exchequer, and the cabinet debates were over the scale and nature of such grants. Finally, with considerable compromise on Chamberlain's part, the bill to reorganize local government and abolish the boards of guardians was introduced in November 1928.[52]

The Local Government bill, of well over 100 clauses, covered many areas in addition to the poor law. In respect to the latter, it abolished the 625 boards of guardians, transferring their powers, duties, and assets to the county councils and county borough councils. Counties were to establish public assistance committees (PACs). Each county was to be divided into relief districts, over which a 'guardians' committee' nominated by the elected councillors was to have control of the dispensing of outdoor relief. Indoor relief was to be handled on a county-wide basis by the PAC in each county or county borough. The Ministry of Health would continue to have jurisdiction on relief policies, and had to formally approve the precise administrative arrangements each county made to comply with the act. Because of the massive size and complexity of the metropolis, somewhat greater flexibility was given to the London County Council in devising its arrangements and policies. The substantial derating of industry previously negotiated within the cabinet was incorporated into the bill, as was the total derating of agricultural land. To make up for the shortfall caused by derating, block grants from the Exchequer (an estimated £24 million annually) were to be made to the councils.[53]

With some show of resistance by Labour MPs, who argued that the bill did not go far enough, and that a fully national system of relief was required, the bill passed into law. On 31 March 1930, the final day of the poor law, a writer in *The Times* noted that at midnight, 'a page of English local history will be turned over'.[54] When the new system came into effect on 1 April, there was a clear sense that an era had passed. Institutions and practices, many of them deeply ingrained in the social and political fabric of the country for a century or more, had been swept aside. What was not clear was the impact that this transformation would have on the lives of the poor.

The Persistence of the Poor Law

On 1 April 1930, boards of guardians, a central feature of the New Poor Law, ceased to exist. Their functions were transferred to the public assistance committees (PACs) and guardians' committees of county and county borough councils. How significant a change was this? Many of the former guardians found places on these committees, bringing with them much the same mindset that had prevailed on the defunct boards of guardians. Their activities were still overseen and regulated by the Ministry of Health, many of whose officials had begun in the Poor Law Division of the Local Government Board. Most importantly, relief applicants were still scrutinized closely according to the hated household means test. An inquisition into all the resources of family members and lodgers to determine eligibility and amount of relief, the means test represented to the poor the continuation of the poor law. The same might be said of the workhouse, though it had long since shed that designation. It still tended to loom as a dreaded and shameful terminal residence for many of the poor. So too, for vagrants, for whom the workhouse, or 'spike', as it was still called by the homeless, was as repellent as ever. George Orwell's vivid description of workhouse casual wards in 1930 in *Down and Out in Paris and London* would have been instantly recognizable to any Victorian vagrant. Although an inquiry by the Labour government of 1929–31 led to somewhat improved conditions in casual wards after 1931, the 'spike' lived on through the decade.[55]

On the other hand, there was a much greater degree of centralization, especially after the Unemployment Act of 1934 was passed. This statute removed relief to the unemployed, indeed to any of the outdoor poor not receiving unemployment insurance payments, from the county councils, transferring it to a new central authority, the Unemployment Assistance Board, which operated its own local offices. This was not always to the advantage of the unemployed, for it was found that in some districts the elaborate scales devised by the authority resulted in relief payments considerably below those provided by the boards of guardians. This situation was remedied by allowing the local unemployment offices to raise their payments to the old levels, but it is ironic that the reviled poor law had to be invoked for any improvement to take place.[56]

The Second World War was even more productive of planning for an enlarged apparatus of social programmes than the First. The Beveridge Report of 1942, in calling for an array of new or greatly enhanced central government services, provided a revised definition of the duties of the state and called for a broadening of the rights of citizenship. Close in spirit to the Webbs' totalizing vision, it began to be implemented soon after the end of the war, thanks to Labour's electoral landslide. The resulting Welfare State, providing universal social security and free medical care, as well as greater educational opportunities, seemed to put an end to those aspects of the poor law that had survived the abolition of the boards of guardians. The National Assistance Act of 1948 most directly took over those elements of relief formerly handled by poor law guardians and county councils. Yet within the new state apparatus, elements of the old suspicion and ill treatment of 'paupers' could still be discerned, partly a function of former poor law officials still in government service. This was one legacy of the poor law, though one that diminished with time. The workhouse was another, often transformed into a National Health Service medical facility, with attendant cosmetic changes to make it as bright and cheerful as possible. Still, for years afterwards it was not uncommon to find it referred to by the elderly, especially in small towns and country districts, as simply the 'workhouse'. It is unnecessary to pursue this line of inquiry into recent decades to realize that certain aspects of poor law thinking and policy survived into the era of the Welfare State, indeed to the present. Thatcherite praise of Victorian attitudes and values in regard to government policy shows that 1834 is not necessarily remote from us.

8

CONCLUSION

The poor laws deeply etched the character of English government and society, and their echoes are with us still. Attempting to discern some patterns in poor law history, we are confronted with a tangled and complex picture. Seen through the lens of Whiggish linearity, it is less tangled. There seems to be a progression, if a sometimes halting one, from highly localized mechanisms for dealing with the indigent to greater and greater accretions of authority by central government. Simultaneously, there appears to be an ever-expanding array of provisions that attach themselves to the poor law, primitive versions of modern social services. There is also an evident movement from harsh policies towards more humane ones. It is quite natural to look for the historical antecedents of present-day institutions and practices, nor is it without merit. In important ways, we can locate such progressions. The trouble with this approach is that, unless tempered by a strong sense of the contingency and fluidity of past events, as well as the persistence of older attitudes and values, it can lead to a naive triumphalism. That is, we end by celebrating the modern Welfare State, validating it by conjuring up an apparently inevitable chain of events leading to the present. Such a mental framework becomes a straitjacket in two ways. First, it leads us to ignore or distort past events that do not fit into the evolutionary paradigm. Second, it obscures the many different ways the past might have unfolded. Applying these cautionary notes, let us try alternate modes of making sense of the poor law history recounted in this book. The best way to break the thrall of the evolutionary model that is unintentionally enhanced by a largely chronological study such as this is to view the English poor law experience as simultaneously consensual, contested, and contingent.

For a good part of the period covered in this book, most people accepted the necessity of a public relief system, administered by members of the local community. They agreed on the need to maintain the aged, the infirm, abandoned children, and others unable to care for themselves. As for the able-bodied, there was broad assent to the proposition that those rooted in the community who were temporarily unable to find work (or work at a sufficient wage to support themselves and their families) had to be maintained at public expense. Of course, there was a statutory requirement to do these things, and there was a legal system, beginning with the local magistracy, to enforce it. From time to time, recalcitrant or negligent overseers and other local officials had to be enjoined to perform their duties. On the whole, however, relatively little coercion had to be employed, because there was a broad social consensus about relieving the poor. A remarkably consistent pattern in regard to this locally based consensus prevailed during the history of the poor laws. While different material standards were in play at various times, in a major sense the basic attitudes of community members towards their less fortunate neighbours was not much different in the mid-nineteenth century than it had been in 1700. And there are detectable elements of the traditional poor relief ethos in operation right up to the end of the system.

However, if we need to keep this *longue durée* of the poor laws in mind, it is also important to consider the often sharp, even bitter, debates over the poor laws that characterized the period since 1700. For the most part, these debates grew out of wider social, economic, and intellectual currents. Often involving highly abstract modes of thinking about poverty, they were the work of those of a more intellectual and cosmopolitan bent. We have seen numerous examples of the ways in which new sets of ideas challenged the traditional values and practices of poor relief. The emergence and refinement throughout the eighteenth century of economic analysis, such as that of Bernard Mandeville, Adam Smith, or Joseph Townsend, challenged and destabilized the traditional paternalism that underlay the poor laws. The grim population theories of Thomas Malthus had an even more corrosive effect on the traditional system, threatening for a while to eradicate mandatory poor relief altogether; they certainly powerfully influenced the adoption of harsh and punitive measures towards the poor. Jeremy Bentham's visionary schemes for restructuring government and reconfiguring the character of the poor through the use of Panopticon – his 'simple idea in architecture' – came to at least partial fruition following the passage of the New Poor Law.

Countering these powerful intellectual challenges, all of which embraced an atomistic individualism, were a welter of conservative and radical writers, defending in their distinctive ways the right of the poor to mandatory relief of a decent standard. Figures as different as William Cobbett, Samuel Taylor Coleridge, and Charles Dickens all championed tradition and the wisdom of the local community in opposition to abstract theory and centralized authority. From the 1830s, however, there emerged a radicalism far less tethered to traditional rights than that of Cobbett. The Chartists, in their spirited opposition to the New Poor Law, operated from a democratic egalitarianism that was itself the product of abstract reasoning. By the turn of the twentieth century, democratic and socialist advocates of a forward-looking national system of social services had become more than a match for those still grounded in philosophical individualism and laissez-faire economics. The proliferation of enhanced poor law services, plus the fashioning of new social programmes independent of the poor law by the Liberal government between 1906 and 1911 signalled the magnitude of the shift. By the time the poor law was formally ended in 1930, it was accompanied by anticipations of further development towards a comprehensive network of government services.

While it is important to understand this clash of ideas in poor law history, it can, if due care is not taken, lead to both a naive intellectual history and a further bolstering of Whiggish linearity. The antidote to the first is to insist that there is wisdom in the Marxist claim that ideas are not disembodied, autonomous entities, but are grounded in economic and social relations. Thus we must bear in mind that the ideological struggle over the poor laws is connected to England's often painful transition from agrarian to industrial, from rural to urban, and from aristocratic to democratic. The antidote to allowing even this socially grounded sense of ideological conflict to bolster Whiggish triumphalism is a sense of contingency. Things could have turned out differently, perhaps substantially so. To cite but two examples: (1) the Malthusians nearly succeeded in abolishing mandatory poor relief altogether in the early nineteenth century, and the change of relatively few votes on critical motions could have tipped matters the other way; (2) the odd alignment of a general election and the Swing riots in 1830 resulted in the coming to power of a reform ministry willing, and because of Swing, able, to carry through a sweeping overhaul of the poor law. It does not require an extravagant reach into the airy realm of counterfactual history to assert that such turning points could have had dramatically different results.

Finally, it should be pointed out that there was no steady advance in poor law history in regard to 'humane' policies. The New Poor Law itself is the strongest argument against that proposition, for it was widely perceived by those best able to judge, the poor themselves, to be inhumane. And while the New Poor Law did seem to develop a somewhat greater ameliorative character in a few decades, there were many retrograde steps, such as the Campaign against Outdoor Relief of the 1870s. Indeed, the treatment of vagrancy, right up to the end of the poor law in 1930, represents a counter-current, towards ever more punitive measures. Ebb and flow seems a more apposite model for many aspects of poor law history than evolution.

NOTES

1 INTRODUCTION: APPROACHING ENGLISH POOR LAW HISTORY

1. Charles Chaplin, *My Autobiography* (New York: Simon and Schuster, 1964), 26–32.
2. On the Webbs' poor law programme, their role as reformers, and the effect of this on their writing, see M. E. Rose, 1977–80 and Kidd, 1999.
3. Dozens of books and articles constitute this body of work. Three of the major books are by MacDonagh, 1961, Roberts, 1960, and Lubenow, 1971.
4. Some of the major scholars addressing these issues are Redford, 1926, Blaug, 1963, Baugh, 1975, Landau, 1988, 1990, 1991, 1995, Holderness, 1972, Taylor, 1976, 1989, 1991, Huzel, 1989, Snell, 1985, 1992, King, 1997, Boyer, 1990, and M. E. Rose, 1976. The last of these is one of the most prolific and wide-ranging of poor law historians, and therefore difficult to categorize.
5. On the economists and the poor laws, see Coats, 1958, 1975, Cowherd, 1977, and Fetter, 1980. For a wider approach, encompassing leading philosophers of the age like Bentham and Burke, see Himmelfarb, 1970, 1984, and Winch, 1996. The full intellectual ferment of the period is addressed by Poynter, 1969, who examines not only the major thinkers but a host of pamphleteers and obscure voices. Dean, 1991, provides a valuable critique of the thinkers of this era, with insightful tie-ins to present-day values and structures.
6. See, for example, Soffer, 1978, and Meacham, 1987.
7. Brundage, 1972, 1978, Dunkley, 1979, 1981, 1982, Mandler, 1987, 1990, and Eastwood, 1994, are central. For a debate on the question of the nature and extent of the landed interest's involvement in poor law reform, see Brundage, Eastwood, and Mandler, 1990.
8. The classic work on the village labourer by J. L. and Barbara Hammond, 1911, is the start of this literature. Digby's works (1975, 1976, 1978) on the rural poor law are germane to these issues, as they are to some of the economic historical issues. Edsall, 1971, and Knott, 1986, are concerned with resistance to the New Poor Law. Other works of interest are David Williams, 1955, Reay, 1990, Hobsbawm and Rudé, 1968, and Randall and Newman, 1995, on the major riots of the 1830s and 1840s, which were fuelled in part by maladministration of the poor law.
9. See Fraser, 1970, 1976, Harris, 1972, 1983, 1993, Ryan, 1978, 1985, and Gilbert, 1966, 1970.
10. Lees, 1990, 1998, Thane, 1978, 1982, Cody, 2000, Marks, 1993, and Levine-Clark, 2000, are of note here.
11. Medical care has been an especially active field, and the key works are Hodgkinson, 1967, Richardson, 1987, 1993, Richardson and Hurwitz, 1997, Flinn, 1976, E. G. Thomas, 1980, and Tomkins, 1999. For education, see Duke, 1976, and Pallister, 1968. There is little directly on poor law emigration policy

(but see Franzén, 1996 and Howells, 1998). Malchow, 1979 covers the wider dimensions of emigration policy. The poor law's treatment of lunatics is addressed by Bartlett, 1998, 1999, and in an article by Melling, Adair, and Forsythe, 1997. Vagrancy forms a sub-topic in many books. There are also important articles on vagrancy by Vorspan, 1977, and by Matthews, 1986.

12. On Bentham's Panopticon scheme and related commercial venture, see Semple, 1993, Dandeker, 1990, Bahmueller, 1981, and the section on Bentham in Himmelfarb, 1984. Crowther, 1981, is the most comprehensive study of the workhouse system, though Longmate, 1974, is incisive and highly readable. F. Driver, 1993, breaks fresh ground, employing Foucauldian perspectives without being chained to the theory. Crompton, 1997, is quite satisfactory on the treatment of workhouse children.

13. Owen, 1964, is still highly valuable, as are Prochaska, 1980, and Himmelfarb, 1991. Humphreys, 1995, and Kidd, 1999, are important additions. See also McCord 1976, Brundage, 1998, the treatment of philanthropy and the Victorians in Harrison, 1982, and the chapter on the poor law and charity in Daunton, 1995.

14. Oxley, 1974, and Slack, 1990, are highly useful surveys of the Old Poor Law.

2 THE POOR LAWS IN THE EIGHTEENTH CENTURY

1. For the antecedents, see Slack, 1990.
2. Ibid., 28.
3. Styles, 1963.
4. Landau, 1988 and Ely, 1986.
5. Landau, 1988, 398.
6. Landau, 1988, 414. See also the other articles by Landau in the bibliography. Her views, challenged by Snell (see his book and articles), have recently been supported by Song, 'Agrarian Policies on Pauper Settlement', 1998.
7. Oxley, 1974, 80–1.
8. Webb, 1927, 103–5.
9. De Schweinitz, 1943, 58–9.
10. D. Marshall, 1926, 28–9.
11. 9 Geo. I, c. 7.
12. D. Marshall, 1926, 129–30.
13. Thomas Alcock, *Observations on the Defects of the Poor Laws, and on the Causes and Consequences of the Great Increase and Burden of the Poor. With a Proposal for redressing these Grievances, in a Letter to a Member of Parliament* (London: R. Baldwin, 1752), 62.
14. Webb, 1927, 277.
15. Ibid., 277–308.
16. D. Marshall, 1926, 92–4.
17. Breconshire Quarter Sessions Order Book, Michaelmas 1767, Powys County Archives B/QS/O/5. http://history.powys.org.uk/history/ COMMON/SUPPORT.HTM
18. Lees, 1998, 52.
19. Slack, 1990, 25.
20. D. Marshall, 1926, 221.
21. Webb, 1927, 308–13.
22. M. B. Rose, 1989, 8.
23. Crompton, 1997, 4–5.
24. Owen, 1964, 14–15.

25. Thomas, 1980, 2.
26. Ibid., 2–5.
27. Tomkins, 1999.
28. Thomas, 1980, 7.
29. Ibid., 6.
30. Oxley, 1974, 71.
31. Thomas, 1980, 6.
32. Semple, 1993, 67.
33. Webb, 1927, 266.
34. Ibid., 265–6.
35. Digby, 1978, 34–5.
36. Ibid., 35–47.
37. D. Marshall, 1926, 10.
38. Digby, 1978, 36.
39. Webb, 1927, 267.
40. Ibid., 264–72.
41. Ibid., 270.
42. In 1781, Thomas Gilbert unsuccessfully promoted a massive public works project designed to absorb returning veterans. Cowherd, 1977, 5.
43. Webb, 1927, 272–6.
44. Owen, 1964, 86.
45. *A Letter to Thomas Gilbert, Esq.; On his Intended Reform of the Poor Laws, by a Country Gentleman* (London: J. Debrett, 1787), 37–8.
46. Holderness, 1972, 128.
47. See, for example, Coats, 1958, and Cowherd, 1977.
48. Lees, 1998, 83–7.
49. Carter, 1995, 170.
50. J. S. Taylor, 1969, 142–3.
51. Song, 'Continuity and Change in English Rural Society', 1998, 380.
52. Kidd, 1999, 168.
53. Eastwood, 1994, 79–80.
54. Ibid., 117.
55. 36 Geo. III, c. 23, s. 6.
56. *Considerations on the Subject of Poor-Houses and Work-Houses, Their Pernicious Tendency, And their Obstruction to the Proposed Plan for Amendment of the Poor Laws; In a Letter to the Rt. Hon. W. Pitt from Sir William Young, Bart., F.R.S.* (London: John Stockdale, 1796), 8.
57. Ibid., 29.
58. M. E. Rose, 1971, 36–7.
59. Webb, 1927, II, 38.
60. Eastwood, 1994, 111.
61. Webb, 1927, 175–6.
62. Ibid., 178.
63. M. E. Rose, 1971, 34.
64. Neuman, 1969.
65. Boyer, 1990, 31–43.
66. Snell, 1985, 58–64.
67. Boyer, 1990, 85.
68. Adam Smith, *An Inquiry into the Nature and Causes of the Wealth of Nations* (New York: Modern Library, 1937, 1776), 141.

69. Himmelfarb, 1984, 61.
70. Joseph Townsend, *A Dissertation on the Poor Laws by a Well-Wisher to Mankind* (Berkeley: University of California Press, 1971, 1786), 17, 35.
71. Harrison, 1982, 229.
72. Himmelfarb, 1984, 66–73.
73. M. E. Rose, 1971, 43.
74. Cowherd, 1977, 16–17.
75. Poynter, 1969, 116–17.
76. M. E. Rose, 1971, 46.
77. Himmelfarb, 1984, 100–32.
78. Ibid., 85.
79. Quinn, 1994, 85.
80. Ibid., 86–7.
81. Poynter, 1969, 108–9.
82. Himmelfarb, 1984, 79.
83. See, for example, Bahmueller, 1981 and Himmelfarb, 1984. For a recent defence of Bentham against charges of 'totalitarianism', see Quinn, 1994.
84. Bahmueller, 1981.
85. Roberts, 1960, 29–31.
86. Dean, 1991, 137.

3 DEBATES, EXPERIMENTS AND REFORMS, 1800–1832

1. Kidd, 1999, 70–1.
2. 'Village Politics, Addressed to all the Mechanics, Journeymen, and Labourers in Great Britain', in *The Works of Hannah More: with a memoir and notes* (London, 1853), Vol. 2, 226.
3. Digby, 1982, 9.
4. Eastwood, 1994, 139.
5. Poynter, 1969, 187–90.
6. Webb, 1929, Vol. 2, 25.
7. Poynter, 1969, 210.
8. Brundage, 1978, 8.
9. Poynter, 1969, 213.
10. Ibid., 217.
11. Ibid., 200–7.
12. Webb, 1927, 423–4.
13. Starting with the work of Blaug, 1963. The revisionist case was amplified by Huzel, 1969, Snell, 1985, and Boyer, 1990, though there are important differences of emphasis and interpretation in their work.
14. Boyer, 1990, 150–72, challenging the views of Huzel, 1969.
15. Solar, 1995.
16. King, 'Poor Relief and English Economic Development Reappraised', 1997.
17. Eastwood, 1994, 139.
18. Poynter, 1969, 226–7.
19. Ibid., 228.
20. Ibid., 229–31.
21. Ibid., 234.
22. Ibid., 251.

23. Ibid., 235–7.
24. Brundage, 1998, 104–5.
25. Davis, 1979, 92.
26. James MacPhail, *Observations Exhibiting the Propriety and Advantageous Tendency of the Poor Laws, Their Policy Vindicated, etc.* (London: Geo. Cowie and Co., 1819), 7, 10.
27. Mandler, 1987, 144–6.
28. Poynter, 1969, 240–1.
29. Ibid., 237–9.
30. M. E. Rose, 1971, 50.
31. Poynter, 1969, 247.
32. *British Parliamentary Papers* 1819, II, 308–9.
33. Poynter, 1969, 248.
34. *British Parliamentary Papers* 1818, V, 37.
35. Hansard, *Parliamentary Debates*, 1st ser., XXXVI, 523–4 (21 Feb. 1817).
36. Ibid., XXXVIII, 573 (7 May 1818).
37. M. E. Rose, 1971, 68.
38. Neuman, 1982, 176.
39. Ibid., 181–2.
40. Ibid., 183.
41. Digby, 1982, 7.
42. Eastwood, 1994, 175.
43. Ibid., 177.
44. Ibid., 178.
45. J. D. Marshall, 1961, 384–6.
46. Ibid., 387.
47. Wood, 1991, 60.
48. J. D. Marshall, 1961, 394–5.
49. Nicholls and Mackay, 1898, Vol. 2, 179.
50. Webb, 1927, 256.
51. George Nicholls, *Eight Letters on the Management of the Poor* (London: James Ridgeway, 1822), 24.
52. Ibid., 15.
53. Webb, 1927, 258–9.
54. Ibid., 231–3.
55. Eastwood, 1994, 171–2.
56. M. E. Rose, 1971, 57.
57. Webb, 1927, 192–3.
58. Ibid., 193–6.
59. Mandler, 1987.
60. Hobsbawm and Rudé, 1968, 104–6.
61. Ibid., 111.
62. Ibid., 119.
63. Randall and Newman, 1995, 210, 215.
64. Ibid., 222.
65. Hobsbawm and Rudé, 1968, 262–3.

4 THE NEW POOR LAW TAKES SHAPE, 1832–1847

1. Mandler, 1990, 131–41.
2. Brundage, 1978, 17.

3. Webb, 1929, Vol. 1, 46–7.
4. Lees, 1998, 109.
5. Brundage, 1978, 19–20.
6. Lees, 1998, 118; Brundage, 1978, 21–2.
7. Brundage, 1978, 21.
8. Lees, 1998, 118.
9. John Walter, *A Letter to the Electors of Berkshire on the New Management of the Poor. Proposed by the Government* (London: J. Ridgway, 1834), 14.
10. Blaug, 1964.
11. *Report from His Majesty's Commissioners for Inquiring into the Administration and Practical Operation of the Poor Laws* (London: B. Fellowes, 1834), 54, 240.
12. Ibid., 128.
13. M. E. Rose, 1971, 85.
14. *Report from His Majesty's Commissioners for inquiring into the Administration and Practical Operation of the Poor Laws* (London: B. Fellowes, 1834), 99–198.
15. Brundage, 1978, 47–54.
16. Brundage, 1988, 29–33.
17. Brundage, 1978, 55.
18. Roberts, 1960, 41–2.
19. *The Times*, 2 May 1834.
20. Brundage, 1978, 60.
21. Ibid., 69.
22. Cody, 2000, 144–5,
23. Ibid., 138–42.
24. Brundage, 1978, 65–6.
25. Henriques, 1967.
26. Brundage, 1978, 71–2.
27. Webb, 1929, Vol. 1, 105–7.
28. Brundage, 1978, 78–9.
29. Brundage, 1988, 40–1.
30. Brundage, 1978, 78–103.
31. *First Annual Report of the Poor Law Commissioners* (London: HMSO, 1835), 19.
32. Brundage, 1972.
33. For examples, see Brundage, 1978, 105–44.
34. Choomwattana, 1986, 89–92.
35. Song, 1999. Song differs on this point from Eastwood, who claims that the redrawing of petty sessions boundaries 'curtailed the effective independence of the magistracy ...', Eastwood, 1994, 92.
36. Brundage, 1978, 55.
37. Ibid., 155–6.
38. Edsall, 1971, 209.
39. Brundage, 1978, 152–4.
40. Edsall, 1971, 27–9.
41. Reay, 1990, 77.
42. Knott, 1986, 71–2.
43. Randall and Newman, 1995, 216.
44. Brundage, 1978, 148.
45. Edsall, 1971, 35–44.
46. Ibid., 79–80.
47. Webb, 1929, Vol. 1, 122–3.
48. Brundage, 1978, 94–5.

49. F. Driver, 1993, 59.
50. Ibid., 61.
51. Ibid., 59.
52. Fowler, 1991, 4, 15.
53. Anstruther, 1984, 76.
54. F. Driver, 1993, 48.
55. Longmate, 1974, 76.
56. For examples see Edsall, 1971, and Hagen, 1998–99.
57. M. E. Rose, 1966.
58. Kidd, 1999, 168.
59. Crowther, 1981, 41.
60. Thomson, 1983, 57.
61. Levine-Clark, 2000, 122.
62. Thomson, 1983, 54–5.
63. This was the dietary adopted by the Andover workhouse in Hampshire. Anstruther, 1984, 86.
64. Henriques, 1968, 365.
65. Longmate, 1974, 251–2.
66. Levine-Clark, 2000, 121–2.
67. Richardson, 1987, 170.
68. Brundage, 1978, 158.
69. See the superb biography of Oastler by C. Driver, 1946.
70. Webb, 1929, Vol. 1, 163.
71. Brundage, 1988, 42, 48.
72. F. Driver, 1993, 61.
73. Brundage, 1978, 162–3.
74. Ibid., 163–8.
75. Ibid., 173–9.
76. Webb, 1929, Vol. 1, 202–3.
77. Brundage, 1978, 97.
78. Webb, 1929, Vol. 1, 203–4.
79. Boot, 1990, 225.
80. Roberts, 1963, 98–9.
81. Ibid., 102.
82. Griffin, 1974.
83. Anstruther, 1984, 85.
84. Longmate, 1974, 122–6.
85. Brundage, 1988, 115–18.
86. Longmate, 1974, 133–5.

5　MID-VICTORIAN POOR RELIEF, 1847–1870

1. Longmate, 1974, 127.
2. Brundage, 1988, 133–56.
3. M. E. Rose, 1971, 145–8.
4. F. Driver, 1993, 50–7.
5. Wood, 1991, 142–3.
6. Webb, 1929, Vol. 1, 319.

7. Duke, 1976, 68.
8. Crompton, 1997, 107–16.
9. Tanner, 1998.
10. Duke, 1976, 68–72.
11. Crompton, 1997, 155–9.
12. Duke, 1976, 72–3.
13. Pallister, 1968, 280.
14. T. Thomas, 1992, 95.
15. Crompton, 1997, 172.
16. Ibid., 141.
17. Duke, 1976, 75.
18. Webb, 1929, Vol. 1, 266.
19. Duke, 1976, 77–82.
20. Webb, 1929, Vol. 1, 267–9.
21. Flinn, 1976, 48.
22. Brundage, 1988, 79–85. Chadwick has recently been criticized for diverting attention away from the long-standing insistence by many medical doctors that poverty itself was the chief threat to public health. See Hamlin, 1997.
23. Webb, 1929, Vol. 1, 152–3.
24. Ibid., 221.
25. Ibid., 332.
26. Richardson and Hurwitz, 1997, 219–20.
27. Ibid., 221–2.
28. Hodgkinson, 1967, 482.
29. Ibid., 484.
30. Ibid., 486–9.
31. Webb, 1929, Vol. 1, 339–40.
32. Roberts, 1960, 62.
33. Bartlett, 1998, 423.
34. Hodgkinson, 1967, 575–88.
35. 4 & 5 Will. IV, c. 76, s. 62.
36. Finer, 1952, 123–4.
37. Franzén, 1996, 70–1.
38. Ibid., 85.
39. Ibid., vi.
40. Howells, 1998.
41. Franzén, 1996, 167.
42. Malchow, 1979, 28–9.
43. Webb, 1910, 35.
44. 5 & 6 Vict., c. 57.
45. Fowler, 1991, 67.
46. Lees, 1998, 225.
47. Caplan, 1978, 274.
48. Nicholls and Mackay, 1898, 3: 351–3.
49. Caplan, 1978, 277.
50. Ashforth, 1985, 80.
51. Caplan, 1978, 279–83.
52. Frances Power Cobbe, 'The Philosophy of the Poor-Laws and the Report of the Committee on Poor Relief', *Fraser's Magazine* 70 (1864), 380.
53. M. E. Rose, 1985, 10.

54. M. E. Rose, 1976, 43.
55. Lees, 1998, 234.
56. Finlayson, 1994, 105.
57. Lees, 1998, 235–6.
58. K. Williams, 1981, 237–77.
59. Nicholls and Mackay, 1898, Vol. 3, 520.
60. Tanner, 1999.
61. *The Poor Laws Unmasked: Being a General Exposition of our Workhouse Institutions, with Special Reference to the Laws of Settlement and Removal of the Poor, Together with Notes and Remarks upon the Present System of Levying the Poor Rate*, by a Late Relieving Officer (London: Thomas Day, 1859).
62. MacKinnon, 1987, 610–11, 624–5.
63. M. E. Rose, 1971, 227–8.
64. Nicholls and Mackay, 1898, Vol. 3, 504–13.

6   THE REVIVAL OF DETERRENCE AND THE EXPANSION OF SERVICES, 1870–1900

1. Bellamy, 1988, 111–14.
2. Ibid., 116–17.
3. Sir John Simon, *English Sanitary Institutions, Reviewed in Their Course of Development and in Some of Their Political and Social Relations* (London: Cassell and Company, 1890), 348.
4. Hodgkinson, 1967, 449.
5. Bellamy, 1988, 233.
6. Webb, 1910, 151.
7. Herbert Preston-Thomas, *The Work and Play of a Government Inspector* (Edinburgh and London: William Blackwood and Sons, 1909), 152–7.
8. Bellamy, 1988, 167–79.
9. Brundage, 1998, 106–7.
10. Caplan, 1984, 15–16.
11. McCord, 1976, 102–3.
12. Prochaska, 1980, 151, 178–9.
13. Humphreys, 1995, 22.
14. Jones, 1971, 241–61.
15. Florence Nightingale, 'A Note on Poverty', *Fraser's Magazine* 79 (1866), 287–8.
16. R. N. Thompson, 1979, 123.
17. Owen, 1964, 220.
18. Ibid., 222.
19. Humphreys, 1995, 159.
20. Owen, 1964, 236–7.
21. Wood, 1991, 46.
22. For an excellent discussion of casework in practice, see Fido, 1977.
23. Lees, 1998, 260–1.
24. Wood, 1991, 45.
25. Finlayson, 1994, 149.
26. Gregson, 1985.
27. Humphreys, 1995, 144–74.

28. Lees, 1998, 265.
29. Thane, 1978, 39.
30. Kidd, 1999, 49.
31. Lees, 1998, 265.
32. Bruce, 1966, 107.
33. Finlayson, 1994, 135.
34. Kidd, 1999, 65–159.
35. Finlayson, 1994, 150.
36. Albert Pell, *The Reminiscences of Albert Pell* (London: Murray, 1909), 287.
37. Vorspan, 1977, 60.
38. London: Chapman and Hall, 1887.
39. Lees, 1998, 250–8.
40. Tanner, 1999, 196.
41. Ibid., 199–200.
42. Vorspan, 1977, 74–5.
43. M. E. Rose, 1971, 211–13.
44. Land, 1990, 74–5.
45. Vorspan, 1977, 61–2.
46. Ibid., 66–7.
47. Matthews, 1986, 108.
48. Vorspan, 1977, 70–1.
49. Herbert Preston-Thomas, *The Work and Play of a Government Inspector* (Edinburgh and London: William Blackwood and Sons, 1909), 337.
50. F. Driver, 1993, 87–9.
51. Ibid., 96.
52. Ibid., 97.
53. T. Thomas, 1992, 102.
54. F. Driver, 1993, 99–101.
55. K. Williams, 1981, 108–9, 116–18.
56. Thane, 1978, 39.
57. Ibid., 41–3.
58. Webb, 1910, 241.
59. Robin, 1990, 210.
60. Lees, 1990, 83–5.
61. Melling, Adair, and Forsythe, 1997, 385–9.
62. Lees, 1990, 86–8.
63. Brundage, 1975, 208–9.
64. Crocker, 1987, 35.
65. Ryan, 1985, 151.
66. Rodgers, 1956, 194.
67. Brundage, 1975, 208–10.
68. Ibid., 209–10. See also Hurren (2000).
69. Hansard, *Parliamentary Debates*, 4th ser., XVIII, 188 (3 Nov. 1893).
70. Brundage, 1975, 212–13.
71. Albert Pell, *The Reminiscences of Albert Pell* (London: Murray, 1909), 356.
72. K. Williams, 1981, 104–5.
73. John Martineau, *The English Country Labourer and the Poor Law in the Reign of Victoria* (London: Skeffington and Son, 1901), 27.
74. R. A. Leach, *The Evolution of the Poor Laws* (Great Malvern, 1924), 4.
75. Crowther, 1981, 77.

76. Caroline A. Biggs, *Some Notes upon the Election of Guardians of the Poor*, reprinted from *The Englishwoman's Review*, March 15th, 1887 (London: the Society for Promoting the Return of Women as Poor Law Guardians, 1887).

77. Louisa Twining, *Workhouses and Pauperism and Women's Work in the Administration of the Poor Laws* (London: Methuen, 1898), 121.

78. Richardson, 1993, 63.

79. Gertrude Green, *The History of the Poor Law* (London: Greenwich and Deptford Labour Guardians' Election Committee, 1893), 16.

80. Emmeline Pankhurst, *My Own Story* (London: Eveleigh Nash, 1914).

81. *Women and the Parish Councils Act. The Past, Present and Future of Parochial and Poor Law Government. A Lecture Delivered by Mrs. McIlquham (Poor Law Guardian) to the West Bristol Women's Liberal Association on the 4th of October, 1894* (Congleton: Women's Emancipation Union, 1894).

82. British Parliamentary Papers 1907, LXXII, 441.

83. Longmate, 1974, 191.

84. Crowther, 1981, 78.

85. Webb, 1929, Vol. 1, 220.

86. Soffer, 1978, 75–6.

87. M. E. Rose, 1971, 237.

88. Harris, 1993, 119.

89. Meacham, 1987.

90. M. E. Rose, 1971, 236–7.

7   THE ECLIPSING AND TRANSFORMING OF THE POOR LAW, 1900–1930

1. Harris, 1983, 71–2.

2. George Haw, *From Workhouse to Westminster: The Life Story of Will Crooks, M.P.* (London: Cassell and Co., 1911).

3. Ryan, 1978, 67.

4. Ryan, 1985, 164.

5. Ryan, 1978, 67–8.

6. Ibid., 68.

7. British Parliamentary Papers, 1906, CIV, 9, 24.

8. Ryan, 1978, 69–70.

9. Webb, 1929, Vol. 2, 649–51.

10. Ibid., 471–3.

11. Woodroofe, 1977, 141.

12. Webb, 1929, Vol. 2, 477–88.

13. Kidd, 1987, 406–7.

14. Lees, 1998, 320–1.

15. Vincent, 1984.

16. Lees, 1998, 321–2.

17. Woodroofe, 1977, 155–9.

18. 'The New Charter of the Poor', London School of Economics, Pamphlet Collection, fHV/66.

19. Kidd, 1996.

20. *The Poor Law Minority Report. Report of Debate between George Lansbury, L.C.C. and H. Quelch on September 20 and 21, 1910* (London: Twentieth Century Press, 1910), 4.
21. Sir William Chance, Bart., *Poor Law Reform. Via Tertia. The Case for the Guardians* (London: P. S. King and Son, 1910).
22. *The Reports of the Poor Law Commissions of 1834 and 1909* (London, 1909). London School of Economics, Pamphlet Collection, Microfilm HV/57.
23. Thane, 1978, 47.
24. Gilbert, 1966, 161–80.
25. Robin, 1990, 208.
26. Thomson, 1983, 64.
27. *Old Age Pensions and Poor Relief* (London, 1899), 1. London School of Economics, Pamphlet HD 7/179, Microfilm Pamphlets, Reel 93.
28. Gilbert, 1966, 202–7.
29. Ibid., 229–30.
30. Jones, 1997.
31. Thane, 1982, 91.
32. Laybourn, 1995, 176.
33. Longmate, 1974, 275.
34. Andrea Smith, 'The Pathologization of Old Age and its Impact on Poor Law Policy for the Aged Workhouse Pauper, 1880–1913', paper presented to the annual meeting of the North American Conference on British Studies, Colorado Springs, 17 October 1998.
35. Crowther, 1981, 92–4.
36. Gilbert, 1970, 208–9.
37. Bellamy, 1988, 258.
38. Lees, 1998, 329.
39. Gilbert, 1970, 215–18.
40. Webb, 1929, Vol. 2, 888–9.
41. Feiling, 1970, 130–8.
42. Webb, 1929, Vol. 2, 918–25.
43. Ibid., 926–9.
44. Gilbert, 1970, 221.
45. Jeremy, 1977, 68. See also Sian Williams, 1979.
46. Jeremy, 1977, 69–71.
47. *A Public Scandal: Glaring Cases of Abuses under the Administration of Socialist Poor Law Guardians*, published by the National Union of Conservative and Unionist Associations (London: Chancery Lane Printing Works, n.d.).
48. *The Times*, 26 September 1927.
49. Gilbert, 1970, 222–3.
50. Ibid., 223–4.
51. British Parliamentary Papers, 1929, XVI, 797.
52. Gilbert, 1970, 225–9.
53. Ibid., 229–30.
54. Longmate, 1974, 280.
55. Crowther, 1981, 265.
56. Gilbert, 1970, 180–6.

BIBLIOGRAPHY

Secondary sources are listed here. Primary source citations are in the endnotes.

Anstruther, Ian. *The Scandal of the Andover Workhouse*, 2nd edn. Gloucester: Sutton, 1984.

Apfel, William, and Peter Dunkley. 'English Rural Society and the New Poor Law: Bedfordshire, 1834–1847'. *Social History* 10, no. 1 (1985): 37–68.

Ashforth, David. 'Settlement and Removal in Urban Areas: Bradford, 1834–71'. In *The Poor and the City: the English poor law in its urban context, 1834–1914*, ed. Michael E. Rose, 57–91. New York: St. Martin's Press, 1985.

Ashforth, David. 'The Urban Poor Law'. In *The New Poor Law in the Nineteenth Century*, ed. Derek Fraser, 128–48. London: Macmillan, 1976.

Bahmueller, Charles F. *The National Charity Company: Jeremy Bentham's silent revolution*. Berkeley: University of California Press, 1981.

Bartlett, Peter. 'The Asylum, the Workhouse, and the Voice of the Insane Poor in 19th-Century England'. *International Journal of Law and Psychiatry* 21, no. 4 (1998): 421–32.

Bartlett, Peter. *The Poor Law of Lunacy: the administration of pauper lunatics in mid-nineteenth-century England*. London: Leicester University Press, 1999.

Baugh, D. A. 'The Cost of Poor Relief in South-East England, 1790–1834'. *Economic History Review* 28, no. 1 (1975): 50–68.

Bellamy, Christine. *Administering Central–local Relations, 1871–1919: the local government board in its fiscal and cultural context*. Manchester: Manchester University Press, 1988.

Blaug, Mark. 'The Myth of the Old Poor Law and the Making of the New'. *Journal of Economic History* 23, no. 2 (1963): 151–84.

Blaug, Mark. 'The Poor Law Report Reexamined'. *Journal of Economic History* 24 (1964): 229–45.

Boot, H. M. 'Unemployment and Poor Law Relief in Manchester, 1845–1850'. *Social History* 15, no. 2 (1990): 217–28.

Boyer, George R. *An Economic History of the English Poor Law, 1750–1850*. Cambridge: Cambridge University Press, 1990.

Bruce, Maurice. *The Coming of the Welfare State. With a comparative essay on American and English welfare programs*, rev. edn. New York: Schocken Books, 1966.

Brundage, Anthony. *England's 'Prussian Minister': Edwin Chadwick and the politics of government growth, 1832–1854*. University Park: Pennsylvania State University Press, 1988.

Brundage, Anthony. 'The Landed Interest and the New Poor Law: a Reappraisal of the Revolution in Government'. *English Historical Review* 87 (1972): 27–48.

Brundage, Anthony. *The Making of the New Poor Law: the politics of inquiry, enactment, and implementation, 1832–1839*. New Brunswick, NJ: Rutgers University Press, 1978.

Brundage, Anthony. 'Private Charity and the 1834 Poor Law'. In *With Us Always: a history of private charity and public welfare*, ed. Donald T. Critchlow and Charles H. Parker, 99–119. Lanham, Md: Rowman and Littlefield, 1998.

Brundage, Anthony. 'Reform of the Poor Law Electoral System, 1834–1894'. *Albion* 7 (1975): 201–15.

Brundage, Anthony, David Eastwood, and Peter Mandler. 'Debate: The Making of the New Poor Law *Redivivus*'. *Past and Present* 127 (1990): 183–201.

Cage, R. A. *The Scottish Poor Law, 1745–1845*. Edinburgh: Scottish Academic Press, 1981.

Caplan, Maurice. *In the Shadow of the Workhouse: the implementation of the New Poor Law throughout Nottinghamshire, 1836–1846*. Nottingham: University of Nottingham Department of Adult Education, 1984.

Caplan, Maurice. 'The New Poor Law and the Struggle for Union Chargeability'. *International Review of Social History* 23, no. 2 (1978): 267–300.

Carter, Paul. 'Poor Relief Strategies: Women, Children, and Enclosure in Hanwell, Middlesex, 1780 to 1816'. *Local Historian* 25, no. 3 (1995): 164–77.

Chinn, Carl. *Poverty amidst Prosperity: the urban poor in England, 1834–1914*. Manchester: Manchester University Press, 1995.

Choomwattana, Chakrit. 'The Opposition to the New Poor Law in Sussex, 1834–1837'. Ph.D. dissertation, Cornell University, 1986.

Coats, A. W. 'Economic Thought and Poor Law Policy in the Eighteenth Century'. *Economic History Review* 2, no. 1 (1958): 39–51.

Coats, A. W. 'The Relief of Poverty, Attitudes to Labour, and Economic Change in England, 1660–1782'. *International Review of Social History* 21, no. 1 (1975): 98–115.

Cody, Lisa Forman. 'The Politics of Illegitimacy in an Age of Reform: Women, Reproduction, and Political Economy in England's New Poor Law of 1834'. *Journal of Women's History* 11, no. 4 (2000): 131–156.

Collins, Harry. 'The Pattern of Poor Law Removals in Nottinghamshire in the Early Nineteenth Century'. *Local Population Studies* 27 (1981): 71–78.

Cowherd, Raymond Gibson. *Political Economists and the English Poor Laws: a historical study of the influence of classical economics on the formation of social welfare policy*. Athens: Ohio University Press, 1977.

Crocker, Ruth Hutchinson. 'The Victorian Poor Law in Crisis and Change: Southampton, 1870–1895'. *Albion* 19, no. 1 (1987): 19–44.

Crompton, Frank. *Workhouse Children*. Stroud: Sutton, 1997.

Crowther, M. A. *The Workhouse System, 1834–1929: the history of an English social institution*. London: Batsford, 1981.

Cuttle, George. *The Legacy of the Rural Guardians: a study of conditions in mid-Essex*. Cambridge: W. Heffer & Sons, 1934.

Dandeker, Christopher. *Surveillance, Power, and Modernity: bureaucracy and discipline from 1700 to the present day*. New York: St. Martin's Press, 1990.

Daunton, M. J. *Progress and Poverty: an economic and social history of Britain, 1700–1850*. Oxford: Oxford University Press, 1995.

Davis, Stephen P. 'The Concept of Poverty in the Encylopedia Britannica from 1810 to 1975'. *Labor History* 21, no. 1 (1979): 91–101.

Dean, Mitchell. *The Constitution of Poverty: toward a genealogy of liberal governance*. London: Routledge, 1991.

De Schweinitz, Karl. *England's Road to Social Security, from the Statute of Laborers in 1349 to the Beveridge Report of 1942*. New York: A.S. Barnes, 1972 [first published 1943].

Digby, Anne. 'The Labour Market and the Continuity of Social Policy after 1834: The Case of the Eastern Counties'. *Economic History Review* 28, no. 1 (1975): 69–83.

Digby, Anne. *Pauper Palaces*. London: Routledge and Kegan Paul, 1978.

Digby, Anne. *The Poor Law in Nineteenth-century England and Wales*. London: Historical Association, 1982.

Digby, Anne. 'The Rural Poor Law'. In *The New Poor Law in the Nineteenth Century*, ed. Derek Fraser, 149–70. London: Macmillan, 1976.

Driver, Cecil. *Tory Radical; the life of Richard Oastler*. New York: Oxford University Press, 1946.

Driver, Felix. *Power and Pauperism: the workhouse system, 1834–1884*. Cambridge: Cambridge University Press, 1993.

Duke, Francis. 'Pauper Education'. In *The New Poor Law in the Nineteenth Century*, ed. Derek Fraser, 67–86. London: Macmillan, 1976.

Dunkley, Peter. *The Crisis of the Old Poor Law in England, 1795–1834: an interpretive essay*. New York: Garland, 1982.

Dunkley, Peter. 'The Hungry Forties and the New Poor Law: A Case Study'. *Historical Journal* 17, no. 2 (1974): 329–46.

Dunkley, Peter. 'Paternalism, the Magistracy, and Poor Relief in England, 1795–1834'. *International Review of Social History* 24, no. 3 (1979): 371–97.

Dunkley, Peter. 'Whigs and Paupers: The Reform of the English Poor Laws, 1830–1834'. *Journal of British Studies* 20, no. 2 (1981): 124–49.

Eastwood, David. *Governing Rural England: tradition and transformation in local government, 1780–1840*. Oxford: Clarendon Press, 1994.

Edsall, Nicholas C. *The Anti-Poor Law Movement, 1834–44*. Manchester: Manchester University Press, 1971.

Ely, James W. Jr. 'The Eighteenth-Century Poor Laws in the West Riding of Yorkshire'. *American Journal of Legal History* 30, no. 1 (1986): 1–24.

Englander, David. *Poverty and Poor Law Reform in Britain: from Chadwick to Booth, 1834–1914*. New York: Addison-Wesley Longman, 1998.

Feiling, Keith. *The Life of Neville Chamberlain*. Hamden, Conn.: Archon Books, 1970 [first published 1946].

Fetter, Frank Whitson. *The Economist in Parliament, 1780–1868*. Durham, NC: Duke University Press, 1980.

Fido, Judith. 'The Charity Organisation Society and Social Casework in London 1869–1900'. In *Social Control in Nineteenth Century Britain*, ed. A. P. Donajgrodzki, 207–30. London: Croom Helm, 1977.

Finer, S. E. *The Life and Times of Sir Edwin Chadwick*. London: Methuen, 1952.

Finlayson, Geoffrey B. A. M. *Citizen, State, and Social Welfare in Britain 1830–1990*. Oxford: Clarendon Press, 1994.

Flinn, M. W. 'Medical Services under the New Poor Law'. In *The New Poor Law in the Nineteenth Century*, ed. Derek Fraser, 45–66. London: Macmillan, 1976.

Fowler, Simon. *Philanthropy and the Poor Law in Richmond, 1836–1871*. Richmond: Richmond Local Historical Society, 1991.

Franzén, Katharine Mary Grigsby. 'Free to Leave: Government Assisted Emigration under the 1834 Poor Law'. Ph.D. dissertation, University of Virginia, 1996.

Fraser, Derek. *The New Poor Law in the Nineteenth Century*. New York: St. Martin's Press, 1976.

Fraser, Derek. 'Poor Law Politics in Leeds, 1833–1855'. *Publications of the Thoresby Society* 53 (1970): 23–49.

Gilbert, Bentley. *British Social Policy 1914–1939*. Ithaca: Cornell University Press, 1970.

Gilbert, Bentley. *The Evolution of National Insurance in Great Britain: the origins of the welfare state*. London: Joseph, 1966.

Gorsky, Martin. 'Experiments in Poor Relief: Bristol, 1816–1817'. *Local Historian* 25, no. 1 (1995): 17–30.

Gregson, Keith. 'Poor Law and Organized Charity: the Relief of Exceptional Distress in North-east England, 1870–1910'. In *The Poor and the City: the English poor law in its urban context, 1834–1914*, ed. Michael E. Rose, 93–131. New York: St. Martin's Press, 1985.

Griffin, Colin P. 'Chartism and Opposition to the New Poor Law in Nottinghamshire: the Basford Union Workhouse Affair of 1844'. *Midland History* 2, no. 4 (1974): 244–9.

Gutchen, Robert M. 'Masters of Workhouses under the New Poor Law'. *Local Historian* 16, no. 2 (1984): 93–9.

Hagen, Grace. 'Women and Poverty in South-West Wales, 1834–1914'. *Llafur. Journal of Welsh Labour History* 7, nos. 3–4 (1998–99): 21–33.

Hamlin, Christopher. *Public Health and Social Justice in the Age of Chadwick. Britain, 1800–1854*. New York: Cambridge University Press, 1997.

Hammond, J. L., and Barbara Hammond. *The Village Labourer, 1760–1832: a study in the government of England before the Reform Bill*. London: Longmans, Green and Co., 1911.

Hampson, Ethel Mary. *The Treatment of Poverty in Cambridgeshire, 1597–1834*. Cambridge: Cambridge University Press, 1934.

Harling, Philip, 'The Power of Persuasion: Central Authority, Local Bureaucracy, and the New Poor Law'. *English Historical Review* 107(1992): 30–53.

Harris, Jose. *Private Lives, Public Spirit: Britain 1870–1914*. Harmondsworth: Penguin, 1993.

Harris, Jose. 'The Transition to High Politics in English Social Policy, 1880–1914'. In *High and Low Politics in Modern Britain: ten studies*, 58–79. Oxford: Clarendon Press, 1983.

Harris, Jose. *Unemployment and Politics; a study in English social policy, 1886–1914*. Oxford: Clarendon Press, 1972.

Harrison, Brian Howard. *Peaceable Kingdom: stability and change in modern Britain*. Oxford: Clarendon Press, 1982

Henriques, Ursula. 'Bastardy and the New Poor Law'. *Past and Present* 37 (1967): 103–29.

Henriques, Ursula. *Before the Welfare State: social administration in early industrial Britain*. London: Longman, 1979.

Henriques, Ursula. 'How Cruel was the Victorian Poor Law?' *Historical Journal* 11, no. 2 (1968): 365–71.

Hilton, Boyd. *The Age of Atonement: the influence of evangelicalism on social and economic thought, 1795–1865*. Oxford: Clarendon Press, 1988.

Himmelfarb, Gertrude. 'Bentham's Utopia: the National Charity Company'. *Journal of British Studies* 10 (1970): 99–107.

Himmelfarb, Gertrude. *The Idea of Poverty: England in the early Industrial Age*. New York: Knopf, 1984.

Himmelfarb, Gertrude. *Poverty and Compassion: the moral imagination of the late Victorians*. New York: Knopf, 1991.

Hindle, Steve. 'Power, Poor Relief, and Social Relations in Holland Fen, c. 1600–1800'. *Historical Journal* 41, no. 1 (1998): 67–96.

Hobsbawm, E. J., and George Rudé. *Captain Swing*. New York: Pantheon Books, 1968.

Hodgkinson, Ruth G. *The Origins of the National Health Service; the medical services of the new Poor law, 1834–1871*. London: Wellcome Historical Medical Library, 1967.

Holderness, B. A. '"Open" and "Close" Parishes in England in the Eighteenth and Nineteenth Centuries'. *Agricultural History Review* 20 (1972): 126–39.

Howells, Gary. '"For I Was Tired of England, Sir": English Pauper Emigrant Strategies, 1834–60'. *Social History* 23, no. 2 (1998): 181–94.

Humphreys, Robert. *Sin, Organized Charity, and the Poor Law in Victorian England*. New York: St. Martin's Press, 1995.

Hurren, Elizabeth T. 'Labourers Are Revolting: Penalising the Poor and a Political Reaction in the Brixworth Union, Northamptonshire, 1875–1885'. *Rural History* 11, no. 1 (2000): 37–55.

Huzel, James P. 'The Labourer and the Poor Law, 1750–1850'. In *The Agrarian History of England and Wales*, Vol. VI, *1750–1850*, ed. G. E. Mingay, 755–810. Cambridge: Cambridge University Press, 1989.

Huzel, James P. 'Malthus, the Poor Law, and Population in Early Nineteenth-Century England'. *Economic History Review* 22, no. 3 (1969): 430–52.

Jeremy, Paul. 'Life on Circular 703: the Crisis of Destitution in the South Wales Coalfield during the Lockout of 1926'. *Llafur* 2, no. 2 (1977): 65–75.

Jones, Gareth Stedman. *Outcast London: a study in the relationship between classes in Victorian society*. Oxford: Clarendon Press, 1971.

Jones, Margaret. 'The 1908 Old Age Pensions Act: the Poor Law in New Disguise?' In *Social Conditions, Status, and Community, 1860-c.1920*, ed. Keith Laybourn, 82–103. Stroud: Sutton, 1997.

Kidd, Alan J. 'Historians or Polemicists? How the Webbs wrote Their History of the English Poor Laws'. *Economic History Review* 40, no. 3 (1987): 400–17.

Kidd, Alan J. 'The State and Moral Progress: the Webbs' Case for Moral Reform c. 1905 to 1940'. *Twentieth Century British History* 7, no. 2 (1996): 189–205.

Kidd, Alan J. *State, Society and the Poor in Nineteenth-century England*. Basingstoke: Macmillan, 1999.

King, Steve. 'Poor Relief and English Economic Development Reappraised'. *Economic History Review* 50 (1997): 360–8.

King, Steve. 'Reconstructing Lives: the Poor, the Poor Law, and Welfare in Calverley, 1650–1820'. *Social History* 22, no. 3 (1997): 318–38.

Knott, John. *Popular Opposition to the 1834 Poor Law*. New York: St. Martin's Press, 1986.

Land, Neville. *Victorian Workhouse: a study of the Bromsgrove Union Workhouse, 1836–1901*. Studley: Brewin Books, 1990.

Landau, Norma. 'The Eighteenth-century Context of the Laws of Settlement'. *Continuity and Change* 6, no. 3 (1991): 417–39.

Landau, Norma. 'The Laws of Settlement and the Surveillance of Immigration in Eighteenth-Century Kent'. *Continuity and Change* 3, no. 3 (1988): 391–420.

Landau, Norma. 'The Regulation of Immigration, Economic Structures and Definitions of the Poor in Eighteenth-Century England'. *Historical Journal* 33, no. 3 (1990): 541–72.

Landau, Norma. 'Who Was Subjected to the Laws of Settlement? Procedure under the Settlement Laws in Eighteenth-Century England'. *Agricultural History Review* 43, no. 2 (1995): 139–59.

Laybourn, Keith. *The Evolution of British Social Policy and the Welfare State*. Keele: Keele University Press, 1995.

Laybourn, Keith, ed. *Social Conditions, Status and Community, 1860–c. 1920*. Stroud: Sutton, 1997.

Lees, Lynn Hollen. *The Solidarities of Strangers: the English poor laws and the people, 1700–1948*. Cambridge: Cambridge University Press, 1998.

Lees, Lynn Hollen. 'The Survival of the Unfit: Welfare Policies and Family Maintenance in Nineteenth-Century London'. In *The Uses of Charity: the poor on relief in the nineteenth-century metroplois*, ed. Peter Mandler, 68–91. Philadelphia: University of Pennsylvania Press, 1990.

Leonard, E. M. *The Early History of English Poor Relief*. New York: Barnes & Noble, 1900.

Levine-Clark, Marjorie. 'Engendering Relief: Women, Ablebodiedness, and the New Poor Law in Early Victorian England'. *Journal of Women's History* 11, no. 4 (2000): 107–30.

Lewis, Jane. 'The Boundary between Voluntary and Statutory Social Service in the Late Nineteenth and Early Twentieth Centuries'. *Historical Journal* 39, no. 1 (1996): 155–77.

Lewis, R. A. 'William Day and the Poor Law Commissioners'. *University of Birmingham Historical Journal* 9 (1964): 163–96.

Longmate, Norman. *The Workhouse*. London: Temple Smith, 1974.

Lubenow, William. *The Politics of Government Growth: early Victorian attitudes toward state intervention 1835–1838*. Newton Abbot: David and Charles, 1971.

McCord, Norman. 'The Implementation of the 1834 Poor Law Amendment Act on Tyneside'. *International Review of Social History* 14, no. 1 (1969): 90–108.

McCord, Norman. 'The Poor Law and Philanthropy'. In *The New Poor Law in the Nineteenth Century*, ed. Derek Fraser, 87–110. London: Macmillan, 1976.

MacDonagh, Oliver. *A Pattern of Government Growth*. London: MacGibbon, 1961.

MacKay, Lynn. 'A Culture of Poverty? The St. Martin in the Fields Workhouse, 1817'. *Journal of Interdisciplinary History* 26, no. 2 (1995): 209–31.

MacKinnon, Mary. 'English Poor Law Policy and the Crusade against Outrelief'. *Journal of Economic History* 47, no. 3 (1987): 603–25.

MacKinnon, Mary. 'Poor Law Policy, Unemployment, and Pauperism'. *Explorations in Economic History* 23, no. 3 (1986): 299–336.

MacKinnon, Mary. 'The Use and Misuse of Poor Law Statistics, 1857 to 1912'. *Historical Methods* 21, no. 1 (1988): 5–19.

Malchow, Howard L. *Population Pressures: emigration and government in late nineteenth-century Britain*. Palo Alto, Calif.: Society for the Promotion of Science and Scholarship, 1979.

Mandler, Peter. *Aristocratic Government in the Age of Reform: Whigs and Liberals, 1830–1852*. Oxford: Clarendon Press, 1990.

Mandler, Peter. 'The Making of the New Poor Law Redivivus'. *Past and Present* 117 (1987): 131–57.

Mandler, Peter. 'Tories and Paupers: Christian Political Economy and the Making of the New Poor Law'. *Historical Journal* 33, no. 1 (1990): 81–103.

Marks, Lara. 'Medical Care for Pauper Mothers and Their Infants: Poor Law Provision and Local Demand in East London, 1870–1929'. *Economic History Review* 46, no. 3 (1993): 518–42.

Marshall, Dorothy. *The English Poor in the Eighteenth Century; a study in social and administrative history*. London: Routledge & Sons Ltd, 1926.

Marshall, J. D. 'The Nottinghamshire Reformers and Their Contribution to the New Poor Law'. *Economic History Review* 13, no. 3 (1961): 382–96.

Marshall, J. D. *The Old Poor Law 1795–1834*, 2nd edn. London: Macmillan, 1985.

Martin, E. W. 'From Parish to Poor Law Union: Poor Law Administration, 1601–1865'. In *Comparative Development in Social Welfare*, ed. E. W. Martin, 25–56. New York: George Allen & Unwin, 1972.

Matthews, Glen. 'The Search for a Cure for Vagrancy in Worcestershire, 1870–1920'. *Midland History* 11 (1986): 100–16.

Meacham, Standish. *Toynbee Hall and Social Reform 1880–1914: the search for commmunity*. New Haven: Yale University Press, 1987.

Melling, Joseph, Richard Adair, and Bill Forsythe. '"A Proper Lunatic for Two Years": Pauper Lunatic Children in Victorian and Edwardian England: Child Admissions to the Devon County Asylum, 1845–1914'. *Journal of Social History* 31, no. 2 (1997): 371–405.

Midwinter, Eric C. *Social Administration in Lancashire, 1830–1860: poor law, public health and police*. Manchester: Manchester University Press, 1969.

Mowat, Charles Loch. *The Charity Organisation Society, 1869–1913: its ideas and work*. London: Methuen, 1961.

Mullineux, C. Elise. *Paupers and Poorhouse: a study of the administration of the poor laws in a Lancashire parish*. Pendlebury: Swinton and Pendlebury Public Libraries, 1966.

Neal, Frank. 'Lancashire, the Famine Irish, and the Poor Laws: a Study in Crisis Management'. *Irish Economic and Social History* 22 (1995): 26–48.

Neate, Alan R. *The St. Marylebone Workhouse and Institution, 1730–1965*. London: St. Marylebone Society, 1967.

Neuman, Mark. *The Speenhamland County: poverty and the poor laws in Berkshire, 1782–1834*. New York: Garland Pub., 1982.

Neuman, Mark. 'A Suggestion Regarding the Origin of the Speenhamland Plan'. *English Historical Review* 84 (1969): 317–92.

Nicholls, George, and Thomas Mackay. *A History of the English Poor Law, in Connection with the State of the Country and the Condition of the People*, 3 vols. New edn. London: P.S. King & Son, 1898 [first published 1854].

Owen, David. *English Philanthropy, 1660–1960*. Cambridge, Mass.: Belknap Press of Harvard University Press, 1964.

Oxley, Geoffrey W. *Poor Relief in England and Wales, 1601–1834*. Newton Abbot: David & Charles, 1974.

Pallister, Ray. 'Workhouse Education in County Durham: 1834–1870'. *British Journal of Educational Studies* 16, no. 3 (1968): 279–91.

Pashley, Robert. *Pauperism and Poor Laws*. London: Longman Brown Green and Longmans, 1852.

Polanyi, Karl. *The Great Transformation: the political and economic origins of our time*. Boston: Beacon Press, 1957 [first published 1944].

Poynter, J. R. *Society and Pauperism: English ideas on poor relief, 1795–1834*. London: Routledge & Kegan Paul, 1969.

Preston-Thomas, Herbert. *The Work and Play of a Government Inspector*. Edinburgh: Blackwood, 1909.

Prochaska, Frank. *Women and Philanthropy in Nineteenth-Century England*. Oxford: Clarendon Press, 1980.

Quinn, Michael. 'Jeremy Bentham on the Relief of Indigence: an Exercise in Applied Philosophy'. *Utilitas* 6, no. 1 (1994): 81–96.

Randall, Adrian, and Edwina Newman. 'Protest, Proletarians, and Paternalists: Social Conflict in Rural Wiltshire, 1830–1850'. *Rural History* 6, no. 2 (1995): 205–27.

Reay, Barry. *The Last Rising of the Agricultural Labourers: rural life and protest in nineteenth-century England*. Oxford: Clarendon Press, 1990.

Redford, Arthur. *Labour Migration in England, 1800–50*. Manchester: Manchester University Press, 1926.

Richardson, Ruth. *Death, Dissection, and the Destitute*. London: Routledge & Kegan Paul, 1987.

Richardson, Ruth. 'Middlesex Hospital Outpatients Wing: the Strand Union Workhouse'. *History Today* 43 (1993): 62–3.

Richardson, Ruth, and Brian Hurwitz. 'Joseph Rogers and the Reform of Workhouse Medicine'. *History Workshop Journal* 43 (1997): 218–25.

Roach, John. *Social Reform in England, 1780–1880*. London: B. T. Batsford, 1978.

Roberts, David. 'Dealing with the Poor in Victorian England'. *Rice University Studies* 67, no. 1 (1981): 57–74.

Roberts, David. 'How Cruel was the Victorian Poor Law?' *Historical Journal* 6, no. 1 (1963): 97–107.

Roberts, David. *Victorian Origins of the British Welfare State*. New Haven: Yale University Press, 1960.

Robin, Jean. 'The Relief of Poverty in Mid-Nineteenth-Century Colyton'. *Rural History* 1, no. 2 (1990): 193–218.

Rodgers, Brian. 'The Medical Relief (Disqualification Removal) Act, 1885'. *Parliamentary Affairs* 9, no. 2 (1956): 188–94.

Rose, Mary Beth. 'Social Policy and Business: Parish Apprenticeship and the Factory System, 1750–1834'. *Business History* 31, no. 4 (1989): 5–32.

Rose, Michael E. 'The Allowance System under the New Poor Law'. *Economic History Review* 19 (1966): 607–20.

Rose, Michael E. 'The Crusade: the Webbs and the Campaign to Break up the Poor Law'. *Memoirs and Proceedings of the Manchester Literary and Philosophical Society* 120 (1977–80): 72–89.

Rose, Michael E. *The English Poor Law, 1780–1930*. Newton Abbot: David & Charles, 1971.

Rose, Michael E. *The Poor and the City: the English poor law in its urban context, 1834–1914*. New York: St. Martin's Press, 1985.

Rose, Michael E. *The Relief of Poverty, 1834–1914*, 2nd edn. Studies in Economic and Social History. London: Macmillan, 1986.

Rose, Michael E. 'Settlement, Removal, and the New Poor Law'. In *The New Poor Law in the Nineteenth Century*, ed. Derek Fraser, 25–44. London: Macmillan, 1976.

Rushton, P. 'The Poor Law, the Parish, and the Community in North-East England, 1600–1800'. *Northern History* 25 (1989): 135–52.

Ryan, Pat. 'Politics and Relief: East London Unions in the Late Nineteenth and Early Twentieth Centuries'. In *The Poor and the City: the English poor law in its urban context, 1834–1914*, ed. Derek Fraser, 133–72. New York: St. Martin's Press, 1985.

Ryan, Pat. 'Poplarism'. In *The Origins of British Social Policy*, ed. Pat Thane, 56–83. London: Croom Helm, 1978.

Searby, Peter. 'The Relief of the Poor in Coventry, 1830–1863'. *Historical Journal* 20, no. 2 (1977): 345–61.

Semple, Janet. *Bentham's Prison: a study of the panopticon penitentiary*. Oxford: Clarendon Press, 1993.

Slack, Paul. *The English Poor Law, 1531–1782*. Basingstoke: Macmillan, 1990.

Snell, K. D. M. *Annals of the Labouring Poor: social change and agrarian England, 1660–1900*. Cambridge: Cambridge University Press, 1985.

Snell, K. D. M. 'Settlement, Poor Law, and the Rural Historian: New Approaches and Opportunities'. *Rural History* 3, no. 2 (1992): 145–72.

Soffer, Reba N. *Ethics and Society: the revolution in the social sciences, 1870–1914*. Berkeley: University of California Press, 1978.

Solar, Peter M. 'Poor Relief and English Economic Development; a Renewed Plea for Comparative History'. *Economic History Review* 50 (1997): 369–74.

Solar, Peter M. 'Poor Relief and English Economic Development before the Industrial Revolution'. *Economic History Review* 48 (1995): 1–22.

Song, Byung Khun. 'Agrarian Policies on Pauper Settlement and Migration, Oxfordshire, 1750–1834'. *Continuity and Change* 13, no. 3 (1998): 363–89.

Song, Byung Khun. 'Continuity and Change in English Rural Society: the Formation of Poor Law Unions in Oxforshire'. *English Historical Review* 114 (1999): 314–38.

Song, Byung Khun. 'Landed Interest, Local Government, and the Labour Market in England, 1750–1850'. *Economic History Review* 51, no. 3 (1998): 465–88.

Stevenson, John. *Popular Disturbances in England, 1700–1832*, 2nd edn. London: Longman, 1992.

Styles, P. 'The Evolution of the Law of Settlement'. *University of Birmingham Historical Journal* 9 (1963): 33–63.

Tanner, Andrea. 'The Casual Poor and the City of London Poor Law Union, 1837–1869'. *Historical Journal* 42, no. 1 (1999): 183–206.

Tanner, Andrea. 'A Troublesome Priest: a Victorian Workhouse Chaplain in the City of London'. *London Journal* 23, no. 1 (1998): 15–31.

Taylor, Geoffrey. *The Problem of Poverty, 1660–1834*. Harlow: Longmans, 1969.

Taylor, James Stephen. 'A Different Kind of Speenhamland: Nonresident Relief in the Industrial Revolution'. *Journal of British Studies* 30, no. 2 (1991): 183–208.

Taylor, James Stephen. 'The Impact of Pauper Settlement 1691–1834'. *Past and Present* 73 (1976): 42–74.

Taylor, James Stephen. 'The Mythology of the Old Poor Law'. *Journal of Economic History* 29 (1969): 292–7.

Taylor, James Stephen. *Poverty, Migration, and Settlement in the Industrial Revolution: sojourners' narratives*. Palo Alto, Calif.: The Society for the Promotion of Science and Scholarship, 1989.

Thane, Pat. *Foundations of the Welfare State*. London: Longman, 1982.

Thane, Pat. 'Women and the Poor Law in Victorian and Edwardian England'. *History Workshop Journal* 6 (1978): 29–51.

Thomas, E. G. 'The Old Poor Law and Medicine'. *Medical History* 24, no. 1 (1980): 1–19.

Thomas, Tydfil. *Poor Relief in Merthyr Tydfil Union in Victorian Times: based on a study of original documents*. Cardiff: Glamorgan Archive Services, 1992.

Thompson, E. P. *The Making of the English Working Class*. New York: Vintage Books, 1963.

Thompson, Kathryn. 'Apprenticeship and the New Poor Law: a Leicester Example'. *Local Historian* 19, no. 2 (1989): 51–5.

Thompson, R. N. 'The Working of the Poor Law Amendment Act in Cumbria, 1836–1871'. *Northern History* 15 (1979): 117–37.

Thomson, David. 'Workhouse to Nursing Home: Residential Care of Elderly People in England since 1840'. *Ageing and Society* 3, no. 1 (1983): 43–69.

Tomkins, Alannah. 'Paupers and the Infirmary in Mid-Eighteenth-Century Shrewsbury'. *Midland History* 43 (1999): 208–27.

Treble, James H. *Urban Poverty in Britain, 1830–1914*. New York: St. Martin's Press, 1979.

Vincent, A. W. 'The Poor Law Reports of 1909 and the Social Theory of the Charity Organization Society'. *Victorian Studies* 27, no. 3 (1984): 343–63.

Vinson, A. J. 'Poor Relief, Public Assistance, and the Maintenance of the Unemployed in Southampton between the Wars'. *Southern History* 2 (1980): 179–225.

Vorspan, Rachel. 'Vagrancy and the New Poor Law in Late Victorian and Edwardian England'. *English Historical Review* 92 (1977): 59–81.

Walsh, Vincent J. 'Old and New Poor Laws in Shropshire, 1820–1870'. *Midland History* 2, no. 4 (1974): 225–43.

Weaver, Stewart Angas. *John Fielden and the Politics of Popular Radicalism, 1832–1847*. Oxford: Clarendon Press, 1987.

Webb, Sidney, and Beatrice Webb. *English Poor Law History. Part I: The Old Poor Law*. London: Longmans Green, 1927.

Webb, Sidney, and Beatrice Webb. *English Poor Law History. Part II: The Last Hundred Years*. 2 vols. London: Longmans Green, 1929.

Webb, Sidney, and Beatrice Webb. *English Poor Law Policy*. London: Longmans Green, 1910.

Williams, David. *The Rebecca Riots, a Study in Agrarian Discontent*. Cardiff: University of Wales Press, 1955.

Williams, Karel. *From Pauperism to Poverty*. London: Routledge & Kegan Paul, 1981.

Williams, Sian Rhiannon. 'The Bedwellty Board of Guardians and the Default Act of 1927'. *Llafur* 2, no. 4 (1979): 65–77.

Williams, Sydna Ann. 'Care in the Community: Women and the Old Poor Law in Early Nineteenth-Century Anglesey'. *Llafur* 6, no. 4 (1995): 30–43.

Wilson, M. D. *The Paupers of Leigh: their persecution and poor relief, 1660–1860*. Leigh: Leigh Local Historical Society, 1976.

Winch, Donald. *Riches and Poverty: an intellectual history of political economy in Britain, 1750–1834*. Cambridge: Cambridge University Press, 1996.

Wood, Peter. *Poverty and the Workhouse in Victorian Britain*. Wolfeboro Falls, NH: Alan Sutton Pub., 1991.

Woodroofe, Kathleen. 'The Royal Commission on the Poor Laws, 1905–09'. *International Review of Social History* 22, no. 2 (1977): 137–64.

INDEX